SO LITTLE TIME

So Little Time

ESSAYS ON GAY LIFE

MIKE HIPPLER

CELESTIAL ARTS
Berkeley, California

The author gratefully acknowledges the following: "Anatomy of a Murder Trial" and "The Vigil: A Profile in Gay Courage" originally appeared in *The Advocate*. "Portrait of a Drug Dealer" originally appeared in the *San Francisco Bay Guardian*. "Chariot of Fire: Tom Waddell and the Gay Games," "Captain of the Campus," and "Hymn to The River" originally appeared in the *New York Native*. All others originally appeared in the San Francisco *Bay Area Reporter*.

CELESTIAL ARTS
P.O. Box 7327
Berkeley, California 94707

Cover design by Ken Scott
Author photo by Steve Savage
Text design by Sal Glynn
Composition by Wilsted & Taylor, Oakland, California

Library of Congress Cataloging-in-Publication Data

Hippler, Mike.
So little time: essays on gay life / Mike Hippler.
p. cm.
ISBN 0-89087-609-6:
1. Homosexuality, male—United States. 2. Gay men—United States—Psychology. 3. Gay men—United States—Sexual behavior.
I. Title.
HQ76.2.U5H56 1990
305.38'9664—dc20 90-2071
CIP

First Printing, 1990
0 9 8 7 6 5 4 3 2
94 93 92 91
Manufactured in the United States of America

FOR MARK,
AND FOR MY FAMILY,

and in memory of
DENNIS, LIONEL,
RUSSELL, PAUL,
and MICHAEL

CONTENTS

Foreword

SO LITTLE TIME. Ten years ago, for most gay men (most I knew, at any rate), the phrase meant one thing only: so many men, so little time. Now it means something else entirely: the threat of impending death. This shift in meaning reflects the phenomenal transition my friends and I have undergone during this decade. The phrase, therefore, is an appropriate symbol, a linguistic bridge to span the gap between the way life used to be and the way it is now.

But for me it means so much more. It is my habitual complaint that there are never enough hours in the day for all I want to do. Despite AIDS, despite temporary periods of boredom, anxiety, or despair, life remains for me an exhilarating affair, and I am all too aware that in the grand scheme of things, my own singular life is but a fleeting moment, a gust of wind in a season of storms. The least I can do is make the most of it.

It is difficult to encompass the hopes and fears of a generation in a weekly newspaper column, or in a book of essays drawn primarily from that column. But at the risk of sounding ridiculously pompous, that's exactly what I've tried to do. To me, the greatest compliment of all is the acknowledgment, "You've written what I feel." For a writer who focuses so often on his own personal experiences, this is more than appreciation: it is justification.

Because I came of age during a period of tremendous flux, when fundamental social and political questions were impossible to avoid, I've always felt a great responsibility to address these kinds of issues. But ever since I was old enough to keep a diary I've been equally drawn to the personal—in all our lives, not just my own. Even if I wanted to, I couldn't write about AIDS, for example, *all* the time. In spite of the epidemic, people still fall in love, pursue careers, and search for fulfillment. These things too deserve attention.

In assembling these essays, I've attempted to do what I do in my column: to strike a balance not only between the public and the private, but also between the educational and the entertaining, the sublime and the ridiculous. If I err, it is on the side of frivolity. To me, nothing is sacred, including myself. Try as I might, I can never be serious for long. This doesn't mean, of course, that I don't care passionately about things. Like my more somber friends, naturally I get frustrated and angry at times. But it's easy to shout and depressing to cry. If at all possible, I'd rather laugh.

Mike Hippler
San Francisco
April 1990

Introduction

IF SOME ARCHAEOLOGIST from some millennia in the future were seeking a document that could offer the definitive insight into what it meant to be a gay man in the last decades of our twentieth century, I could think of no better volume of instruction than *So Little Time.* In matters great and small, Mike Hippler has encapsulated the agonies and ecstasies of all of us in this difficult time.

For readers of San Francisco's gay press, this assessment will not be surprising. Mike Hippler has long chronicled the travails of the fledgling gay minority in weekly columns for San Francisco's largest gay weekly, the *Bay Area Reporter.* His work has underscored a paramount, though little understood, truth of journalism: In reporting, subject matter is all. Readers will tolerate bad writing if it's about an interesting subject while entirely reject the finest of writing—if it's about a boring topic. Mike Hippler's genius is in hitting upon terrific topics, the subjects that you've always wondered about. What *do* those strippers think when they're up on stage, getting ready to climax on cue? Read Hippler from week to week and you'll find out.

The most striking reportage from Hippler, however, comes in his first-person pieces. I can think of no other gay writer today whose work so unpretentiously portrays something of a (gulp) gay Everyman. I know that sounds ostentatious, but the following pages prove me right.

It wasn't until I read Mike that I realized there were probably tens of thousands of other Eagle Boy Scouts with taboo yearnings who eagerly read and reread that section of the Scouting handbook about "wet dreams." When Mike wrote about his first love, I could have sworn he was talking about mine.

By talking about the little issues in life, he also strikes at those that are larger. How do you explain to your eight-year-old nephew what it means to be gay? What will happen when he takes your San Francisco/Castro Street explanation back to the nuns at his parochial school?

The bonus in Hippler's oeuvre is that he also writes well. This is not self-conscious prose from a recovering English major in Manhattan. This is writing that communicates clearly, concisely, and honestly.

The honesty, in fact, can get quite searing in Mike's work, particularly as he delves into the AIDS epidemic. I don't know of any other writer with the courage to enumerate all his past sexually transmitted diseases. Should he have canceled the gambling trip to Reno to attend a friend's memorial service? (He didn't.) And then there's the pain: scanning the obituaries to look for friends, saying that last good-bye to a former lover, and suffering through each T-cell test while the numbers drop lower and lower.

Such is the stuff of modern gay life. These are trying times, far more trying than many of us find it useful to admit as we struggle through each day surrounded by the dead and dying. Make no mistake about it: someday, archaeologists and historians will be asking how we, gay men struggling both against a virus and against prejudice, were able to survive in this time. In this book, the answers can be found: that we survived and even became enriched through courage, community, and, of course, humor.

Randy Shilts
Guerneville, California
May 1990

THE FAMILY

Dear Abby, Am I Too Gay?

FEBRUARY 1984

"YOU'RE TOO GAY," my stepmother told me the last time I was in Los Angeles. "You write for a gay newspaper, you work in a gay restaurant, and you go to a gay gym. All your San Francisco friends are gay. All you ever talk about is gay this and gay that. Don't you realize that you are living in a fantasy world, totally isolated from the *real* world about you? You are losing your ability to relate to that world, Mike. Wake up and smell the coffee."

"That's not true," I replied. "I do have one straight friend in San Francisco. Besides, I'm no more gay than you are straight and upper middle class. All your friends are straight, well-to-do people. Everything you do, you do with straight, well-to-do people. When was the last time you set foot outside this suburb? We all confine ourselves to the environment in which we feel most comfortable, Phyllis. Mine is simply different from yours, no better or worse."

So I argued. But inside I felt a little guilty, for much of what Phyllis said was true, and she didn't even know the half of it. Yes, I write for a gay newspaper and go to a gay gym, although I no longer work in a gay restaurant. Lots of my old friends are straight, and I still keep up with them, but since moving to San Francisco 99 percent of the people whom I see regularly are gay, and, what is worse, 99 percent of those are male. I bank at Hibernia on Eighteenth and Castro, and I buy my food in the heart of the Castro at Cala Foods. When I want to see a movie, Castro Theater is always my first choice. If I go to the beach, it's usually Land's End. I drive a car that I've named after Jayne Mansfield. Oscar Wilde is my patron saint.

My apartment is as gay as it could be. In the living room hang framed posters of Nureyev, Baryshnikov, Christopher Isherwood, and the Gay Olympic Games. The Calvin Klein underwear model faces the Eagle man in the bedroom. In the kitchen Sister Boom Boom's campaign poster presides. (I didn't vote for her, mind you. I just like the poster.) I have a collection of gay books that would make the owner of Walt Whitman Bookstore proud. Tchaikovsky records litter the music cabinet. The Gay Engagement Calendar rests near the phone, and in the closet an aqua prom dress hangs by my black leather motorcycle jacket. I save everything even remotely gay: my scratch 'n' sniff card from the movie *Polyester,* the *National Enquirer* cover featuring a picture of Liberace and his boyfriend, and a collection of sequin and lace wedding garters from various female relatives. Oh yes, and what gay apartment, mine included, would be complete without the poppers in the refrigerator?

Everything I do is gay. I go to the Gay Film Festival, the Gay Rodeo, gay dance concerts at the Falcon Dance Theater, and gay plays at Theater Rhinoceros.

I attend the Lesbian/Gay Freedom Day parade, the Castro Street fair, and the Harvey Milk birthday celebration. I catch gay comedians at the Valencia Rose and gay cabaret artists at Fanny's or 132 Bush. Once in a while I even go to gay bars.

Am I *too* gay?

My friend Martha prefers to call it limited. Every year I write a lengthy Christmas letter to about fifty of my nearest and dearest, describing the year's events in merciless, unabashed detail, and this year Martha, who has known me since at least the sixth grade, was kind enough to point out that approximately 80 percent to 90 percent of the references I made in my letter were to matters entirely gay. "Dad and I read it," she wrote, "but we did not show it to Mother, who truly believes that you are sweet and innocent, and we do our best not to shatter her illusions, as it is tough to be in menopause. . . . I realize that you were being entertaining in your newsletter and that it went only to dear friends who knew you, loved you, and accepted you unequivocally as yourself, no matter what. But *please* do not lose your objectivity. . . . I think you might be in danger of losing your perspective, because you live in and are a major part of a self-contained community in San Francisco."

Martha went on to compare me to her sister, Libby, who was not gay, but who was nuts for Jeanette MacDonald. "You see," she continued, "Libby is a member of the J. M. Fan Club, which meets annually in LA. She is almost obsessive compulsive on this, as she was with Susan Hayward, and then Ginger and Fred, etc. Don't get me wrong. My parents are this way about Judy Garland, and my husband is this way about Sean Connery. I think it's great that this makes Libby happy and that she is going for it. But not everyone in the free world is into J. M., and it becomes tedious to friends and family when she discusses this long-deceased movie star ad infinitum to ad nauseum. . . . Do you get my point? I'm only saying that you presented a very limited viewpoint in your letter. Not everyone is wrapped up in the abuses against homosexuals."

Is she kidding: "Do you get my point?" Do I feel it when I am hit on the head with a sledgehammer? Even my stepmother didn't come on that strong. And Martha isn't the only one. My friend Susan says the same thing, and although with most people I might be tempted to attribute this attitude to homophobia pure and simple, I know it isn't homophobia with them. Susan was practically the first person I ever told I was gay, the day after I fucked a man for the first time. She was also a fag hag once upon a time, for Christ's sake, and still has an engagement ring from one of her old gay boyfriends. And Martha—well, Martha was in the theater for years. Need I say more?

After I received Martha's letter, fearing that perhaps I *was* in danger of losing my perspective on things because I lived in San Francisco, I began to think about why I had come here in the first place. When I had graduated from college ten years ago I had had four priorities: live in the mountains and play the part of a nature boy, complete with a horse and a dog, the whole bit; teach; move to a big city and be gay gay gay, as gay as I possibly could be; and travel shirtless in Greece, picking olives and ambling over sun-drenched marble ruins. I decided the first two were most important, so I combined them by teaching in the mountains of Virginia for two years. Then I feared that love was passing me by as I tended my garden, so I fled to the big city, to LA, and there discovered Boy's Town, U.S.A. LA gave way to New York; New York gave way to San Francisco. I never did make it to Greece. I wound up in San Francisco and never wanted to leave.

I had always known I'd make it to here, to mecca, eventually. Why? Because being gay was important to me, and I wanted to be at the center of things. I wanted to know the people who made things happen, I wanted to be among the best and the brightest, I wanted to have a hand in creating the new world. Most of all, I knew I would be comfortable here. In San Francisco no one would look twice, I thought, if I walked down the street arm in arm with a lover. No one would call me a faggot, and no one would make fun of me if I wanted to go to the ballet rather than to a football game. No one would think I was a borderline transvestite if I said, "Oh, girl!" from time to time. And people would understand, empathize, identify with, all my very gay emotions, from heartbreak when yet another didn't love me to exhilaration when hundreds of thousands of us marched down the street together. It didn't turn out to be exactly as I had thought it would be, but it came awfully close.

Exhilaration, yes, that's the word for life in San Francisco. My friend Lionel agreed with me when he remembered his first Lesbian/Gay Freedom Day parade in San Francisco in 1979: "I'd never been in a place where there were so many other homosexuals in my life. There must have been four hundred thousand of us. I was overwhelmed. I climbed up on a newsstand at the corner where the parade turned up toward the Civic Center, and it was incredible. I flew back to Houston the next day, packed up my things, and moved out here for good five days later." I felt the same way during my first parade. And my second and my third. Although I now take so much for granted, I still feel that way from time to time, for example, when I came back from a week's trip to the mountains and noticed that for the first time in days everyone around me was gay. What a delight that was. Or when I went to the first Moscone party and was surrounded by a surging sea of homosexuals. I hadn't thought there could be that many gay people in the world, much less in one room in San Francisco.

There are drawbacks to life in the ghetto, of course. Although I always wanted us to create a new world, I'm not sure I like the world we've created very much. It's too much like the old one. Consumerism is rampant, as is an emphasis on youth and beauty. Too many of us devote all our time and energy to infantile and pointless pursuits: drugs and partying, partying and drugs. And sex—well, I'm as obsessed as the rest of my friends, but I do get tired of big dick stories every now and then. Sometimes, when I'm at my gym working hard to look like everyone else, I get so sick of it I nearly scream. Mary, I think, let me out of here! But all of these shortcomings are simply a reflection, perhaps a magnification, of the same faults in American society at large, and we've heard it all before. Boring. Besides, with all our faults, I'd still rather be in this gay ghetto than elsewhere. And if I were in a lifeboat, and it came to a choice between saving some empty-headed, conformist gay boy wearing a form-fitting *Dreamgirls* T-shirt and Calvin Klein underwear beneath his 501s, struggling to keep his head above water so his hair wouldn't get wet, and almost *anyone* else who was not gay, I think I'd save the gay boy. (No, no, I don't really mean it, Grandma.)

But why? Why is being gay so important to me? I still haven't reached the heart of the matter. I still haven't answered Phyllis's accusation that I'm *too* gay. Goddamnit, Phyllis, it just *is* important. I'll admit that being gay has had an inordinate effect on my life. If I had grown up in a world where being gay was no big deal, just another sexual preference, I'm sure my life would have been completely different. I wouldn't be living in San Francisco, for one thing, and I wouldn't be pouring my heart out as a writer for a gay paper. There would have been no need. But the fact is that I didn't grow up in such a world. Being gay *was* a big deal, and it was not me who made it that way. I didn't put the label on it, after all. Straight people did. They were the ones who called me a faggot. I didn't think of myself as someone gay. I just wanted to love people of my own sex. I didn't grow up wanting to be part of a separate community. It was straight people who excluded me from theirs, who forced me out.

But I really don't expect Phyllis, Martha, or Susan to understand that. I don't expect them to understand that unless we form our own communities, our needs and desires will be ignored. I don't expect them to see that everywhere we look—on TV, in magazines, on the street—we are bombarded by straight this and straight that. When have you seen a magazine ad featuring two men living in the same house or a TV program showing two women kissing, Martha? When has your bridge club (okay, okay, your encounter group) welcomed a lesbian couple or your church admitted a screaming queen? I used to think, when black separatists in the 1960s told me that I couldn't possibly understand what it was like to be black, that they were full of shit. But now I understand their point of view, and I say to my straight friends, "Don't tell me I'm too gay. My world is hardly gay enough."

So does all this make me a separatist? Because I feel the need for a gay ghetto and enjoy, even prefer, living with those with whom I feel most comfortable, does this make me a radical? There are millions of gay people, after all, who have not migrated to San Francisco, millions who are presumably content to lead their provincial, possibly closeted, lives. I'll never understand them, I confess. I *am* a different sort of creature. But living in San Francisco has not made me a different kind of human being entirely. I have not lost my ability to relate to the outside world. I still enjoy my sister's kids; I still talk about airplanes with my cousin. When my uncle talks about his vacation in England, I care; when a friend describes the new house he has bought, I am excited for him. We are moved by the same things, straight people and I: sunsets, Mozart, and plays about love. The things that are important to them are important to me. I still love straight people, I do. So what is this crap about "too gay"?

A question occurs to me: Will there ever come a time when I no longer feel the need for reinforcement from others like me? Will there ever come a time when I leave mecca willingly? My friend Randy, who is gay, left this city. After five years in San Francisco, he returned to the place whence he came, New Orleans. Listen to him: "Why did I leave San Francisco? Disillusionment. The city is so pregnant with promise, so spectacularly beautiful, so very liberated, that I felt, as have many, that just living there would make me happy. And it did—for several years. . . . But after a while I began to feel lonely. I had few friends in San Francisco, and friendship had always been more important to me than anything else. . . . The only people I knew were emigrés, like myself, and the emigré culture was hopelessly one-dimensional. Bodies, drugs, sex, gay rights, and the price of real estate were the only things of moment. I guess that's why I left, really. I was lonely and I wanted to experience and belong to a more traditional and cohesive community. . . . Leaving San Francisco, however, was one of the hardest things I've ever done. Living there spoiled me in many ways. . . . Having found paradise, who could be foolish enough to leave it? But there came a time for me when it was no longer important to live in the gay capital of the world, and when I began to realize that the very uniqueness of San Francisco was working to limit, rather than to expand, my consciousness and personal experience." Unlike Randy, I do not feel limited by San Francisco's "one-dimensional" gay culture, and I have no desire to leave it. I find it invigorating rather than limiting, but I include his comments just so you will know that there are others of us who agree with my friend Martha. The criticism that many of us are "too gay" comes not only from outside the community.

I went to the Valencia Rose again last night, and as I listened to comedian Danny Williams talk about his experience in a mental hospital—he was put there for being gay, not *too* gay but just gay—I understood at once why I lived in this city, why I immersed myself in the gay subculture, and I wondered why I had been foolish enough to question for one moment whether I was too gay. As Danny made clear, despite the things we share with straight people, we *are* different from them in many ways. We share a special sense of humor and a unique attitude, perhaps born of oppression, perhaps not, which set us apart. We share a common bond, a mutual set of experiences, that makes us different. And rather than ignore that difference, I celebrate it, and I want to continue celebrating it. When Phyllis, Martha, and Susan accept me wholly and respect my priorities, perhaps then that difference won't mean so much and those priorities will change. But until then I will keep on living in San Francisco, spending mornings on Castro Street, afternoons at the gym, and evenings at Valencia Rose. As Danny would say, "I don't know. Makes sense to me."

Does Your Mother Know?

JULY 1984

I DON'T KNOW when my parents first suspected I was gay: when, at six years old, I asked for a Jenny doll instead of a GI Joe for Christmas, or later, when I refused to participate in Little League? Was it in the third grade, when I organized the neighborhood's first amateur theatrical production, or in the seventh, when I decorated the walls of my bedroom with posters of Marilyn Monroe and Barbra Streisand? It might have been anytime. They certainly had enough clues throughout the years. But they couldn't have known absolutely until I told them at twenty-two years of age, only two years after I finally had told myself. Telling them wasn't easy—it had been hard enough to tell myself, after all—but it was something I knew I had to do. My homosexuality was too important a part of my life to keep secret from those I loved.

My family had always been a close-knit one. We all loved and respected each other a great deal. But unfortunately, my homosexuality set me apart. I always felt a little as if I did not belong. My sisters, for example, always brought their boyfriends along on vacations with us, but I did not. I could not. I remember one vacation in particular, when, after an evening on the beach, my older sister and her husband decided to take a moonlit stroll north along the beach, and my younger sister and her boyfriend decided to wander south. Mom and Dad decided to retire to the beach house for the night, and I—well, what was left for me?

Only to disappear alone into the ocean, and that night I felt like it. I knew I wouldn't feel that way if only my family knew about me, if only they understood and accepted my gayness. And I knew that if this was to be brought about, then it was up to me to arrange it.

Unfortunately, I was afraid. Ever since I had first slept with a man on August 14, 1972—a date I still celebrate, a date second in importance on my calendar only to my own birthday—I had wanted to tell them. Hell, I figured I owed it to them, for it was in the back seat of my mother's station wagon that the long-awaited event had finally taken place. But I was afraid. I didn't know how my family would react. Oh, I knew they loved me, and I recognized that they were all intelligent, rational people, but I also knew that when it came to homosexuality, there were no guarantees. Often love and intelligence were not enough, and it was impossible to predict how people would react. So I laid low and postponed the inevitable.

Eventually I concocted a plan. I would tell my parents, I decided, when I had graduated from college and established a home of my own. Then, if anything went wrong, the consequences would be minimal. If my parents could not understand or accept my homosexuality, then I would not be around to bear the burden of their disapproval. This plan had both advantages and disadvantages. The chief advantage was that I was not due to graduate from college for two years. That gave me two years to refine my arguments, to perfect my attack. Unfortunately, those two years were also the plan's chief disadvantage: I had two years to hide, two years of subterfuge and lying whenever I was at home and wanted to go out. It also didn't allow for much follow-up once I had told them. It did seem rather rude, after all, to hit them with that bombshell and then to disappear without giving them time to ask questions, time to adjust. But I decided to minimize that problem by telling them at Christmas, when I would be at home for two weeks: ample time for questions and answers. It would also give me the opportunity to tell them in person, and I very much wanted the confrontation—if confrontation it was to be—to be face to face. It seemed to me heartless to impart the information by letter. The only thing more unkind would be to tell them by telegram—or not to tell them at all.

A year and a half before the big date arrived, however, I decided to practice on my older sister and her husband. The three of us were in England at the time—I was spending part of my junior year abroad—and it was a perfect opportunity to test the family waters. Like the rest of my family, my sister expected a great deal from me, and I was afraid that the things she expected were not the things I had to offer. But in England I sensed that Judy had changed a bit and had come to value many of the same things I did—art, music, beauty—typical faggot stuff. Yet did this mean that she would value a faggot younger brother? I had always respected her a great deal, but would she respect me once she found out?

I don't remember how I told her—I think it just spilled out one night after dinner—but I do remember how she reacted. Quietly. She didn't say much—I didn't give her a chance—but at least she didn't scream or pull her hair. Her husband, on the other hand, was extremely supportive. He asked a thousand questions and wanted to know what it was like to be gay, what it was like to experience what I had experienced. Later, over the course of the next few months, I found that my sister too was interested in what I was feeling. She was not appalled and *did* continue to love me. But it took her longer than my brother-in-law to accept my gayness, for she wanted to be sure that I would be happy with the "choice" I had made. She was concerned that, for a person as family oriented as I was, homosexuality wasn't going to be a very fulfilling "lifestyle."

After I had returned from England and six months before the date I had set to tell my parents, I almost blew it. I almost spilled the beans too soon. It would have been all right, I suppose, except that only my mom and my little sister were at home. Dad was out in California for the summer, planning to relocate the family, or what was left of it, to Los Angeles. My mom, my sister, her boyfriend, and I were sitting around the living room one night, when we began one of our usual "heavy" discussions about God, drugs, sex, what-have-you. I was usually fairly open about most things, having long since confessed to atheism and drug use, and as the discussion intensified, I found myself saying, "Mom, you've accepted all our differences so well over the years, yet if you only knew the biggest difference of all, concerning one of the most important facets of my life, you'd never be able to deal with it."

"I'll bet I know what it is," Mom replied immediately.

"No, you don't," I countered. "You couldn't know. And I'd tell you, but I have to wait until Christmas, when Dad is with us."

"I do know," she said. "And to prove it, I'll write it down and seal it in an envelope, and when you come to California at Christmas, I'll show you. I know what it is."

She was right, of course. I had dropped enough hints along the way that she did know what I was talking about. And when I did tell my parents and my younger sister at Christmas, there were no tears or recriminations. Far from it. My parents were as supportive as they could be, and they gave me all the love and understanding I could have desired. Nevertheless, they weren't entirely at ease with the situation, and, like my older sister, they did have their concerns. I recognized that it would take them a while to get used to the idea, so to help them adjust, I gave them a book about homosexuality and twenty or thirty pages of typed excerpts from my journal, excerpts having to do with my feelings about my homosexuality. If they could see written proof of my own anxiety and ultimate adjustment, I reasoned, perhaps it would help them to deal with their own fears and worries.

In January, immediately after that Christmas vacation, I received a letter from my mother, in which she told me, "I'm glad you finally shared your story with us. It's so much better to have things like that out in the open with those you love. It still took great courage to tell us, I'm sure. I hope our reaction wasn't too disappointing to you. Somehow I've known for quite a long time—long before our discussion this summer. Then this summer I felt I knew for sure. . . . I hope we can be more understanding of your feelings and emotions. Your journal has helped a great deal. I think the book will too. [It did not. It was a stupid idea to give them that book, which was full of the strident, aggressive gay liberation rhetoric typical of the period.] It's a different concept of love for us, so you must try to bear with us while we adjust. We love you so much and you're so great that you make this much easier for us to accept. I honestly wish I could say that I'm happy for you, but I can't do that yet, Michael. Maybe in time that will come. I can say that I pray you find the person—be it woman or man—with whom you can share great love. . . . Being your mother, I can't help but worry about your happiness. I'll try to let go, however, and let you lead your own life as you see fit. We'll always need you, though, and we hope that to some degree you'll always need us. Mainly I want you to know that no matter what, we love you deeply and always will. And we'll always be glad to claim you as our only son."

Regardless of what Mom and Dad may actually have felt, they went out of their way during the next few months and years to show me they cared. Mom began to include clippings from the LA newspapers concerning homosexuality and the gay community in her letters to me. She chose items she thought would be of interest, including a series of articles on the notorious 1975 LAPD raid on a gay "slave" auction. Later she began to scout out potential husbands for me. When one of my younger sister's best friends, a gorgeous hunk of man, an All-American boy who had completely charmed my mother, came out, Mom wrote me a letter exclaiming, "Have I got the man for you!" Dad was no less remarkable. When I began to study dance in LA in 1977, he came down to Hollywood to watch me spin and twirl. Later, in 1979, after I had moved to San Francisco, he visited and attended the Castro Street fair with my lover and me. He enjoyed it so much (especially dunk-a-hunk, the cookie ladies, the "nuns" on roller skates, and the man with transparent vinyl overalls) that he wrote his entire family, including his eighty-four-year-old mother, about it.

Of course, I expected as much acceptance from my parents and demanded even more. To this day it amazes me how much I did expect. What I must have put my parents through! When I came down with my first case of the clap, Dad was the first to know. I also told him about my nights out on the town: where I had gone, whom I had met, and generally what we had done. Mercifully, I spared him the sexually explicit details. Later, when I finally did snare a husband and brought him home to meet the folks, the first thing my lover and I did when we arrived at the house was to push the twin beds together and set up the poppers and the grease on the night table for all the world to see. I held nothing back. But my family learned to cope with my confessional excesses. And although I may have gone too far at times, it was better to share too much than too little.

I was not the first obvious homosexual ever to enter my parents' lives, by the way. When they were growing up in central Florida in the 1930s, they had a friend by the name of Barton Sumac. Barton's mother had a good deal of money, and because she was interested in dance, she used her influence to persuade the famous modern dancer Ted Shawn to establish his winter headquarters near my parents' hometown. Naturally, Mrs. Sumac encouraged her son to participate in Shawn's company, and Barton, it seems, took to dancing like a duck to water. Soon, according to some accounts, he and the rest of the Ted Shawn dancers were dancing "naked in the woods." (I tend to doubt it, however. There are too many palmettos, sandspurs, and other prickly things in the Florida woods for nude dancing to be very comfortable there.) At any rate, Barton, who had the time of his life organizing amateur dance productions after Shawn left town, was "that way." Everyone knew it, but as long as nobody drew attention to it, it was all right.

There was also another boy, Barry Heywood, who was my father's best friend for a while as well as one of my mother's boyfriends. In fact, on the first day of first grade, my mother came home from school and announced, "I am going to marry either Jack Hippler or Barry Heywood." It's a good thing my mother chose my dad, for shortly after they all graduated from high school in 1942, Barry was court martialed by the Army for homosexual conduct. My father's father, a lawyer, defended him, but I have no idea how the trial came out. All I know is that my parents never saw Barry again. Supposedly he got married, had kids, and became a college professor in New England. Poor Mrs. Heywood. Poor kids. But lucky Barry. Think of all those college boys!

I suspect that Barry Heywood never learned how wonderful coming out can be. For me it was like a fever. Once I got started it was impossible to stop. The exhilarating rush of freedom felt so good that I wanted to tell the whole world. The next step for me, after telling my immediate family, was to tell the other relatives. Most people wouldn't even consider informing their aunts, uncles, and cousins of their homosexuality, I suppose, but in a family such as mine, where the extended ties were strong and lasting, it was important to tell them. We had spent many of our vacations together in the past. I knew we would continue to see each other in the future. And I didn't want to have to endure a repeat of scenes such as the one at Daytona Beach in 1973, when my cousin's boyfriend, a football player at the University of Georgia, dressed up in my cousin's nightgown and pranced around the motel room, pretending to be a queer, much to the delight or disgust of everyone there—everyone but me, who found it tiresome and unoriginal.

I chose first a favorite aunt and uncle. Although they were as conservative as the rest of the family—Reaganites, all—these particular relatives were renowned for their sense of humor, and I figured they could handle it. This time I did write a letter, and in reply my aunt wrote back, "The truth is, I hate it! I know if we could talk face to face I would probably say stupid things based on my narrow vision of the subject, but then that's all I have to go on. I am glad, however, that you are happy and content with your life as it is. I have read and reread your letter and feel you really do believe in yourself, and that's how it should be. But you've had years to get used to the idea, so please bear with me. At least now we won't be bugging you to get married, but we won't promise not to slip in a gay joke now and then. You know we love you, and there is no reason for your news to change anything." Added my uncle, an accountant, "You got any more bombs to drop, kid, save 'em for after tax season. It's 1:00 A.M., for cryin' out loud!"

Another aunt and uncle, right wing, Bible-toting Baptists, found out in a most unusual manner before I had had a chance to tell them. This aunt was a teacher, as I was once upon a time, and she had the misfortune to read in a teachers magazine an article I had written about what it was like to be a gay teacher. She was not amused. I heard through the grapevine that she had read the article, and I immediately wrote her a letter, apologizing for not telling her sooner and expressing my hope that this discovery wouldn't make any difference in our relationship. A few days later she and my uncle called to tell me what everyone else had already said: "We don't approve, but we still love you." I would have preferred approval as well as love, but I decided to settle for what I could get. This aunt and uncle still try to convert me from time to time by sending me Bible verses and warning me about "sickness" and "perversion," but I have ways of retaliating. When their twenty-eight-year-old daughter, my cousin, came to visit me in San Francisco a year ago, I took her to a gay dance concert. She liked the tap dancers, but oh, those boys in G-strings!

It may seem inconsistent with all that I have said, but I never have told my sole remaining grandparent, my father's mother, that I am gay. There just doesn't seem to be any point. Sure, it would be nice if she knew, if we could talk about it, but the woman is eighty-eight years old, two generations removed from me. I don't think she could possibly understand. Why should I traumatize her final years? Besides, I think she knows already. Remember the letter my father sent her about the Castro Street fair? The woman is no dummy. She can figure out why her unmarried grandson is watching dunk-a-hunks on Castro Street. And if she still has any doubts, she could ask. I would tell. But all this is pathetic rationalization on my part. I am simply afraid to tell her, and my fear causes me to perpetuate an undesirable situation. In this one instance, I am a coward. (Or is it that I have learned to respect the right of certain individuals not to know? Does anyone have that right? Not if he or she desires an honest relationship.)

I understand that many gay people do not share my overwhelming need to discuss their homosexuality with their families. Their family situations more closely resemble the relationship I have with my grandmother rather than the one I had with my parents: their homosexuality is understood, but it is never openly discussed. "Why should I tell my parents?" they ask. "It's not their concern. They don't tell me about their sex lives. Why should I tell them about mine? It's better to leave well enough alone." I can only respond that I have found life to be infinitely richer because I can share matters closest to my heart with my family, and I think the same would be true for these people if only they opened up to their families as well. The longer the subject is avoided, the larger the barriers become. I waited two years to talk to my parents. Had I waited a few more, I would have had no one to tell, for within seven years they were both dead. (And no, my telling them was not what did them in.) Certainly I could have lived with myself had they died before I had had a chance to be honest with them, but I would not have the many fond memories that I have now. And I would never have been certain that the love they had for me was the kind I had to have, one that was total and all-encompassing.

I realize also that not all parents react the same way mine did to news of their child's homosexuality. I've known numbers of people whose parents kicked them out of the house when they learned their child was gay. And I've read or heard of countless other horror stories. The mother of one of my friends actually chased her son around the house with an ax when he told her. But in the long run most parents adjust. They really do. Even the ax lady relented eventually and now treats her son's lover as a favored son-in-law. The happy endings far outnumber the sad ones, and in any case the risk is worth it, I believe, for a parent who rejects a gay child entirely isn't a parent worth having.

In his wonderful book *Familiar Faces, Hidden Lives,* the late Harold Brown writes, "Telling his parents is one of the most emotional and significant events in the life of a homosexual man. It is, perhaps, at least in our society now, the ultimate test of love, both for the parents and their son." For the most part I agree, and I have always been grateful that my parents passed that test. I am sorry, however, that such a test was necessary in the first place. For future generations of my family, perhaps it will not be. My older sister is raising two sons now. If they turn out to be gay, will they have as much difficulty coming out to their parents as I did to mine? I hope not. With me as an example—a role model, if you will—they should not. But at this point the question is academic. After all, they haven't asked for Jenny dolls—yet.

At a Family Reunion

OCTOBER 1985

I DON'T KNOW how many gay people at age thirty-three choose to spend their vacations with their families. Most families have a difficult time dealing with an avowed homosexual or lesbian in their midst; yet mine copes fairly well with me, and I am as avowed as they come. At times I *have* noticed a certain amount of latent hostility, especially from the conservative Baptist sector of the family, but this does not, oddly enough, seem to interfere with their love for me. At any rate, no amount of hostility, latent or otherwise, would have kept me from attending my grandma's ninetieth birthday party and family reunion in Florida this past Labor Day.

My family is a fairly large and close-knit one, but, to the best of my knowledge, I am the only homosexual. As there are thirteen grandchildren on this side of the family, this defies Kinsey's odds, I am aware, but I still have hopes for one of my cousins. He was a difficult child—egocentric, overbearing, and infinitely too sensitive—much like me, in fact, which is why I was once convinced that he would eventually turn queer. As I learned on this vacation, however, he is still dating girls, alas, and although he has known about me for years, he has yet to turn to me for cousinly (sisterly?) advice.

My other cousins are hopelessly straight. A couple are too cute for words, but I keep my hands off. I used to have the hots for my cousin Dan, but last year he got married, and besides, he went prematurely bald, so I recently transferred my affection to a younger cousin. This one has thighs men die for, thighs made to envelop and smother faces, and he has the butchest of haircuts, but the man is far too conservative. Quite the entrepreneur, he recently opened his own business while still a student. This I simply do not understand. It seems to me that any normal, healthy boy would be more interested in sex than money, especially when he has to look no further than his cousin to satisfy what should be (and would be if I had anything to say about it) his natural desires.

Naturally I kept quiet about these unrequited longings at the reunion. It was not the only thing I kept quiet about. My family knows I write for a small "neighborhood" newspaper, for instance, and they know that I am gay, but they do not know that the two have anything to do with one another—although they suspect. They often ask to see my articles, and when one cousin came to San Francisco recently, she asked to see a copy of the paper, but so far I have managed to evade most of these requests. It is not that I am afraid my articles would offend them (although some would, of course, including this one), but how to explain to them the ads for Long Dong Silver or the numerous pictures of leather queens in studded jockstraps? It is a problem as yet unresolved.

And yet I say I am avowed. Well, I am. I may not talk about condoms and douching with the family, perhaps, but I do talk about other aspects of the gay community: AIDS, for instance. One night two of my aunts and I had a long discussion over dinner, and I told them about friends who have died and others who are struggling. I wanted them to know what this community was facing and how we were dealing with it. I also wanted them to be prepared in case something should happen to me. I have often wondered, If something did, would I return home? At present, I doubt it. God forbid I should ever desert my videotape collection—or the friends here who, unlike my family, can read my articles without blushing.

The AIDS crisis is something my family does not fully understand—yet. Actually, it is only one of the aspects of my life they do not understand. On the day of Grandma's birthday party, one of my aunts had plans to take pictures of each family group dressed in gay nineties drag (for Grandma was born in 1895). She was unsure, however, what to do with me, because I was single. "Let's make the nineties really gay," I suggested, and I offered to put on a dress and join my sister and her husband as a nagging mother-in-law. My aunt did not think this was funny. Instead, she paired me with a distant relative I did not even know, and the two of us posed—ridiculously, I thought—as husband and wife. Later my aunt relented and took the picture I had suggested. She was right. It was not funny, at least in the family context.

Nevertheless, in spite of such moments, the family vacation was, as always, delightful. If I once felt like an outsider, when no one was aware of the secret longings raging within me, I no longer do. So what that I don't have kids of my own? I can still take my sister's kids to Disney World and help with my nephew's tennis lessons. So what that I don't share an interest in business promotions and house mortgages? I still play a mean game of beach handball, and I thrive at

Pounce, the family card game. And everyone knows just who makes the most fabulous sand castles in the family. In little ways such as these, and in larger ones as well, I am still an integral part of the family.

Shortly before the end of the vacation, my uncle screened several old home movies for the assembled group, and, until the projector broke, there was no doubt who was the screaming queen of this family. In one scene I saw myself, resplendent in a brilliantly colored Hawaiian shirt, run sweetly down a swinging bridge. In another I waved good-bye to the camera with wrists flopping all over the place. Yet no one laughed; no one made fun of me, for we recognized that we were each somewhat ridiculous in his or her own way. "Ooh, baby, *love* that shirt," was all my brother-in-law said before whistling at a scene of his future wife in her first bikini. As I sat there I realized that the reason I kept going down to Florida for these family vacations was that this was a group who knew me well yet loved me all the same, a group with whom I felt comfortable—even if I couldn't bury my face in my cousin's thighs.

Explaining Boyfriends and Girlfriends to a Kid

DECEMBER 1988

TRADITIONALLY the holidays are all about families. And supposedly families are all about sharing. So this year, while celebrating an early Christmas with my family in Washington, D.C., I decided to share with my eight-year-old nephew Yeats the fact that I was gay.

Ideally I should never have had to make an issue of my sexuality. He should have grown up knowing about it, just as he grew up knowing that stoves are hot and ducks go quack. But during my brief family visits, because I had never appeared with a boyfriend while Yeats was there, there was never an opportunity for my nephew to absorb this knowledge.

Oh, sure, we had discussed gay issues in front of Yeats, but he screened them out as so much adult talk that didn't concern him. And because there were two other single adults in the family besides myself, he never questioned my being single. I was simply Mike. Being gay didn't enter into it.

A year and a half ago, however, Yeats finally gave me an opening to explain things in greater detail. A friend of mine from college, Alice, came to visit, and Yeats pounced.

"Who's this, Mike?" he asked. "Your girlfriend?"

"No, Alice is a good friend of mine. She's not my girlfriend. I don't have a girlfriend."

"I bet she's your girlfriend," he insisted.

"Yeats, listen. Boys and girls don't have to be boyfriends and girlfriends. They can be just good friends."

It didn't sink in. Yeats persisted until I was ready to shout, "Look, you little pest, I'm queer! Q-u-e-e-r! Do you know what that means?" But I couldn't, because I wasn't sure how my sister felt about my telling him. Until I cleared it with her, my options were limited.

When I told my sister what had happened and asked for permission to set things straight, however, she demurred. She didn't want me telling him until he was "old enough to understand."

"But that only means until he is old enough to become prejudiced," I protested. "By then it will be too late. The damage will have been done. Besides, what do I do in the meantime?"

My sister replied that the real reason she wanted to wait was that she had to figure out a way to tell him that it was okay for me to be gay but not for him.

"We want him to know that we love you anyway, but we prefer him to be straight. We think he'll be happier that way."

Stunned, I hesitated before replying. I had had no idea my sister felt that way. What could one say to such a warped (albeit well-intentioned) philosophy, anyway? That neither she nor Yeats had any control over her or his sexual orientation? That even if they did, why should anyone be happier if Yeats was straight? I hardly knew where to begin. Under the circumstances I decided the best thing to do was to let the matter rest for a while.

Yeats didn't ask me about girlfriends again until this month, when, on the first night of my visit, he asked, "Mike, when are you getting married?"

Reluctantly I put him off with some excuse or another, but he asked the same question the next night and again the next. Desperate, I fled to my sister again, and said, "Look, he clearly wants to know what's up. You've got to let me tell him. It's not fair to either of us to keep him in the dark any longer. I promise to break it gently, to keep it low key."

Surprisingly, both my sister and her husband agreed, so the next time Yeats asked, I said, "Okay, I'll tell you, but it's kind of complicated. People get married because they love each other, right? Well, some boys fall in love with girls, and some boys fall in love with boys. And boys can't marry boys, although they can live together and make commitments to each other—which is almost the same thing."

Yeats cut through my confusing, long-winded, and evasive explanation with the question, "So you love boys?"

Immediately I wished I had used the words *men* and *women* rather than *boys* and *girls*, but I let that pass. Instead I simply answered yes, as I felt an irrational, gut level fear take control for a moment. The question was so direct, so elemental, that it called forth reservoirs of guilt and shame that I had thought no longer existed. Suddenly I had to confront, for the first time in years, my own homophobia, and I hated myself for allowing the past to haunt me so.

I attempted to get back on track and to make things clearer for Yeats by explaining that I too had a mate, just as my sister had her husband. I reminded Yeats that he had eaten dinner with my boyfriend a few months ago, but I hadn't been there, so Yeats wasn't able to make the connection—and he didn't really remember anyway. I decided to call it a day by asking, "So does any of this make sense to you, Yeats?"

"Not really," he answered.

"Well, someday it will," I assured him, relieved to have broached the subject at last.

"Yeah, sure," he replied. Then he asked what I was giving him for Christmas.

It would be nice to conclude that the battle has been fought and won, but I know this is only the beginning. Assuming Yeats remembers this conversation, there will certainly be more questions in the future.

Unfortunately, there will also be conflicts. What happens when he tells his friends about boys loving boys, for instance? Or, worse yet, tells the nuns at the parochial school he attends? What happens when he hears the word *fag*, or learns that, according to some people, homosexuality is a sin? Will my sister explain things for him the way I would like for her to do?

I don't know. All I know is that at last we have made a first step. And that's better than no step at all.

ON THE TOWN

Dancing in Jockstraps

MAY 1985

FRANKLY, CONTESTANT number one doesn't do all that much for me. His skin is too pale, his tattoos adorn all the wrong places, and his waist spills over his jockstrap. Contestant number two is a refugee from Polk Street. He has a smooth, slim body, long, blond hair parted in the middle, and a gold chain around his neck. (The only other thing he wears is his jock, of course.) Number three, the short one in the black jock, has tight, rippling muscles and a nice smile. Unfortunately, he bears a striking resemblance to the diminutive Academy Award–winning actress Linda Hunt, and is a long shot at best. I cannot wait to see what the rest of the competition looks like. It is Sunday night at nine o'clock, and I *could* be home watching "Masterpiece Theater," but instead I am at the End-up on Sixth and Harrison watching another long-running series, the infamous biweekly jockstrap contest. It is as good a way as any to spend a Sunday night.

The End-up has been holding these contests for fourteen years now, according to Randy Johnson, the contest's popular cohost—the gay Johnny Carson. Established by Paul Bentley (otherwise known as Luscious Lorelei and a former member of the Imperial Court) as a promotional gimmick for the bar, the series is the oldest contest of its kind in the gay community. "It began as a dance contest," explains Johnson, who has been running the show for the past ten years, "but soon it became a *sexual* dance contest. And that is what it is today." Indeed—with an emphasis on the sexual, I think.

The rules of the contest are simple. Contestants volunteer from the crowd. (On slow nights volunteers must be recruited, Johnson admits.) Then they strip to jockstraps or other suitable attire. One by one, Johnson introduces them to the audience, for whom they dance as a group. Then Johnson and his cohost, Diamond John, take turns interviewing each individual. Next the audience has a chance to ask questions, and the contestants dance some more. Finally the nearly naked young men venture into the crowd with large paper bags in order to collect as many tickets as possible. (These tickets have been issued to each bar patron in advance.) The person who collects the most tickets wins and takes home $175 in prize money. The first runner-up takes home $125, and the third-place winner garners $75. All three are eligible to compete in the contest's celebrated finals, held twice a year at the bar. And that's all there is to it.

Contestants range in number from three to twenty-five—"but we like to have ten or fewer to keep the show shorter than two hours," Johnson says—and range in age from twenty-one on up. Twenty-one is the minimum age for the obvious reason—the legal one. (The only other legal requirement is that there be no nudity, which is the reason for the jocks in the first place.) All kinds of people participate—this night's contest includes an accountant at C & H Sugar, a manager of a Mrs. Fields' cookie store, an unemployed landscapist, and a Navy corpsman—and they participate for all kinds of reasons. "Some are exhibitionists, some do it on dares, others are encouraged by friends, and still others do it for money," says Johnson. "Most are young and figure, Hell, you only live once, right?"

I suppose. But I don't think I would ever get up onstage and subject myself to that kind of public scrutiny, and I feel a little sorry for those who do when the question-and-answer period arrives. Many of the questions are harmlessly routine and would not be out of place at a Miss America pageant: "Where are you from?" "Where do you work?" "Do you have a boyfriend?" "What do you like best about yourself?" But others are personal, suggestive, even graphic, and Johnson and Diamond John can be relentless at times: "What do you like to do most in bed?" they may ask. "What kind of man turns you on?" "Are you a top or a bottom?" "What makes your dick hard?" "Is that all you, or is there something stuffed in your jockstrap?" The crowd often encourages Johnson and Diamond John to excess (if such a word has any meaning in a situation such as this). When someone in the crowd asks contestant number two, "Are you a natural blond?" Diamond John, without missing a beat, says, "Bend over and let me look at your roots." Amazingly enough, number two does, spreading his asshole for all the world to see. Even John is taken aback. "I didn't mean *those* roots," he says. "What have you got up *here?*"

Although they may not seem it at times, both Johnson and Diamond John can be surprisingly sensitive. They have to be. "We can tell in a minute," claims Johnson, "if a contestant is a son of a bitch, if he's nervous, if he's going to play to the crowd, or whatever. So we know how to treat them, what kinds of questions to ask, whether to have fun, be serious, get dirty, or cut them off." Neither Johnson nor Diamond John will probe if the contestant is uncomfortable. "The point is to have a good time, after all," says Johnson. "There is a belt, and there is below the belt, and we try not to hit below the belt. We don't laugh *at,* we laugh *with,* the people onstage."

Nevertheless sometimes the crowd gets a little rude, and things get out of hand. Such was the case recently when an unattractive, fifty-year-old fat man with glasses got up to participate. Explains Johnson, "I knew this could get ugly, so I did my best to build the man up. 'You only live once,' I said. 'It takes balls to get up here. You're a good sport.' The crowd came around. It usually does. We have a lot of regulars here, and they don't let things get too out of hand. Besides, most people are here only to have a good time, to see and hear a little porno. They're voyeurs at heart, not sadists."

The crowd does have a good time, it is true, and there are moments of genuine hilarity. When Diamond John asks contestant number four, clearly the crowd favorite, "What sexual fantasy do you jack off to the most?" someone in the crowd shouts out, "Ann Miller tap dancing!" But Diamond John wants a serious answer. "What makes your dick hard?" he persists. "Bondage!" number four answers with pride. "Band-Aids?" asks John. "You're into Band-Aids?" Later, when Johnson asks contestant number five, a black Navy corpsman, "How many inches do you have?" the corpsman, who has evidently misunderstood, replies, "I have a lot of interests." Johnson only deadpans, "I'll bet."

Occasionally the contest takes an odd twist. When contestant number six appears, someone in the crowd shouts, "It's a woman!" "You'd better believe it," answers Diamond John. "This is what you always wanted to look like, honey." Indeed it is a real woman, a gorgeous, divinely endowed black woman wearing black-and-red jungle print panties, a white tank top, and red spike heels. She is here with her straight boyfriend, a man named Angel, and she has entered the contest, she says, because, "I'm an exhibitionist." Because she is frank and self-assured, the crowd loves her. She admits, when questioned, that she likes penetration and she likes to give blow jobs. When asked if she ever goes to glory holes, she says, "I don't have to—men come to me." Later she sings a Billie Holiday song a capella, and when she dances, she struts and poses like a professional.

Women often enter the jockstrap contest, acknowledges Johnson. (I remember one in particular from years past—a truck-driving bull dyke named Animal with the ugliest ass I have ever seen—but a charming personality, I hasten to add.) "They get the biggest hands but usually don't win. The guys here love them, but they vote for the ones they want to go to bed with." And the one they want to go to bed with this night is not number six, the real woman, but slim, tanned, mustachioed contestant number four instead.

It is contestant number four, who says he has entered the contest "for fun!" and who only smiles when Diamond John says, "Where is this number four? Where is this ugly thing?" who collects the most tickets and is declared the winner at the end of the night. Like contestants one through three and five through seven, he is not someone I would go to bed with (if he is wise, he would not go to bed with me either), but there *have* been contestants in the past for whom I would willingly have sacrificed my right arm—nay, my entire body. One I remember was a gymnast from New Zealand. Others have included Chippendale dancers and porn stars such as Leo Ford and Jack Wrangler. But in general—and this is what you really want to know, you merciless things—the contestants at the End-up are hardly picture postcard perfect. Rather, they are about as attractive as the average Joe on the street: no more, no less. But they *are* superlative in one way: they are certainly far braver.

At contest's end I smile as a volunteer from the audience shoves $175 in cash down the front of number four's jockstrap, but secretly I am glad that my stepmother and my grandmother are not here to witness this (although I did bring my sister once, and she enjoyed it). It is not so much that I worry about what kind of image the contest would present to the outside community, but that there is something in the spectacle that I find inherently, if slightly, degrading. I look at these unclothed men parading in front of others, fully clothed and leering, and I am reminded of heterosexual wet T-shirt contests, which my feminist friends tell me (and I believe them) are a scourge and a blight upon the name of humanity. If my relatives could see the same thing, they would be reminded of something far worse: Sodom and Gomorrah, perhaps. Now, I don't give a fuck about Sodom and Gomorrah, but I do care about dignity, and I can't help wondering whether jockstrap contests are the surest path to self-respect.

If I am bothered by such questions, no one else seems to be. Naturally, neither of the show's cohosts sees the contest as the least bit degrading. They seem genuinely surprised that I even mention the matter, as if it is something they have not considered before. Although Johnson admits that he would not appear onstage in any other capacity than that in which he now serves, he says he might have done so ten years ago. "Degrading?" he ponders. "I don't think so. There are no put-ons, no fixes. Anybody can come out and win. The contest has been going on for fourteen years now, so we've gotta be doing something right."

Even if Johnson's response does not directly answer the question, I concede that perhaps my reservations are unwarranted. I am usually embarrassed and uncomfortable, I admit, only when the unattractive appear. I feel for them as I would feel for someone at a party with a lampshade on his head. When a chiseled god appears, however, I feel only lust—that and a bit of envy. But perhaps that is my problem and not theirs. At any rate, I suddenly realize that, in addition to the contest's stated purpose of providing a little "harmless" fun, it also serves a deeper need. Through a keyhole, it allows us to vent subliminal anxieties—it gives us a chance to appreciate what we have, be grateful for what we don't have, and long for what we might have—all in the name of fun.

Fun, after all (it bears repeating), is the bottom line at the aptly named Endup. "Did you have a good time?" Johnson asks the crowd as the deejay plays "Invitation To Dance." Few respond, although the smiles are broad and the answer is obvious. Perhaps they are taking the deejay's invitation seriously and are considering dancing in the next jockstrap contest two weeks hence. I can almost see it written on their faces: If *he* can do it . . .

27

SO LITTLE TIME

My Night with Kitten

DECEMBER 1985

THE OLDER I get, the more certain I am that straight people are as bizarre as—if not more bizarre than—the gay people I know. Take Joe Wheelan, for instance. He is a straight bartender at the restaurant where I work, a former punk rocker with a shaved head who thinks that Ronald Reagan is God's gift to America and that Andy Warhol's *Bad* is one of the greatest movies ever made. Nevertheless, despite his seeming contradictions and fascist political views, I admire Joe a great deal, partly because he is one of the few straight men I know who seems to have little problem relating to gay men. Beyond that, he is simply a nice guy.

I do find it hard to relate to him sometimes, however, such as the time a couple of months ago when Joe began raving about his favorite movie star, Miss Kitten Natividad.

"Kitten who?" I asked.

"Kitten Natividad," Joe answered, "the star of the great porn classic *Bodacious Ta-Tas*. I saw her perform the other night at the Mitchell Brothers, live and in person, and she was great."

"And just what does Miss Natividad do?"

"She dances."

"With or without her clothes on?"

"Both."

"And how much did you pay for this dubious pleasure?"

"Twenty bucks—and it was worth every penny. You really ought to see her, Mike. She's terrific."

Somehow I doubted I would think so, but everybody has a right to his or her own opinion, and far be it from me to criticize a friend for the perverted way in which he chooses to spend his time.

I didn't hear about Kitten again until one night a few weeks ago when Joe said to me, "Kitten's back in town, at the Market Street Cinema this time. Only eight bucks. Want to go?"

I paused. A thousand excuses ran through my head, but then I remembered that Joe and I had gone skydiving together twice two summers ago, and a bond such as that creates certain responsibilities that you don't take lightly. After a moment's hesitation, therefore, I agreed, but only after Joe promised to consider going with me someday to see the gay counterpart to Kitten Natividad: Rick "Humongous" Donovan, he of the "bodacious" pee-pee.

A few nights later I met Joe at Jack-in-the-Box on Seventh and Market, just up the street from the Market Street Cinema, where, over a generous helping of greasy fried chicken, Joe filled me in on Kitten's background. He had first seen her in Russ Meyer's *Super Vixens* years ago and later in *Beneath the Valley of the Ultra Vixens*. He became an instant and ardent admirer. It wasn't just her tits that attracted him—although they were a sizable attraction indeed (44DDD, to be precise)—it was her personality as well. "Kitten's articulate, aware, and polite," he said. "Plus she's got a great sense of humor. If she were a politician, she'd win on personality alone."

Kitten has starred in several other movies since her first two, including *My Tutor* and *Wildlife,* and an interesting facet of her movie career is that she does not allow penetration. "She has licked pussy, and she's had her pussy licked by other women on film," admitted Joe, "but there's no insertion. No, sir. Kitten's got class."

Perhaps Kitten's class is the reason why she was selected as Ms. Nude Universe or why Sean Penn chose her to dance at his stag party earlier this year, which resulted in a write-up and photo spread in *People* magazine. This kind of success hasn't spoiled Kitten, however, according to Joe. No way—she remains the same sweet girl she was years ago when Russ Meyer discovered her and turned her into "The Sex World's Biggest Star."

Breathless with anticipation, we entered the theater (impossible to miss—Live Nude Girls! blared the marquee) and seated ourselves in the third row. Onstage the show had already begun, but not with Kitten. No, some other woman with a nice body (but with tits like grapes compared with Kitten's) was dancing around a set decorated to look like a whore's bedroom—lots of red velvet and pink tulle, and rhinestones for days. This woman—Nicole it was—was buck naked except for a strand of imitation pearls and high heels, and her dancing consisted mainly of dropping to her hands and knees, sticking her butt up in the air, spreading her legs, and fingering herself for all the world to see.

I was amazed. "Has she no shame?" I asked Joe. "Thank *God* we didn't sit in the front row."

At last came the moment we were all awaiting. To the strains of "She's Got the Horse and I've Got the Saddle," Kitten—all 44DDD inches of her—strutted onstage wearing a floor-length see-through Frederick's of Hollywood dress slit up to there, high heels, and a black feather boa. All smiles, Kitten greeted the regulars in the audience, jiggled her tits, and began dancing. As Joe promised, Kitten had class—a lot more class than Nicole, certainly—and as she danced she kept up a steady stream of good-natured chatter.

"Look," she said, pointing to Joe's shaved head, "you've got one of my titties on your head."

Soon the see-through dress gave way to a sequined bra and panties and fishnet stockings, and before long that outfit gave way to nothing at all. Then Kitten got down and got dirty, somewhat like Nicole, but not quite so earnestly, I thought.

I turned and whispered to Joe, "Do people ever jerk off to this?"

"Please, Mike. This is like a meeting with the president. You *don't* take your tool out of your pants."

Just then a couple of stagehands dragged a plastic swimming pool onstage and Kitten stepped inside. To the tune of "Splish Splash, I Was Taking a Bath," Kitten poured water all over herself, soaped up, and scrubbed away with a long, stiff brush. Concentrating on certain parts of her body, Kitten looked at one man in the front row and cooed, "Ooh, did you make my pussy wet?" Suddenly she squeezed her thighs together, sending sprays of soapsuds into the audience.

After the bath Kitten took the mike and told us a little about herself. "My latest movie is a comedy," she said, "but then it would have to be, wouldn't it? Who could take tits as big as these seriously?"

Next she asked if anyone had any questions.

"Are they real?" shouted some entirely unoriginal clod.

"Of course!" Kitten beamed. "Every inch."

No one else had any questions, so Kitten wished us a good night and said, "Thank you for coming, and if you have to, please jerk off to me."

As the announcer told us to stick around for the other dancers—"We got lots and lots of tits for you here at Market Street Cinema"—Kitten moved into the lobby to autograph pictures and to meet her fans. For only ten dollars she posed topless with one star-struck couple (a man and a woman, no less), who seemed to be interested in a great deal more than just Kitten's photograph and a few minutes of chit-chat. They were wasting their time. I had known Kitten only a few brief moments, and already I knew that she would *never* agree to what they had in mind.

"You're in such great shape," said the man, desperate to prolong the fleeting contact. "Do you work out?"

"Oh yes, I exercise regularly," Kitten purred.

"Yeah, well, it shows."

"Christ," I thought, "get him out of here." But I said nothing. Instead I browsed through Kitten's promotional literature and learned that this visit to San Francisco was part of her fall tour. Kitten was here direct from Dayton, Ohio, and New York, New York. I also learned that for only six dollars (five dollars plus one dollar postage and handling) I could become a member of the Kitten Fan Klub. This would entitle me to an official membership certificate, one autographed topless eight-by-ten glossy, the *Kitten Klub News/Update*, and a 10 percent discount on the following Kitten kollectibles: Kitten Video Kassettes, Kitten Fantasy Polaroids, the Kitten Kalendar, and the *Kitten Autobiography*.

I nudged Joe. "Such a deal!" I said. But Joe only shrugged. Perhaps he was already a member.

Finally Kitten's fans cleared out, and Joe and I asked for her autograph. "To Mike. Busting with love and kisses for you," Kitten wrote across the top of the picture she gave to me, and I left the theater on Kloud Nine.

"Do you think we can come back sometime?" I asked Joe.

"Sure, kid," he answered.

"And what about Rick Donovan?"

"Who?"

"You know—Humongous. Joe, you promised."

Joe bit his lip. "Yeah, well, I don't know, Mike. Maybe. We'll see."

That's the trouble with straight people. Even the best of 'em let you down. I nearly join the Kitten Klub, and Joe won't even give Humongous a chance. They're bizarre, I'm telling you—bizarre.

VICTIMS OF LOVE

They Do, They Do—
But Would You?

JUNE 1985

IN MANY WAYS it was the most traditional of weddings. Banks of white gladiolas beneath rows of the purest white candles decorated the altar of the cavernous Gothic sanctuary. While the organist in the balcony above the sanctuary played airs by Bach and Pacabel, below, ushers and usherettes dressed in white led guests to pews bedecked with white ribbons. The mother of the groom, resplendent in pink, was the last to be seated, just before the wedding party, all in white, marched up the aisle with slow, measured steps. In the pulpit the minister stood waiting, a beatific smile above his white tuxedo. But when at last he greeted the happy couple, nary a veil—white or any other color—was in sight, for at the altar stood not bride and groom, but groom and groom. It was a logical, though hardly traditional, climax to this particular boy meets boy story.

"Why do you want to go to a gay wedding?" a friend at work asked when he heard that I was planning to attend the nuptials of Ray Hollaway, a young waiter at Castro Gardens Restaurant, and his beloved, Vern Black, an "awareness counselor" who once had worked with Werner Erhard.

"Come on, it'll be the hoot of the year," I replied, ever my romantic, sensitive self.

"I doubt it," my friend scoffed. "But have fun anyway."

Fun was exactly what I intended to have. Because I did not know either of the betrothed very well, I had no idea that I was supposed to take the event seriously. But once I arrived at the church, it quickly became apparent that this wedding, although a joyous occasion, was no laughing matter. After all, you don't spend this kind of dough if you're not serious about the consequences.

To my relief, and, I confess, my amusement, the ceremony was not as traditional as the setting. When the minister, Matt Garrigan, asked us to close our eyes, put our hands over our hearts, and "create a space for Ray and Vern to come into that's full of love, joy, and happiness," I knew we were in the hands of no strait-laced conservative. Matt, whose enthusiasm and energy nearly leaped from the pulpit, spoke of Ray and Vern not as spouses but as "committed life mates," and he charged them to "tell the truth, go for results, maintain your freedom of choice, keep all your agreements," and more. In addition, he spoke a great deal about "ecstasy," something my Southern Methodist preacher back home never mentioned, certainly not before a wedding night, for God's sake; he also referred to "the angels of the Greater Light," beings I have yet to meet.

Ray and Vern departed from tradition too, when they promised to trust each other and to bring each other ecstasy rather than to honor and obey. True, they did exchange rings, but they also exchanged crystals, "a symbol of the energy force that is created by our uniting our energies." (Vern's crystal was placed on a gold chain around his neck; Ray's was mounted on a leather thong.) Unlike the procedure at other weddings, at this one vows were timed to be spoken just before 6:20 P.M., a time selected by the couple's astrologer, and when Ray and Vern were pronounced "committed life mates," it was not in the name of God, but "according to the laws of our hearts, minds, and souls." Nevertheless, even at this wedding more than one motherly soul shed tears.

"So, what did you think?" I asked a fellow guest after the ceremony while standing in line to sign the guest register.

"I don't know. I came here thinking it was all kind of silly, but I really got into it."

"Wasn't it beautiful?" beamed a lovely, well-dressed woman who earlier had leaned over to me and said, "I give it three months." Now she confided, "I just love weddings."

After the inevitable and interminable delay while the wedding party posed for pictures, the guests were ushered through a formal receiving line into a reception hall, where champagne and cake awaited them. And what a cake: a dazzling affair of columns, pink roses, and white swans arranged on four magnificent tiers, topped by two tuxedoed grooms! It was a cake worthy of princes—or princesses—and it was served on delicate napkins imprinted with the grooms' names, the date, and the phrase, And This Our Life, Our Beginning.

At the reception a friend of one of the grooms sang a sea chanty titled "Peter the Pig," and Ray and Vern thanked everybody under the sun, including the photographer, the florist, the astrologer, and every member of the wedding party. Then Vern turned to the crowd and said, "Ray and I have given you our convictions, our feelings, and our love. . . . You could have ridiculed us and you didn't. You came instead to share your love with us. . . . And for that Ray and I thank you from the bottoms of our hearts."

Naturally I felt like a viper in their midst, but not for long, for even I—cynical old *moi*—was beginning to admire the obvious sincerity of everyone present, and, in any case, this speech was soon followed by the cutting of the cake. Like other newlyweds, Ray and Vern couldn't resist shoving cake in each other's faces, but, unlike others, these two also licked it off. Then they ran off under a shower of birdseed (more ecologically correct than rice) to a waiting limousine, which whisked them to their honeymoon suite in the city, chosen by friends and unknown to them.

After a three-week honeymoon in Hawaii, Ray and Vern, who had been lovers off and on for more than six years, tried to explain to me at their home why they had at last decided to get married. Throughout our conversation Vern continually referred to something called the integrity tone scale, which he had invented and had posted on the wall of his office. At the top of the chart were the words, Be Committed—words I was to hear again and again during the next hour and a half.

"[Getting married] was what I wanted. Short-term commitments were a cop-out," said Ray, who twice before had entered into periods of commitment with Vern, one for three months and the other for a year. For one thing, it made it easier to clear up misunderstandings, he explained. When you realized there was no backing out, you *had* to talk.

Vern agreed and added that, according to his philosophy of things, there are two phases we go through: a youth phase, when it is important "to experience all kinds of things in order to determine who you are," and an adult phase. His own youth phase lasted until he was past forty. Then he realized "that wasn't what I wanted anymore. . . . I had had enough experience to say, 'More dick, more sex, more this, more that, is not going to give me any more than I already have. I'm done with it.' . . . The terror of the next phase," he continued, "is that you then pick one person. It's what you want, and yet it's terrifying . . . because what you feel you've done is [that you've] closed off spontaneity, freedom of choice. . . . It took us two years to realize that we were ready to go over the terror of that threshold and move into the adult phase."

When questioned how they could be sure that the youth phase was indeed over and that the marriage would endure, Ray offered the following evidence as proof: "Making the [previous] commitments demonstrated to each other that we could keep our commitments, because we did, completely." Added Vern, the relationship will last because "it has already gone through all the trials that I can see would destroy a relationship—not that there won't be more . . . but I think it's the first eight or ten trials that are the hardest. . . . If you get through them, the rest of them will be easy."

Ray and Vern have learned to overcome those trials by requiring "amendments" of one another or to avoid the trials altogether by allowing room for differences. One such difference that might have led to problems in another relationship concerned the nature of the wedding. Although Vern, who said that he leads with his head and that Ray leads with his heart, admitted that he would not have suggested such a formal and traditional public wedding on his own, he willingly acceded to Ray's wishes in the matter. It was Ray who desired the hoopla. "I'm a very ritual oriented person," said Ray, who described himself as an "enlightened" Mormon. "I was raised with that stuff. If Mormonism sells one thing, it's family, it's relationship. So my culture, my background, is steeped in that, and I love it."

Vern noted, "We're steeped in tradition from the day that we're born . . . and my feeling is that you cannot experience ecstasy in a relationship unless you allow yourself to be who you have learned to be. . . . For Ray and I to have sat down and privately committed ourselves to each other for the rest of our lives wouldn't have been the same. It wouldn't have satisfied that part of us that lies dormant in the subconscious. Therefore, we would have been ripping off some of our capacity for ecstasy."

"It would have been like hiding for us," concluded Ray.

They cautioned, however, that despite its public nature, their wedding was not meant to be a gay political affair, but merely a gathering of friends, most of whom were other awareness counselors, 80 percent straight and 65 percent women. "We did not get married to make any kind of statement," avowed Vern. "It's not about the church . . . or the state. . . . It's not about trying to change what's going on out there. I just want Ray and I and our relationship to be ecstatic, and if out of that ecstasy changes occur . . . I would be very happy to see that."

The kind of changes Vern would most like to see, however, are not political but personal ones. As Matt Garrigan noted during the wedding ceremony, "The purpose of your commitment is to create an ecstatic relationship to empower others to uncover more of whom they are." Does this mean that Ray and Vern try to lead others to commitment, recommend marriage for others?

"Oh, definitely," said Ray. "I think it's necessary. I think it's an experience that people miss out on if they don't take this course."

"I absolutely recommend it to everybody, yes," agreed Vern, "but I know that 90 percent of the population can't handle it, that . . . they won't really be committed. . . . My whole life and all of my work is about moving people, by way of the counseling, up to where they can be committed. . . . So I recommend it, but I say to people, 'Qualify yourself. Get your life together.' "

I left Ray and Vern with a greater understanding of and respect for the depth of their commitment, and on the way home I made a mental note to say a few words about homophobia and broadening one's horizons to my friend at work, gay himself, who had scoffed at the idea of a gay wedding. Nevertheless, I heaved a sigh of relief when I walked through my door—*alone*—that afternoon, and I made no immediate plans to rush down to Macy's to register for a china or crystal pattern of my own. Even if I wanted a husband, there's none in sight, and it's just as well. White is not my best color.

37

SO LITTLE TIME

On Being Single

DECEMBER 1985

AN ACQUAINTANCE I rarely see came up to me on the street the other day and asked, "So who are you dating these days?"

"Nobody," I replied.

"Nobody?" he echoed, aghast. "You *never* have a boyfriend, Mike. What's wrong with you, anyway?"

What's wrong with me? Nothing—not that I am aware of, at any rate, other than a blackened front tooth—the result of a waterskiing accident this summer. But that alone shouldn't explain why I can't attract or hold a man—which is what my friend is implying when he asks what's wrong with *me*.

Actually, the reason why I can't attract or hold a man is that I don't try very hard to meet a man in the first place. I never go out anymore—not for that purpose, anyway—and when I do, I become so uncomfortable with once-familiar mating rituals that I leave the bar (or wherever) in exasperation and disgust. It's not that I don't see anyone I like. I do, I do. It's just that it's been so long since I've tried to pick anyone up that I've forgotten how to do it. Besides, who's got the time or patience?

AIDS has a lot to do with it, of course. Once promiscuity was the main way I met potential boyfriends. Now that promiscuity is a thing of the past (indeed, the very phrase, "tried to pick anyone up," has a quaint, archaic ring to it), I am left high and dry with few alternative paths to matrimony. Had I listened to Mom and saved myself for marriage rather than giving it away for free, perhaps I would have learned some of the skills necessary to attract a man without sex. But, slut that I am, I threw myself into the fray and learned an entirely different set of skills—an education that is useless to me now, when I have only my videotape machine and a few nasty tapes for company.

Perhaps I'm selling myself short. I *do* know ways to meet men other than to thrust myself upon them in Buena Vista Park, after all, and periodically I will pull out all the stops and conduct a full-scale husband hunt. But when I do my efforts invariably prove fruitless. I'll meet someone in the gym, say, or . . . well, the gym, and I'll ask him out. He'll say yes, and we'll have a great time together, even if we don't have sex. Then I'll start building airy fantasies of our future life together. ("Dave and Mike," I'll write, or "Mike and Doug" or "Patrick and Mike": I like to see how the names will look on the wedding invitation.) But then he'll tell me about this other man he just met who is too perfect to be believed, or he'll remember an article I wrote years ago about the rather impressive list of diseases I've had, and that will be that. The romance—if romance it ever was—will be over.

My friends are no help whatsoever. You'd think that if they had any concept of true friendship, they'd help me find a husband by setting me up with other friends of theirs. But no: they're so busy destroying their relationships that they don't have time to help me build one. Wait, I take that back. I forgot Miss P. He brought a friend of his to the gym once to meet me, but it was a disaster. True, the man had tits as big as a house, but he had an ego the size of a barn and a brain the size of a pea: not my type at all. In recompense, Miss P. invited me to meet another friend over coffee and "I Love Lucy" reruns at the friend's house. At first I accepted, but then I thought better of it. Did I really want to fall in love with a man who spent his mornings drinking coffee and watching "I Love Lucy"—or with a man who had a friend named Miss P. in the first place?

Actually, I did have a lover once upon a time. (Time out for definitions here: a lover, to me, is someone a] with whom you live, and b] with whom you plan to spend the rest of your life. Of course, some of my friends have planned to spend the rest of their lives with ten or twelve different people, but not me. I take this love business far more seriously than that.) Anyway, I did have a lover once upon a time, but he was a jerk. Unfortunately, it took me a year to figure that out and another year to leave him, and when I did, I vowed, "Never again." I was bitter, disillusioned, and determined to protect myself from the emotional trauma that serious relationships always seemed to involve.

It took a while, but after a few years of independence—years that took their toll physically rather than emotionally—I finally decided to settle down again. As it happens, I was dating two people at the time—a thirty-one-year-old actor and a twenty-three-year-old porn star—and they actually had the nerve to ask me to choose between them. (Can you believe it?) I opted to go for experience and stability rather than for perfect physical beauty and so chose the older of the two, but as soon as I did, he unleashed months of suppressed resentment and paid me back by promptly deserting me. Ah, me: true love once again eluded my grasp.

You know, if the truth be told, despite years of making a god of love and despite the things I say here, I'm not sure that romance and relationships are really all they're cracked up to be. There is certainly something to be said for being single. My friend Rick, in fact, recently sat down and made a list of all the advantages he found in being single:

1. He doesn't have to worry anymore whom his lover is fucking behind his back.

2. He doesn't have to spend a lot of money on outrageously expensive Christmas gifts.

3. And he doesn't have to wonder whose turn it is to do the laundry this week; it's always his turn.

These are negative virtues, however, and there *are* positive ones. Since I've been single, I've found I have much more time for good friends. I also have more time to pursue the things I like to do: nights at the ballet rather than at movies such as *Godzilla 1985,* trips to Alpine Meadows rather than to the I-Beam, and quiet moments spent reading rather than hallucinating. Furthermore, my "career" is progressing much faster now that I have the time to devote to it. It's hard to write Pulitzer material encumbered by a lover interested only in something baser: sex.

Still, I do get lonely sometimes, and there are nights when I think it would be nice to come home to a pair of warm, loving arms rather than to a cold, empty apartment. Despite the compromises that must be made in a relationship, there is something about the idea of a shared life that I find particularly attractive. But as I'm usually perfectly content with things as they are, I'm not going to waste a lot of time wishing I were part of a twosome, especially when I'm not sure that that goal is at all practical or realistic for me. And I'm certainly not going to make an attempt to answer my friend's question. What's wrong with me? Puh-leeze. It's those potential husbands out there who need to come around, not me. Until I find one who likes the things I like but who still has the good sense to leave me alone half the time, I'll be more than happy to pay the rent by myself.

"With an attitude like that, girl," Miss P. said the other day, "you ain't gettin' nobody."

Maybe not, but fuck it: life's too short to compromise.

Stewing for Love

JULY 1987

I'M NOT VERY good at giving dinner parties, for lots of reasons. For one, I don't really have the facilities. I have no dining room, and the table where I eat is crammed into a corner of the kitchen, an arm's reach from the stove and refrigerator. It's cozy, but hardly elegant; quaint, but not quite roomy. Being able to sauté, serve, and savor without leaving my chair is not a skill that many dinner guests appreciate.

Furthermore, my schedule is hardly conducive to entertaining. Because I work in a restaurant four nights a week and eat out two of the others, the refrigerator is usually unstocked, the larder eternally bare. A trip to the store takes forever and costs a fortune. If I buy groceries for two for one night only, I spend fifty dollars. If I don't, I have nothing to offer but Bran Chex.

Finally, as a chef, I have little experience or imagination. With so little time to cook, and so little practice, I can never decide what to serve or how to serve it. In desperation I fall back upon my one tried-and-true resource, *The Joy of Cooking* (the one my sister inscribed, "For a better bachelor life," thirteen years ago). When that fails me, I turn to an even more dependable guide: the takeout menu from Marcello's Pizza or Hunan on Haight.

I do, however, have the inclination to cook. Even though they are time consuming, troublesome, and expensive, dinner parties, I have found, are a delightful way to celebrate old friends and to make new ones. For the old friends I usually dispense with the formalities and serve spaghetti on the living room floor. For the new ones I try a little harder. I figure I might as well. One of my chief reasons for having dinner parties, you see, is that they are about the only way I have to get laid anymore. And although there are more important matters in life than getting laid, it's still a nice thing to do after the sun goes down.

My first effort in seduction through food was to wine and dine a twenty-four-year-old investment broker whom I had met at an awards ceremony weeks before. Although I usually don't go for brokers, I went for this one, and when a mutual friend assured me that the youngster had been wanting to meet me for ages, I assumed that sex was a foregone conclusion.

Unfortunately, we didn't get together for a few weeks, and by the time we did, things had changed somewhat. I had bought an elegant bottle of wine and cooked steak *au poivre*, but midway through the soup course, my guest informed me that since I had seen him last he had fallen madly in love and had moved in with someone else.

"Does that mean that after dinner you're going home to him?" I asked incredulously.

"Guess so," he replied.

I nearly grabbed the soup spoon out of his hand and shouted, "Then why am I cooking for you? Get the hell out of my house!" Luckily, I remembered one of the first obligations of a host—be charming—and continued with the meal.

The next week I tried again, this time with a different cookbook, *The San Francisco Dinner Party Cookbook,* and a different guest. For Carlo, the twenty-two-year-old waiter who was supposedly straight, I bought *two* bottles of wine and cooked lamb curry—a riskier selection, true, but if he really was straight, then I had nothing to lose.

Carlo arrived at 8:00 P.M and stayed until 2:00 A.M. I told him my life story, which took twenty minutes. He told me his, which covered a period half as long, but took two hours to relate. I was happy to indulge him, however, for I was waiting for the good parts, the true confessions, which I was sure were forthcoming. Alas, I was mistaken.

"You mean you really never have been to bed with a man—and never intend to?" I asked.

"That's right," he replied.

I heaved a sigh and mentioned something about the time. Carlo got the point and made his farewell. Before going to bed, I eyed a leftover cucumber in the refrigerator lovingly, but decided against it. I could wait at least one more week.

The third time is the charmer, they say, and I believe them. Out of the blue one day, while I was fixing chili (a proletarian meal, if ever there was one), an old boyfriend showed up and accepted my invitation to dinner. I had no fancy wine this time, no planned menu or complicated recipe. Oddly enough, I didn't need them. My friend enjoyed the meal, but enjoyed me more (or so I presumed). He even spent the night and enjoyed Bran Chex the next morning. And all this cost me little effort and no subterfuge. It gave me—dare I say it?—food for thought.

I will continue to give dinner parties, of course, regardless of the consequences. Practice makes perfect, and if I don't become an accomplished roué, I may at least learn to prepare a decent roux. Neither skill is something Mother ever taught me.

Going to the Chapel

MARCH 1988

ORDINARILY I DON'T ask boyfriends to marry me after three and a half months, but this one, Mark, was leaving for a new job in Chicago in a week, and I had to think of some way to bind him to me. Besides, we were spending the weekend in South Lake Tahoe, skiing with my sister and her husband, and I was inspired not only by the magnificent mountain scenery but also by the multitude of prefab, minimal-gab wedding chapels. Romance was clearly in the air. If ever there was a place to pop the question, I thought, this is it.

Suspicious that he was being used as fodder for yet another newspaper article, Mark was less than enthusiastic about the prospect of getting hitched, but at least agreed to tour the chapels. We chose as our first stop Love's Wedding Chapel on the Nevada side of the border. We were drawn primarily by the white dove and cross featured on the brightly lit road sign—but intimidated by the group of good old boys drinking beer in the dimly lit parking lot.

Fortunately, one of the local boys proved to be an employee of the place as well as an affable and eager source of information. Ushering us past the sign in the foyer, Rice Is Sold in the Flower Shop, he showed us the chapel, where a ceramic Jesus welcomed us with open arms in front of an altar covered with plastic flowers, bedecked with candy cane–striped ribbons, and bordered by electric candelabras.

The minimum fee to exchange vows in this bower of bliss, explained our host, Scott, was $55, which included the minister's fee—"although you can go as high as $300 for the deluxe wedding ceremony, which includes flowers, pictures, a videotape of the proceedings, and tips." There was an additional $27 fee for a license, which had to be obtained in Reno, Carson City, or the county seat, Minden. "But although you have to go to the courthouse," continued Scott, "there is no blood test or waiting period required."

When Mark asked, "Do you ever marry gay people?" Scott looked surprised for a moment, but quickly recovered and replied, "We don't allow it here." He pointed out that gay marriages were not legal in the state of Nevada, although he did not know whether they were specifically illegal. "In any case," he said, "the minister sets all the rules."

The minister, as it happened, was a certain Reverend Love, and he had owned and operated Love's Chapel as a family business for more than twenty years. Exactly what *kind* of minister he was remained a mystery to Scott: "Protestant, I believe."

Thanking Scott for his time, we decided to inspect at least one chapel on the California side. The next morning, therefore, we stopped at Wedding World, right next door to Chapel of the Bells and down the street from Amour du Lac. Parking the car next to a bed of pink plastic poinsettias planted at Ye Olde Outside Chapel, we entered the Swiss Chalet Wedding Chapel and introduced ourselves to Mary, the receptionist.

Unlike Scott, Mary was a no-nonsense functionary with the sense of humor of a fire hydrant. (Mark later described her as an "indomitable bachelorette.") Mary explained to us that at Wedding World, licenses cost $41 and the chapel rented for between $36 and $100. There was also the minister to consider. "We don't like the word *fee,*" said Mary. But according to a sign on her desk, "A donation envelope will be passed at the conclusion of the ceremony."

The minister who performed services at Wedding World was the Reverend Blaine Bender, a "Christian" minister who was ordained in the Reformed Latter Day Saints faith in 1936. "He is a *Reformed* Latter Day Saint," noted Mary. "He is not a Mormon." Although Mary seemed to imply by this that he was not a self-righteous reactionary, neither was he a trail-blazing reformer. Like Reverend Love, he had never performed a gay or lesbian marriage—at least not at Wedding World.

This does not mean that Wedding World has not been the site of homosexual matrimonials. "We do not provide them with documentation," said Mary, "for the ceremony is not recognized by the laws of the state or in the eyes of God, but we do occasionally allow them in the chapel to exchange meaningful vows—to reaffirm their love and devotion. This has happened twice since I've been here. Both ceremonies were performed by the previous minister, a Wesleyan Methodist. Why do you ask? Are the two of you contemplating marriage?"

"We're thinking about it," Mark answered.

"Then would you like to see our chapel?"

"Yes, but first we'd like to check on the baby. He's asleep in the car."

The baby was my nephew, whom we were watching while my sister and her husband skied. We did not explain this to Mary, however, who, for all I knew, may have assumed that this was a shotgun marriage due to the kid. Whatever she thought, Mary only smiled and said, "How nice. How old is he?"

"Two years," said Mark.

"Eighteen months," said I.

"Hmmm," said Mary.

The chapel was a barren, utilitarian affair, with fake stained glass behind the pulpit, metal folding chairs, and the ubiquitous plastic flowers. Aghast, Mark and I quickly made our excuses and beat a hasty retreat. Resisting the urge to inspect any more chapels, we drove back to the city and temporarily abandoned all thoughts of a High Sierra alliance.

"Tell you what," concluded Mark a few days later. "You find an Elvis impersonator for a minister, and I'll go back. Otherwise, it's ta-ta Tahoe."

"And nay to the nuptials?"

"You got it, honey."

Mark, I have decided, may not deserve me. Sometimes he's nothing but a hound dog.

OBJECTS OF LUST

Wally, I Want You

MARCH 1985

ALL KIDS HAVE heroes. When I was growing up in the late 1950s and early 1960s, those heroes came largely from the TV shows my friends and I watched. Most of my friends idolized James Arness, Sky King, or one of the guys on "Combat," the war show. I, on the other hand, idolized the gorgeous young teenagers who appeared on the so-called family shows, the ones who supposedly represented clean-cut, all-American virtues, but who for me represented pure, unadulterated lust. You know, guys such as David Nelson of "The Adventures of Ozzie and Harriet," whom Boyd McDonald in *Christopher Street* calls "one of Hollywood's premier suck objects. . . . Simply by giving men the right kind of look with his jewel-like eyes," McDonald writes, "David could, had he wanted, have spent his life being licked."

Whether David Nelson would have appreciated such attention, I have no idea. All I know is that when I was a kid, I would have loved to give it to him. There were others as well, guys such as his brother, Ricky; Paul Peterson (Jeff Stone on "The Donna Reed Show," not to be confused with porn star Jeff Stone, who currently appears in *The Punishment of Gary Wilde* on Broadway at Forty-ninth in New York City); Billy Gray (Bud Anderson on "Father Knows Best"); gorgeous Don Grady (the middle son on "My Three Sons," the one with the ripe, sensuous lips); and, of course, Tony Dow, Beaver's older brother.

These young men had much in common. They all had wholesome good looks, sunny dispositions, and beautiful bodies (what I could see of them, at any rate, which admittedly wasn't much). I liked to think of them as my older brothers, and I pictured myself alone in the bedroom with them, or, better yet, in the bathroom. They would shave, clad only in a towel, while I watched, and afterward perhaps they would show me how to catch a baseball—a skill I never did master.

There was another closer to my own age I used to adulate, a choice that may be surprising. This was Jay North, the irrepressible Dennis the Menace. (He was born in 1951; I was born in 1952.) Although Jay's sexual attraction may be described as vanilla at best, I think it was his hair that intrigued me. Jay had beautiful, luxuriant, silken hair that fell across his forehead caressingly. To Jay I owe my lifelong addiction to blonds, who, if Dennis the Menace is any example, do indeed have more fun.

I have often wondered what has happened to these young actors since making their impact on impressionable boys such as myself. Where are they now? What have they done since their TV shows were canceled? As they wandered into obscurity and middle age, did they lose the boyish charms that had so attracted me? More to the point, would I still want to do it with them? And, what I really want to know, could I? 'Fess up, girls: which ones are queer?

We all know what Ricky Nelson is doing these days: still making mediocre records and megabucks in LA. To some he is gorgeous, I suppose, but I liked him better when he was young, and besides, it doesn't make much difference. The man, according to all accounts, is straight. God only knows where his brother, David, is, and of Paul Peterson and Don Grady I could learn nothing.

Thanks to the wave of "Beaver" mania that is currently sweeping the nation, however, Tony Dow is still very much in the news. It wasn't that way in the years immediately following the 1963 cancellation of "Beaver," unfortunately. Although Tony did manage to land a few guest appearances on other shows, as well as a continuing role on the soap opera "Never Too Young" in the mid-1960s, National Guard duty temporarily put an end to his career. Guard duty was followed by journalism school, construction work, and sculpting. Eventually Tony launched a show biz comeback by appearing with Barbara Billingsley (June Cleaver) in a production of *Come Blow Your Horn,* and in 1979 and 1980 he toured the country with Jerry Mathers, the Beav himself, in the play *So Long Stanley*.

These pseudo-"Beaver" connections finally led to full-fledged "Beaver" cast reunions on "Good Morning America," "The Match Game/Hollywood Squares Hour," and "Family Feud," and in March 1983 Tony fulfilled his destiny by costarring in the two-hour TV drama "Still The Beaver"—not exactly a critical blockbuster, but certainly no bomb with the public. In this show, alas, Tony was not only married but impotent as well; nevertheless, the show's popularity was so great that it was picked up by the Disney channel as a weekly series on cable TV. Wallyphiles, rejoice.

According to Irwyn Applebaum in his book *The World According to Beaver* (from which I obtained most of the preceding information), Tony Dow was originally chosen for his role because he was a "good-looking, clean-cut, athletic boy with tremendous ability as a swimmer and diver. He had a natural appeal which played well with Jerry." (I'll bet.) Later, in a description that says as much about Applebaum as it does about Tony, Applebaum states that Tony had "a good head on his shoulders, strong muscles in his arms, good hands, and an almost sweetly shy personality." (Good hands?) Applebaum is particularly interested in the relationship between the two boys. He quotes Beaver as stating, "You know somethin', Wally, I'd rather do nothin' with you than somethin' with anybody else," and he asks, "Why do the boys share a bedroom since the house has a spare guest room?" Applebaum does not say, however, that either Tony Dow or the character he plays is gay. In fact, he takes pains to point out that Tony has been married twice and has a ten-year-old son. If it is any consolation, though, according to Applebaum, Tony "is still in great physical shape" and goes swimming, surfing, or "boogey-boarding" near his home in Venice, California, almost every day. At least the man has retained his interest in water sports.

(Note to Wallyphiles: In *The World According to Beaver,* there is a picture of young Wally shirtless that is a must-see. But do not look for it in the San Francisco Public Library's copy of the book. Someone else has already ripped it out.)

Although Billy Gray wasn't quite as cute as Tony (to me, at any rate), if film credits mean anything, he was a much more successful child actor. Editor John T. Weaver in *Forty Years of Screen Credits* lists eighteen films for Billy from 1943, when he was five years old, to 1962, when he was twenty-four, among them *The Day the Earth Stood Still* and *Some Like It Hot*. The one that interests me most is *All I Desire* (1953)—for obvious reasons. (What exactly *did* Billy desire?) Billy's greatest claim to fame, however, is not his various movie roles but the part of Bud Anderson on "Father Knows Best," a role he landed in 1954, when he was sixteen. The show lasted nine years, but was Billy grateful for the steady employment? Hardly. In *Whatever Became Of?,* Richard Lamparski says that after its demise Billy called the show "an embarrassment from the beginning. . . . I'm so ashamed that I had any part in all that. I wish there was some way I could tell kids not to believe it."

In 1962 Billy was stopped on suspicion of drunk driving by the police, who found marijuana seeds and stems (horrors!) under the front seat of his car. He was given a three-month jail sentence and a three-year probation period as a result. Needless to say, Hollywood wouldn't touch him after that. Only two movies in twenty years followed, *Dusty and Sweets McGee* (1971), in which he played—what else?—a drug dealer, and a "Father Knows Best" reunion special in 1979. Nevertheless, Billy still considers himself an actor.

In the 1973 edition of *Whatever Became Of?* Billy is pictured shirtless at his home in Topanga Canyon. His long, scraggly hair reaching past his nipples is excessive, even for the period, but oh, those nipples! His beautiful, tight body begs attention. We are told, however, that he has been married and divorced. That the divorce means anything significant is doubtful, for in the 1982 edition of the same book, we are informed that Billy remarried in 1981. Sigh. Oh, well, at forty-four years of age (in 1982) the man was still attractive. And, if it is any consolation (which seems to be the only pleasure we get in these matters), Billy has a great fondness for motorcycles. Those who wait for him to appear on Folsom Street on one of his bikes, however, are doomed to disappointment. I doubt his wife would approve of it.

It would be hard to picture Jay North riding a motorcycle at all, unless he was pulling a fast one on Mr. Wilson, out of control and wreaking havoc left and right in Mr. Wilson's living room. Jay was hardly the leather/Folsom/biker type. But he *was* a little cutie, and I suppose that's what Hank Ketcham, the comic strip author, thought when he *personally* selected Jay from a field of five hundred boys to play the part of Dennis the Menace on the TV series, which debuted in 1959. Perhaps Ketcham was impressed by Jay's initial TV appearance on "Queen for a Day": who can say? Whatever the reason, Jay landed the plum role and television history was made. (All this according to Lamparski in *Whatever Became Of?* and embellished by *moi*.)

The series didn't last long. Four years later "Dennis" was off the air, and twelve-year-old Jay was looking for a job. In 1965 he found one in the movie *Zebra in the Kitchen*. This was followed by a role in *Maya* (1966), a movie about two mostly naked young boys (one white, one brown) who roamed the jungles of India astride an elephant. *Maya* the movie was turned into "Maya" the TV series, the cause of many a hard-on on Colebridge Road, Atlanta, Georgia, I can assure you—but not for long, for "Maya" was canceled after only one season.

After a long dry spell there was little else for Jay in the show biz world but porn, and in 1974 he appeared in the R-rated film *The Teacher*. Later he toured in the plays *Butterflies Are Free* and—are you ready?—*Norman, Is That You?* (Two guesses what role he played. No, not Norman: Norman's boyfriend.) Once again, alas, military duty intervened to inhibit a star's career. In 1977 Jay joined the Navy. After his hitch in the service he returned to acting, but he has made only one movie since then, a TV movie called *Scout's Honor,* in which he co-starred with—gasp!—Paul Peterson of "The Donna Reed Show."

Despite his roles in *Norman* and *Scout's Honor,* there is little to indicate that Jay is anything but a closet case—and a fascist closet case at that. For a while he was married to a Playboy bunny. At present he lives alone in a condo in Sherman Oaks. According to Lamparski, he describes himself as "real conservative in every way—a square." Not only does he dislike drugs, long hair on men, and rock and roll, he advocates the death penalty for drug dealing as well. Too bad. But then, what does it matter? Of all my adolescent heroes, Jay has aged the poorest. She ain't even cute anymore. In fact, the girl's a mess.

You know, there *were* a few young stars of the TV shows of my childhood who did not attract me. I'd like to make this clear so that it is evident that I do have *some* taste. Bob Denver was one: Maynard G. Krebs of "The Dobie Gillis Show." Rusty Hamer was another, Danny Thomas's obnoxious brat on "Make Room for Daddy." Topping the list, not surprisingly, was Ken Weatherwax, Pugsley on "The Addams Family." I'd also like to point out that my fondness for adolescents has abated somewhat over the years. The last one I liked (and I'm almost ashamed to admit it) was Christopher Knight, who played Peter Brady, the middle son on "The Brady Bunch." It's just as well, for what was once an attraction for older men would now be chicken lust. My friend John, for instance, tends to drool over Michael J. Fox, the youthful star of today's "Family

Ties," an attraction I find most unbecoming. It is wise, I tell him, to remember his age, as well as the age-of-consent laws in the state of California.

I still don't know much about the whereabouts or sexual inclinations of Paul Peterson or gorgeous Don Grady, but I don't suppose it matters. Neither is likely to invite me to his house for supper. And if either did, would I still want to go? Unlikely. I think I prefer watching them on syndicated reruns instead, ever youthful, ever radiant. There is something to be said for longings unfulfilled, for dreams that never die. Like Beaver, I too would sometimes rather do nothin' with Wally than somethin' with anybody else.

By the way, if anybody finds out what son of a bitch stole that picture of Wally in *The World According to Beaver,* please let me know. I'm still pissed that he beat me to it.

You Got My Number: Obscene Telephone Calls

OCTOBER 1986

THE VOICE WAS matter of fact, direct—yet there was an intensity, an edge, to it. "Do you like to beat off?" the anonymous caller asked. "Would you like to beat off with me?"

The first time he phoned, I was amused and flattered. Like most egoists, I assumed that the call had been placed deliberately rather than randomly. The caller must have seen my picture or read one of my articles somewhere, I reasoned, and fallen in love with me. Why else would he go to such lengths to whisper sweet nothings in my ear? Consequently, although I had no intention of acceding to his request, I answered as politely as I could. "Why, yes, I do like to beat off," I said, "but not this early on a Saturday morning, and certainly not with someone I may or may not know. Thanks, anyway."

Perhaps I was too polite, for the next Saturday morning he called again. "Do you like to beat off?" he asked. This time I was less amused, especially because his call had interrupted me in the middle of a dream. I had been just about to go over Niagara Falls, and Patrick Swayze was trying desperately to save me.

Taking a sarcastic (if unoriginal) approach, therefore, I snapped, "I'd love to, darlin', but I just washed my hair." I considered an uglier line: "I'd love to, darlin', but at the moment I'm suffering from a nasty herpes outbreak at the base of my dick." But, for all I know, that might just have excited him more. There are some sick queens in this town, after all, and at least the hair-washing line was safe (if corny).

The third time he called, I sighed, "Don't you ever give up?" He didn't. The fourth time, I simply hung up. I used the same tactic the fifth, sixth, and seventh times, to no avail. To this day the man still phones, no matter what I do. If he calls again, I may throw caution to the wind and cry, "Fuck you, Mary, I'm callin' the police." (As if the *police* would do anything about it. They probably would find this *column* obscene.) It's either that or the classic line "I'd rather suck the farts out of dead seagulls." Neither line, I fear, will daunt my relentless pursuer.

Although I find these calls tiresome and annoying, I don't really consider them obscene. No, I take that back: they *are* obscene, but the obscenity lies not in the subject matter of the calls but in the manner in which they are placed. I find nothing reprehensible about the suggestion of sexual activity (no matter how sordid), but I deeply resent the invasion of my privacy, especially when I have made it clear that the calls are not welcome.

For that reason I find calls from people asking me to buy insurance or requesting a donation to the Firemen's Ball equally as obscene as the ones from a man asking me to masturbate with him. In some ways they are more obscene, for they entail an element of pressure that the others lack. There is always the implied threat in the case of the Firemen's Ball, for instance, that if I don't contribute, perhaps my house will burn down. But what's the phone sex gentleman gonna do if I don't cooperate? Threaten to plaster my telephone number on public bathroom walls? It's been there before, and although it didn't do me any good, it didn't do me any harm either.

In some ways I sympathize with the sex caller. I did it myself when I was an adolescent, so I understand the urge to interject a little excitement into people's lives via the telephone. Well, actually, I didn't exactly call strangers and ask them to pull their pud with me. My calls were more along the lines of the "I-saw-what-you-did-and-I-know-whom-you-are" variety. It gave me a cheap thrill until one day a woman traced the call and called me back. "Listen, you little brat," she said. "You call again and you'll spend the rest of your life in jail." It put the fear of God in me, I'm tellin' you, and broke me of the habit once and for all.

I also sympathize because I understand that these are hard times we are going through, and we all have to get our rocks off as best we can. But c'mon, guy, if you *must* practice safe sex over the phone, there are any number of ways you can do it without disturbing me. The pages of this very paper, for instance, are chockful of ads for phone sex companies with easy-to-remember numbers such as 976–FIST, 976–SUCK, and 976–MEAT. (My favorite ad—because of the picture only, mind you—is the one promising "the sounds of man sex." My least favorite is the one with the attitude queen sneering, "You want me . . . then call me.")

True, you gotta pay to place these calls, but I've always thought that if you want something bad enough, you ought to be willing to pay for it. (Pride goeth before a fall, remember.) If you don't want to pay, then check the personals. Somewhere between the man asking to hear from people who have been abused and the man begging for "hot Latin men to sit on my face" you will find the man offering "dirty talk" for free. Satisfaction is only a phone call away.

In the meantime, I wish the obscene sex caller would leave me out of it. I've got better things to do with my phone (and my dick). Besides, some of the messages I receive are getting to be a little much, like the one I got the other day: "I wanna cum up your butt." I mean, really, how rude. Couldn't he at least have asked for a date first? Or couldn't he have said something sweet, like the man who left the message, "You don't know me, and I'd be embarrassed to tell you this to your face, but I think you're wonderful"? My friend John, who was with me at the time, said that as far as *he* was concerned, the latter message was the most obscene thing he had ever heard. But then John probably beats off into telephone receivers, so what the hell does he know?

Ready Freddie, Pump-Up Pete, and Bendable Bruce

OCTOBER 1986

IT IS A MYSTERY to me how so many mail order catalogs find their way to my apartment. I think it's because I ordered an assortment of jams and jellies for Grandma at Christmastime a few years ago, and that started the invasion. Now they come pouring in from all directions, from sources as obscure as the Wisconsin Cheeseman and Country Curtains to those as standard as L. L. Bean and Lands' End. Most I throw away; some I save, just in case.

Last week, however, a catalog arrived in the mail that was so much fun that I not only saved it, I also took it to work to share with my friends. It was sent by a company called Mercury Mail Order, located right here in San Francisco (in the Swish Alps, no less). What it offered for sale was not jams and jellies, but leather paraphernalia and sex toys, forty-seven pages' worth, photographed in glorious black and white (although black and blue would have been more appropriate).

Frankly, when I thumbed through the catalog, I was stunned. It's not as if it were my first exposure to leather jockstraps, armbands, tit clamps, handcuffs, cock rings, harnesses, dildos, and the like. As a friend says, "I didn't just fall off the cabbage truck, hon." But I honestly never realized the variety and extent of the products available in this area. And I suspect that the Mercury catalog is just scratching the surface of possibilities.

More than stunned, though, I was amused. The headlines alone made the catalog a veritable collector's item. Tit for Tat, announces the section on tit clamps. "In a bind?" asks the man wearing a dog collar. The studded suspenders are "leatherific." The variable-speed vibrators promise "good vibrations."

As I scanned the catalog copy I saw that whoever wrote it deserved an award: "You'll love the spotlight in this exciting new leather look from Mercury! Our *lace-up posing pouch* is a unique style and is fully adjustable with the rawhide lacing. Top-grade cowhide assures a great look and an irresistible feeling! One size fits all. . . . Buckle up in style! A new way to strut your stuff, this companion to our narrow-top harness is fully adjustable with buckles instead of snaps. . . . Rise to the occasion in this imported latex cock and ball sheath! The ultimate in safe sex!" I could just see the Ford Agency boys modeling this stuff at Bergdorf-Goodman's in New York while Eve Arden narrated from the side of the runway. Simply *too* Fellini.

My friends at work, when I showed it to them, focused not on the copy, however, but on the products themselves. "Oh, Christian and I can make a lampshade base out of that!" said Gerald, pointing to a picture of Ready Freddie, the sixteen-inch dildo. Referring to another shapely piece of plastic, Bendable Bruce, Don asked, "What's that one called?"

"Your next husband," answered Paul.

"Does he come complete with rice and the wedding bouquet?" asked Don. "If so, I'll marry him."

My straight friends, however, were less amused. "Oh, that's real fuckin' normal," said Gail as she perused a picture of a man about to squat on Big Black Bo ("for those who enjoy the ultimate challenge").

Answered Don, "As far as I'm concerned, it's fine to sit on it. But it's an entirely different thing to have your picture taken while you're doing it."

Gail *was* amused, however, by the various sizes of butt plugs (freshman, sophomore, and senior) and by my stories of a friend who wore them on Muni buses just for the thrill of it. But when she saw the pictures of tit clamps, she said, "Ooh, that hurts. Why do they do that?" Then, when she saw the picture of a man in restraints, she freaked. "God, who would let somebody do *that* to him?"

Her boyfriend, Andy, didn't seem so bothered. When Gail showed him the tit clamp pictures, he just shrugged and said, "These can double as roach clips, huh?" Later, thumbing through the catalog himself, Andy came across the dog collar section and remarked, "I thought you guys bought these in pet stores."

At that point I began to feel a little guilty for putting our (well, some people's) lives on display for public scrutiny. "If this is how my straight friends react," I pondered, "what must Jerry Falwell fans think when they see things such as this?" I resolved, therefore, to keep a close guard on my Mercury catalog lest it fall into the wrong hands. But it's also true that somebody such as Nancy Reagan could probably benefit from a close encounter with Pump-Up Pete. Bet she wouldn't just say no to him.

Back at home I decided that although I could easily bypass the lure of whips and paddles, perhaps I might buy one thing from the catalog: a T-shirt designed by Uyvari, the artist famous for his Arena and S. F. Eagle posters. I especially liked the one featuring the man sprawled back with all his goods on display—his *gigando* goods, as my sister would refer to them. It might be fun, after all, to wear it to the San Francisco Airport the next time I go anywhere. Well, call it a kick. It's more fun than the Wisconsin Cheeseman can deliver.

A Jock for Jockey Shorts

NOVEMBER 1988

YOU WATCHED HIM win two gold medals for gymnastic excellence in the 1984 Olympic Games," the Macy's ad said of Bart Conner beneath a picture of the gymnast in his underwear. "Now come and meet him personally as the new spokesman for Jockey—America's championship underwear!"

I would have preferred meeting Greg Louganis, the diving star of the 1984 and 1988 games, but beggars can't be choosers. Besides, I had seen plenty of Greg in his Speedos at the Olympics, and seeing him in Jockey shorts couldn't have been any better.

At 11:45 A.M. on October 26, therefore, I found myself at Macy's in a line stretching out the door and down the street, waiting for Mr. Conner to appear. At least half the people standing with me were gay men. I struck up a conversation with three of them, Steven, Dale, and Leonard.

"Do you think he'll show up in his underwear?" asked Dale breathlessly.

"I hope so," answered Steven. "I didn't come down here for nothing, you know."

"Well, you *do* get a free T-shirt and an autographed poster of Bart," volunteered Dale.

"Not good enough," Steven answered.

"Actually, I don't know why I came," I said. "I don't even like Jockey shorts. It's that stupid little Y-shaped pouch in the middle. It reminds me of a Cross-Your-Heart bra."

"Lifts and separates?" asked Steven.

"Exactly."

Fortunately, there was no requirement to buy anything, although Dale and Steven had brought along several pairs of underwear for Bart to sign, not just for themselves but for friends as well.

"Of course, I'll be glad to buy Bart's *own* underwear, if he asks," Steven confessed. "He always was my favorite member of the 1984 gymnastics team."

Dale and Leonard agreed, pointing out that he was clearly the most intelligent of the lot.

"I also liked Mitch Gaylord," added Steven, "because of the Soloflex ads and the publicity stills from *American Anthem*. But that was a purely visual attraction."

"Sorry," I interjected, "but Bart is too pretty, too clean cut, for my tastes. He looks like he ought to be selling Girl Scout cookies or singing in a church choir on Sundays. Still, I suppose he could sit on my face if he insisted—with or without his underwear."

Behind us a middle-class mom from Berkeley and her nine-year-old son enjoyed our conversation. They too were fans of Bart, but for gymnastic reasons and not sexual ones.

Said Mom, "My son saw the 1984 team win the gold medal on TV when he was four and got hooked. He's been taking private lessons ever since, and now he works out with the Cal team at the university gym. We even took him to Salt Lake City for the Olympic trials. He's determined to make the team himself in the year 2000."

"So what are you doing here now?" I asked. "Isn't this a school day?"

"Yes, but I wrote him an excuse. This is worth it, isn't it?"

The group of Chinese women ahead of us in line certainly agreed. Olympic groupies to a woman, they said they attended appearances of Olympic athletes in the Bay Area religiously, and Bart's visit was no exception. They thought Dale and Steven's idea to have Bart sign their underwear was a great one, and they ran off to buy a three-pack for themselves.

Finally, amid a flurry of applause, Bart appeared—sans underwear, alas. (Or if he *was* wearing any, we couldn't tell for the business suit.) Hugging the women and shaking hands with the men, he signed posters, posed for photographs, and chatted amiably—a consummate professional.

"Oh, look, you even get to touch him!" cooed Steven.

"But will he respect you in the morning?" I asked.

Giving in to peer group pressure, I bought a pair of underwear as well—as a gift for my boyfriend, I told myself—and pondered the questions I would have liked to ask the gymnast if I had the time, to wit:

1. How do you feel about posing nearly naked in a family newspaper for an underwear company? Is this part of the Olympic image, or are you just selling out for the bucks?

2. Do you consider yourself a sex symbol? If so, how do you feel about the legions of gay fans you seem to have attracted?

"You could also ask him, like a certain reporter for another gay newspaper asked George Bush, 'What are you going to do about gay rights?' " suggested Leonard.

"Somehow I doubt that Bart Conner has a clearly defined position on that," I said, "much less a great deal of political influence."

As it was, I didn't get to ask Conner anything. He just shook my hand, signed my poster "To Mike" and my underwear "To Mark," and wished me well. I wasn't disappointed. Bart was a nice guy. I'd buy cookies from him any day.

Ironically, when I got home that afternoon and looked in the afternoon paper, I discovered yet another Olympic invitation, this time in the Nordstrom ad: "Join us as we welcome Olympic gold medalist Greg Louganis, and receive his autograph." Shrugging my shoulders, I marked the date on my calendar.

This could get to be a habit, you know.

DEMON DRUGS

Portrait of a Drug Dealer

JUNE 1983

I'VE CLIMBED these steps before, back in the days when I "used to do" drugs. They lead to the well-appointed, spacious flat of the man who was once my dealer, Roger. Roger's place is quiet, comfortable, secure—not at all like the kind of drug den I read about in *Manchild in the Promised Land* when I was a kid. But then Roger isn't a bit like the "pushers" I used to fear when I was younger. Like myself and most of his customers, Roger is young, educated, middle class—and gay.

I haven't done LSD since my thirtieth birthday, a little more than a year ago, when, after a night of absolute euphoria, I crashed too hard and entertained visions of swan diving off the tallest building in town. I've never done MDA and have never liked crystal. I rarely smoke marijuana, and as for cocaine—well, I try to avoid it, but find it difficult to turn it down when it's offered. Roger, however, is still dealing most of these substances. I may not require his services anymore, but others do. Enough people in the gay community are still so fascinated by the power and allure of drugs that Roger, for one, isn't complaining about the recession.

Roger is only twenty-one years old, but he has been dealing drugs for more than three years now. He started to deal when he first came out in the midwestern town where he'd grown up. "I'd never even heard of most of those drugs before I started going to the bars," he says. "But it was a big thing there, doing drugs and partying. So I started doing drugs too. And then I became good friends with someone who dealt. He introduced me to that aspect of it, and soon I was dealing too."

When Roger moved to the West Coast late in 1980, he planned to stop dealing. But money was tight and he couldn't find a job, so through one of his hometown friend's local contacts he began to sell drugs again. At first he dealt only to his close friends. Then in early 1981 he landed a job at one of the city's major party bars, and his circle of acquaintances—and contacts—grew. Soon he was dealing to everyone in sight—only MDA in the beginning, but later Quaaludes, speed, and acid as well.

"That was a big party summer," Roger says. "And for me, everything was so new: the partying, the dancing. It was so much fun. It was something I'd never experienced. In my hometown a year earlier, going out to have a couple of beers once a week with straight roommates was the highlight of the week. But here a group of twenty-five or thirty of us would go out partying all the time. It was great." Although money was the main reason he dealt, Roger admits that social reasons played a part. It was a great way to meet people and make friends.

Shortly after Roger started to work at the party bar, he set up his own cleaning business as well. Because he then worked five days and six nights a week at his two jobs, drugs became "just a sideline." But it was such a profitable sideline that it eventually cost Roger his bar job. "It got out of hand," he explained. "I was being too careless. And people were being too open about it. They were going up to the bar and asking, 'Where's Roger? We need to get some drugs.' Everybody at the bar knew I was dealing. In fact, it was helping business a lot. On weekends that bar was packed, and I'd say the majority of the people there were high on drugs that I was dealing. But it couldn't go on. The owner had given me three warnings. Finally he fired me and eighty-sixed me from the bar. But I don't blame him. I think he was justified in doing that."

At the end of that summer Roger was shaken up by a major drug bust at a local disco, which for him was a close call. "I was real lucky, for I had been told that it was going to happen. Right as I was leaving, about six cop cars pulled up, and all these plainclothes cops started grabbing people, including the guy I had walked outside with. I think they arrested twenty people in all—some for possession, some for being underage." Had Roger been arrested, he would have been guilty of both. He eluded the cops by retreating to the middle of the dance floor, and as soon as they left he ran home and immediately threw out all the drugs he had in his possession. "I was really afraid my name was going to come up when they interrogated those people. But nothing ever came of it. I think the cops were just trying to make a scene."

Although "nothing came of it," the raid at the disco did lead to major changes in the drug trade, according to Roger. "Things got real tight after that," he explains. "Places like that disco cracked down. Before the raid people got drugs wherever they partied. After it they made sure to get them in advance." Consequently Roger started dealing out of his apartment, and his role as a traveling salesperson came to an end. "I never left the house with drugs on my body after that," he states. "Maybe *in* it, but never on it."

Soon Roger had another scare: his apartment was broken into twice. He believes it was a result of his dealing, because the only things that were taken the first time were the cash box and the drug box. The second time he didn't lose anything, because it was all too well hidden. Although he concluded that the thief was an acquaintance, he was still scared, for he realized that he was losing control of the situation. He therefore resolved to change his life in a number of ways. First he moved to a more secure apartment. Then he eliminated many of his former acquaintances and customers, including his old boyfriend. "I tried to be more discreet, more selective," he states. "And I grew up a lot."

Roger still deals out of his apartment, but most of his customers are people he's been dealing with for a year and a half now. "They're basically pretty regular people—good friends. They don't just come over to pick up drugs. We sit and talk for a while." He's not interested in taking on new people, for he wants to keep a low profile these days, and besides, he makes a good enough living as it is.

How good? "Oh, I don't know how much I make. It depends on what's going on. There are times of the year when it picks up a little. Summers are always more active. I suppose it's between two thousand dollars and four thousand dollars a month. Of course, that's all tax free." In Roger's opinion, he deserves that kind of income. "I work hard for it. People expect me always to be there when they want to get high. So I make myself available. I'm home from four until nine or ten every Wednesday through Saturday. I've always got product, I've always got it ready. I keep my house and myself presentable. I'm nice to people—and I expect something in return. I don't like people running in and out or bringing friends over. I don't like them keeping taxis waiting. After all, I put myself out on a limb for these people's good high."

Roger points out that, like any job, "if you apply yourself, make yourself more available, you'll make more." But he isn't interested in going after the big bucks. "Sure, I could hustle up 150 to 200 more customers, but why should I? I make enough to take care of my needs, to entertain myself, and to put a little away. The trouble with a lot of dealers is that they become money hungry. A lot of the ones who get busted are the ones who want to have it all, who want to be Dealer of the Year."

And what of the ones who get busted? How dangerous *is* his job? Isn't Roger afraid of getting busted himself and spending the rest of his life in jail? He says he is not. "I've never had any problems, any truly close calls, and I've never felt threatened. I try to take as many precautions as I can and to be discreet about it. I'm not really a big dealer, and basically, I think they're after bigger people than me. I'm certainly not paranoid about being busted. If I were, I wouldn't be doing it."

Not only is he not afraid, neither does he feel guilty about dealing drugs. "The people I deal with are bright, on the level," he says. "They know what they're doing. I really don't think they're addicted to it. They just like to have a good time." In addition, Roger doesn't feel responsible for what happens to people when they use his drugs, as long as he provides them with good ones. He compares himself to a bartender or a gun salesperson in this regard, and says, "Why should I feel responsible? If they can't get it from me, they'll get it from someone else." To the best of his knowledge, no one has ever had a bad trip or has overdosed on any of his drugs. Some haven't handled the drugs he's provided them very well, but when he has found out about it, he's refused to give them more. "If they are abusing it, I sure as hell don't want to contribute to it. There were a few who were running speed, but I cut them out," he states.

Roger has seen numerous changes in drug usage and habit within the community since he began dealing. He used to sell an ounce a week of MDA, for example. Now he sells an ounce a month. He also sells much less acid. Instead, he says, people are doing more cocaine and speed these days. Why? "The others are too messy," he replies. He attributes their decline partly to people's health concerns and admits that even he has given up poppers, MDA, and ethyl chloride because of AIDS. In spite of this, he believes that gay people still use a wider range of drugs than straights, and they do them more consistently as well. He sees this as a problem only when people get carried away with the drugs they are taking. "Like drinking and smoking, as long as you do it in moderation, every now and then, I don't think there's anything wrong with it," says Roger. "But drugs can definitely be harmful, and too much is not good."

Eventually Roger would like to graduate from the drug trade. "There are lots of times when I say, God, I'd like to get out of this, but financially I've gotten myself in a position where I have to do what I'm doing in order to maintain my present lifestyle. Sure, I could give it up, move into a cheaper apartment and bus tables—but I'm not going to." Besides the money, there are other advantages that make it difficult for Roger to change: a regular schedule and lots of free time. Roger is very content with all this and can't see any plausible alternative to his present occupation.

What *does* the future hold, then? School, perhaps, but what does an ex–drug dealer study? What does Roger want to be when he grows up? "You'll laugh at me when I say this, maybe, but I'm really serious about it. I want to be a pharmacist. It's something that intrigues me." There's no maybe about it: of course I laugh. But in a way, nothing could be more logical. Heaven help Walgreen's, however, if Roger's on his way. And heaven help Roger too. After a number of years dealing LSD and MDA, I can't imagine that selling Preparation H and A–200 would be all that exciting for him.

65

SO LITTLE TIME

Decline and Fall

MARCH 1989

"JUST WHEN you thought it was safe to go to your mailbox again," my friend Eric began his letter from the state prison at Vacaville. He had been arrested for dealing drugs exactly six months earlier and was writing for the first time to let me know that he was okay. "I work out every day and look as good as I ever have. I'm the picture of health. I'm working as a clerk/typist and have written some schools to see about being admitted when I get out later this year. Time will tell. In the meantime, it's nice being sane and sober. I just want to get all this behind me, so I can get on with my life."

When I first met Eric in June 1981, prison and drug addiction were the last things on our minds. I spotted him at the gym, and, as I wrote in my journal at the time, "This one is a candidate for the Most Gorgeous Body Ever award." It didn't take me long to proposition him, and it didn't take him long to accept. That first night we got stoned at my place, had sex, and settled in for pizza and "High Chaparral" reruns on TV.

For a year or so, Eric and I dated, but never exclusively. We were, in the quaint parlance of the day, fuck buddies. Eventually we weren't even that anymore. We became best friends—"sisters"—instead. When Eric fell hopelessly in love with a young blond named Andre, I was happy for him. The three of us spent countless evenings together, playing Scrabble, watching "Dynasty," dining out, and visiting friends.

We also did drugs: cocaine, mainly. Everybody did. But not everybody seemed to enjoy it as much as Eric and Andre. I began to suspect things were getting out of hand at Eric and Andre's annual Christmas Eve pajama party in 1983, when a Gay Monopoly game where all the players were high lasted all night and led directly to a party at a sleazy dance bar the following morning—we were still all high. As I wrote in my journal a few days later, "It was not my ideal way to spend Christmas."

Two months later Eric and Andre borrowed nearly a thousand dollars from me. They needed it, they claimed, to pay off their Christmas bills and to finance their upcoming ski vacation to Colorado. I didn't want to do it, but what could I say? Eric was my best friend. "Granted," I wrote, "a ski vacation is hardly a dire need, but how he intends to use the money is not my concern. All I care about is whether I'll get it back, and I trust Eric completely."

Perhaps I shouldn't have been so complacent. Four weeks later Eric called on a Tuesday night and talked for forty minutes while waiting for Andre to return from the coke dealer. From my journal again: "I am worried about those two.

This week they started partying on Friday and haven't stopped since—which would be fine once in a while, but every weekend? I had hoped they would grow out of it sooner or later."

Things rapidly began to disintegrate. In April 1984 I concluded, "Eric has become a real mess. Every time I see him he is either fucked up on drugs or recovering from a major debauch. Each time he swears, 'Never again,' but he breaks that vow regularly. He claims to have control, but clearly he does not. He spends all his money on cocaine, falls asleep at work (or misses it entirely), skips the gym for weeks at a time, and picks brutal fights with Andre. Andre, who isn't doing much better himself, says that he has spoken to Eric about enrolling in Cokenders or a similar withdrawal program for addicts. I was shocked. I hadn't ever before heard anyone use the term *addict* with reference to Eric."

One of the worst consequences of Eric and Andre's drug habit was the effect it was having on their relationship. Unable to control themselves—which they might have been able to do otherwise—they initiated a series of not-so-clandestine affairs with other people. The fights that ensued were the stuff of legend. During one, Andre kicked a hole in the bathroom door. During another, he threw a fan across the apartment, through the open sliding glass window, and over the balcony. Fortunately no one was walking in the street below at the time.

As the months passed, Eric and Andre became more and more irresponsible, breaking dates with alarming frequency. Under the circumstances it might have been wiser to have disassociated myself from them completely. Nevertheless, I continued to see them. We even spent Christmas together again that year. But this time, unlike the previous Christmas, when everyone else tooted coke, I refrained.

In January 1985 the shit hit the fan. Eric was fired from his job, Andre was forced to declare bankruptcy, and they were evicted from their apartment. They weren't worried, but I was. They didn't exactly seem to be on top of things.

By July Eric and Andre's lives had become a nightmare. Following a week-long binge on speed, Andre walked out on Eric, and Eric trashed the new apartment for revenge. He smashed the TV, shattered the pictures, slit the couch, and destroyed a closetful of clothes. He even took a hammer to the piano. "I know it's sick," Eric stammered when he finally stopped crying, "but I wanted to do it. Andre destroyed our emotional life. I just destroyed the physical one."

Questions of blame aside, I advised Eric to start anew. I also offered him the use of my apartment for a while. As I wrote to myself, "I hate to see Eric hurting like this. I hate to see anyone lose control."

At my place I tried to keep Eric occupied, but nothing could distract him from contemplating the wreck his life had become. His mood was contagious. When a close friend of ours died of AIDS that same week, I wrote, "Is life really as dismal as it seems at times? As a kid I was told that to be homosexual was to lead a life of despair. This week that prophecy seems to have come true."

Eric stayed with me for only a week, and then it was back to the same old lifestyle—but this time without Andre. By October 1985 I had had enough. "I have no desire to waste my time on people who seem bent on self-destruction," I told a friend. "If Eric needs me, I'll be there, but in the meantime I want no part of him."

My friend replied that Eric wouldn't change until he hit rock bottom. Pointing out that he had already lost a job, an apartment, and a lover, I wondered what more he could lose.

"His self-respect," my friend answered. "He has yet to become so disgusted that he'll give up drugs forever. He could also lose his health, but that is a possibility too frightening for him to consider."

On Christmas Eve I took Eric to dinner and listened to new tales of woe. This time the problem was a bank robbery. Three masked robbers had forced Eric at gunpoint to open the safe of the bank where he worked. It was so traumatic that naturally he had to consume major quantities of drugs all weekend to cope with his feelings. Then he called in sick for three days straight.

In March 1986 Eric quit that job and landed a new one. Unfortunately the day before he was scheduled to start, he dropped three hits of acid and called in sick three days in a row. He placed the third call from my apartment, and his new boss fired him on the spot. I didn't say a word. What good would it have done? Eric knew how I felt about his drug usage, and it was best, I thought, to maintain the illusion that I was not only steadfast and loyal but nonjudgmental as well. Besides, if I *had* said something, it would have been, "Eric, honey, why don't you simply jump off a bridge? It's easier and quicker."

A month later Eric fell madly in love with a new boyfriend, a young man who dealt drugs for a living. Wasting no time, Eric immediately joined his boyfriend, Jimmy, in the drug business. "I need a change," he said. "It's time to reassess my goals. I never wanted to be a banker in the first place." I replied that if he truly was tired of banking, then I was glad for him, but I suggested that perhaps drug dealing wasn't the wisest way to start a new life.

My words proved to be all too true. In June 1986, outside the same sleazy dance bar where we had spent Christmas morning two and a half years earlier, Eric and a friend were arrested for possession of an illegal substance (crystal), intent to sell, resisting arrest, and a slew of other charges. With the help of a lawyer and a bail bondsperson, he was out of jail by midnight, but he had had to spend a great deal of money for his freedom.

Amazingly, Eric seemed undisturbed. "I don't understand it," I mused. "He has completely lost his perspective. He doesn't see what a mess he has made of his life; rather than recognize the extent of his downfall, he focuses his concern and anger elsewhere. He is infinitely more concerned about the abuse of his civil rights, for instance (the police called him a faggot), than he is about his own responsibility in the matter (he *was* breaking the law, after all). Until he recognizes the state he's in, he's just going to keep sinking further down."

A month later Eric dislocated his shoulder and broke his hand in a car accident with Jimmy. A week after that, a fight with Jimmy led to a brief hospital visit. When he caught Jimmy having sex in the car with another man one night, he decided he had had enough. Eric took the advice of a friend and fled the city to recuperate with his parents in the Midwest for a while.

Determined to encourage Eric's resolve, I poured out my feelings in a six-page letter. After professing undying love, I implored him to clean up his act. "I know you think I'm condescendingly smug when it comes to drugs," I confessed. "It's true that I've become somewhat intolerant and decidedly negative, but there are reasons for it, good ones. I've seen the lives of too many friends spiral downhill because of drugs. Even if I didn't have their examples to follow, my own experience has taught me as much as I ever need to know."

After several more pages of this, I continued, "You may hate me for writing all this, but it's something I had to do. I've never been a fan of people who say, 'I'm only telling you this for your own good'—which is exactly what I'm doing—but what alternatives do I have? I could keep silent, I suppose, and then hate myself forever when you do lasting damage to yourself."

After warning him, "I half-expect to be writing your obituary before long—and *not* because of AIDS," I reiterated the same old plea: "Anyway, *get your shit together, girl,* and when you do, come back and start over again. You can always stay with me, of course, provided you don't bring those devil drugs with you."

Big mistake, huh? Within a week Eric was back in town, doing drugs and fighting with Jimmy again. Jimmy responded by hitting him on the head with a marble ashtray and having the police haul him away. So Eric took me up on my offer and moved in with me. My friends thought I was crazy, and even I thought I was carrying loyalty beyond the bounds of reason, but I took him in anyway, waving farewell to peace, serenity, and privacy for the indefinite future.

The less said about that period, the better. Eric was in and out of my house at all hours of the day and night—asleep during the day and fried to the tits at night. I spent most of my time trying to avoid him; eventually I abandoned my apartment to him. Then one day he left me the following note: "I'd be too embarrassed to say this to your face. I've been using crystal again so life won't seem so bad. The problem is more with me, though, than with the drugs. I need to find a reason for living with myself. I think I would have killed myself already if I wasn't so afraid that the next life would be worse. I need counseling and I need a friend. I'll be back soon, ready to cooperate if you want to help. Otherwise, you can put my things on the stoop."

I tried to help. Really I did. I found Eric a counselor, but it didn't do any good. He met with the counselor once, maybe twice, and that was it. Then he found a new boyfriend, Vance, who proved to be a disastrous influence. Vance had two things that Eric didn't need: good drugs and the money to buy even more. Soon Eric was talking of moving in with Vance.

I wasn't surprised. "Since breaking up with Andre," I wrote, "Eric has developed a habit of depending on people to make things easy for himself. He is determined to avoid the 'real world' for as long as possible. He is a weakling and a user, and I am a weakling too, for letting him use me."

I didn't allow Eric to use me for long. When he returned to drug dealing, I merely said, "Fine. Be that stupid." But when I found him cutting drugs for a customer in my apartment, we both decided it was best for him to move elsewhere. By that time I didn't care whether Eric solved his problems. I only wanted him out of my hair.

I wish the story ended here, but it doesn't. For the next year and a half, Eric periodically reentered my life. One night he showed up at 3:00 A.M. in the company of a police officer, rambling incoherent nonsense about the Mafia and attempted murder. I wanted to say to him, "Get a grip," but he was too far gone. Following another, similar encounter with Eric, it briefly crossed my mind that if only Eric would overdose, I wouldn't have to worry about him anymore.

In June 1987 Eric at last admitted he was an addict. But he added, "So what's wrong with that? I've accepted it. Lots of people are addicted to all kinds of things, and they lead happy, productive lives. But just because I use speed, that's supposed to make me bad. I'm sick of the hypocrisy of it all."

The flaw in Eric's argument, of course, was that there was nothing happy or productive about his life. He was broke and homeless, and his health was beginning to suffer. I couldn't believe he didn't see that for himself. Yet, as I noted, "The man is hardly the most rational creature in the world at this point."

A few months later all hell broke loose. Eric and his boyfriend, Vance, were arrested when twenty plainclothes officers armed with search warrants burst into Vance's bedroom looking for drugs. Eric and Vance were watching porn movies and having sex at the time. Eric fled to the closet, but he didn't escape the clutches of the cops. And news of his fate hit the front page of the papers the very next day.

To my dismay, Eric was actually pleased; he enjoyed the attention. Furthermore, despite his previous arrest, he was convinced he would emerge from this latest fiasco unscathed. When a friend asked if he had used drugs since his arrest, he replied, "Are you kidding? I'm always on drugs. But I'm happier taking drugs than trying to get off of them, so it doesn't bother me."

It bothered him, however, when he went to jail pending his court appearance a few months later. He asked me to visit, but after contacting a few people whom I thought might be able to help Eric, I wrote him instead. "This is something you're going to have to work out for yourself," I advised him. "The last time I offered help, it didn't do any good. So can you blame me for feeling somewhat detached from the present situation?

"For a long time now, I haven't understood the direction your life has taken, and I don't think you do either. If this sounds harsh, sorry. For what it's worth, I do care. And naturally I'm looking forward to all the sordid stories that are going to come out of this. Who knows? You may even provide the subject for a column or two. After all, the daily papers hardly did you justice."

Perhaps I shouldn't have been so flip. Eric didn't answer my letter, and I didn't hear any more about him until I ran into a friend in September 1987, who told me that at his trial Eric had pleaded guilty and had been sentenced to five years in the state prison. Despite all I had witnessed during the previous few years, I was shocked and angry. Sure, Eric was a mess, but did he really deserve jail? I didn't think so.

"It's all so pathetic," I concluded. "What a good life Eric used to have. How rapidly his life deteriorated! No, it's worse than pathetic. In an era when so many are fighting for their lives, it's disgusting, really, to see Eric throw his away."

I am well aware that by writing about Eric, I may destroy what remains of our friendship (which may not be worth preserving anyway). But it is a risk worth taking. If Eric's decline and fall cause one person to reconsider his or her own involvement with drugs, this story, as wretched as it is, may be worth the telling.

A friend, when referring to Eric, says, "There but for the grace of God goes you or me." I don't believe this, and I don't think it's the lesson I want to teach. We are not all potential addicts. For that matter, Nancy Reagan and her Just Say No campaign notwithstanding, drugs aren't necessarily evil. Yet enough of us are prone to destruction, and drugs are sufficiently dangerous, that it is wise to be wary. The time to abandon ship is before it sinks, not after.

So has Eric's ship sunk? I don't know. He may be deluding himself to think that he can stay clean once he gets out of prison. Then again, he may still have a chance. No matter how disillusioned I become, I never give up entirely. Even for Eric, there is always room for hope.

POLITICS: OPPRESSION

Reflections on Violence: Confessions of a Fag Bashee

JULY 1983

LAST FRIDAY night I was physically assaulted for the first time in my life. I was thrown through a plate glass window on Haight Street. Two friends and I were walking home from a movie at the Red Victorian about 11:30 P.M., and as we crossed Belvedere Street, we saw three belligerent teenagers walking toward us. As they passed, one deliberately bumped into me and said something about "fucking faggots." Oh Christ, I thought. Ironically, the movie we had just seen was *Track Two,* a movie about hostility toward gay people in Toronto. Now I was being confronted with the same sort of hatred in my own city, supposedly a haven for lesbians and gay men.

Ordinarily I would have ignored the provocation and walked on, but I was angry this time. I rarely receive this kind of abuse, yet several times in the past month I've been called a faggot by hostile straight people: kids at the river, punks in the Castro, even a male executive on Market Street. I was sick of hearing it. So this time I turned and told them that they were fucking assholes and to get the fuck out of my neighborhood, or something to that effect. They responded in kind, strode toward me, and assumed threatening postures. It became immediately apparent that this verbal war was rapidly escalating into a physical confrontation.

My friends tried to get me to leave—surely the wise thing to do—but before I could even consider the option, one of the beefier kids (much bigger than me, of course) looked at his friends and said, "Let's get him." All of a sudden he tackled me—the others helped—and threw me against the plate glass window of Mommie Fortuna's restaurant. The glass came shattering down around me in huge, vicious shards, and I stood there in a state of shock, trying to recover my balance and ascertain whether I had been cut. Another kid then began punching me in the face, and I did my best to punch back.

I wasn't at all afraid. I would have been years ago, when I was a childhood coward, but I have long since lost that fear. I go to the gym five days a week, after all, and I have lived in New York City, which makes anyone a streetwise survivor. I had therefore thought I could handle myself if this situation ever arose. Unfortunately, going to the gym and learning to avoid dark alleys and doorways doesn't teach you much about fighting. I had been in only one fight in my life before this, in fact, back in the eighth grade in 1965, when I tried to defend a friend who was being bullied by nasty Jimmy Hammer. I won that fight, simply because I ducked when Jimmy tried to hit me ("Not the face, not the face!"), and he rammed his hand into the brick wall behind me, breaking four of his fingers. But this time I wasn't so lucky. I forgot to duck and I have never known anything about blocking. Consequently, I ended up with a fist in my eye and found myself on the ground in a matter of seconds. I don't think I did my assailant any damage at all.

As soon as I was down, the three fled. It happened so quickly that my friends hardly had time to react, but Alex swore he got a good kick in. They helped me up, and we stood there, staring at the ruins of the restaurant window, amazed that I wasn't cut to ribbons. Outside of a few facial cuts and a black eye, I seemed to be okay. Then we wondered what to do. Should we call the police? Should we just leave? Should we leave a note for Mommie Fortuna's restaurant? As we stood there, someone ran up, a witness to the assault. "They caught one of the guys," he informed us. "They're holding him down the street in a grocery store." "They" were several bystanders who had immediately blown whistles and screamed, "Stop those assholes!" when the teenagers fled. So John, Alex, and I walked down the street to stand sentinel by the grocery store and to wait for the police.

When the police arrived they took the suspect into custody and questioned him. He said he hadn't done anything and refused to implicate his friends. Then the police questioned us, and we told our version of the incident. When I asked what would happen to the kid—would he be charged with anything?—the police explained that because they hadn't been present to witness what had happened, and because the kid was accused of only a misdemeanor, there was nothing they could do, really. They would take his name and address and probably write the incident up as "mutual combat," but no, they could hardly take the kid down to the station and lock him up or "beat the information out of him." When I asked for a case number, they said there wouldn't be one, unless I made a citizen's arrest. "A citizen's arrest?" I asked. The police then explained that I could charge the kid with assault, fill out a brief form, and then follow it up on my own through the district attorney's office. It seemed that I was being asked to bear the burden of ensuring justice, but as I had no other option, I agreed to do it. Throughout, the police were polite and respectful, but not exactly helpful. If I hadn't persisted in asking what exactly would happen with the kid, I'm sure they would have let him go. Luckily, I knew enough to ask for a case number and badge numbers when dealing with the police.

I was afraid I might be getting into more trouble than I cared to deal with, but what else could I do? I didn't want the kid to go entirely unpunished. I didn't want him to rot in jail either, but I did want him to get in a hell of a lot of trouble. I wanted his parents to find out, I wanted to implicate his friends, and I wanted all three kids to suffer the time, expense, and trouble of judicial proceedings. At the very least, I wanted them to pay for the window. Furthermore, I wanted them to think about what they had done and to question whether attacking me was worth it. Above all, I wanted them not to do it again. I didn't want them to attack other faggots.

My fear in pursuing this matter is that it won't do any good, that those kids will blame me for getting them in trouble and that this experience will only serve to enrage them further. But I can't worry about that. Even if it doesn't do any good, the purpose of justice is not only to reform—the ideal—but it is also to punish. Am I too severe? Is my sense of justice being overwhelmed by a desire for vengeance? I don't think so. Fuck, man, those kids pushed me through a plate glass window. They *wanted* to hurt me—all because they didn't like faggots. Screw them. I was the one who was violated, not them. They deserve to be punished.

I do feel some sense of guilt, however, for the incident might so easily have been avoided. I could have walked on, after all. John and Alex wanted me to. "You were so stupid, Mike," they said. "What if they had had knives? What if that glass had cut you to smithereens?" Luckily, they didn't, and it didn't. In retrospect I agree with them, of course. But at the time I was enraged. What right had they to accost me? All I could think about was my sense of pride, my dignity. If we let these fuckers say what they will and do what they want, they'll walk all over us. They'll never cease to oppress us until we stand up to them and fight back. They've got to learn that gay people aren't going to take this crap. A friend at work, however, said that fighting back didn't do any good. "They'll never understand or respect you anyway," he said. "Besides, what does it matter what they think? Your pride and self-respect can't possibly depend on what they think of you, can it?" No, of course it can't. I have to admit he's right. Violence only results in more violence. All I got from fighting back was a swollen black-and-blue eye and a lot of sympathy. But it did feel good to stand up to those assholes. I have to admit that too. I don't regret it at all, and I might even do it again. Who knows?

After the incident I called Randy Schell of Community United Against Violence and found that the burden of enforcing justice will not be mine entirely. Thanks to CUAV, we have an agency in our community that is adept at handling situations such as this. Randy assured me that he will investigate the episode and follow it up for me. Along with a colleague of his in the district attorney's office, they will see that the kid must attend a general arraignment and then, in all likelihood, a pretrial hearing. I will be subpoenaed and have to go to court, but that can't be much of a burden. I have to follow through with this. And it's nice to know that others are there to help me do it.

My eye is healing nicely now, and Mommie Fortuna's restaurant has already replaced its window—to the tune of six hundred dollars. I went over there a few days after the incident and told them about it, so that they could try to collect from the kids if they wanted. There will soon be nothing left to show that this incident ever occurred. Even my anger is gone, mostly. But I *have* learned something. I used to think that I was immune to this sort of thing. I know now that anyone can be attacked. People get accosted every day for the same reason I was and for a hundred others as well, and some get hurt a lot worse than I was. But only some of them become victims. And that I refuse to be.

Confessions of a Fag Bashee, Part II: The Workings of Justice

DECEMBER 1983

IN EARLY JULY I was accosted by a group of belligerent teenage thugs and thrown through a plate glass window on Haight Street as I was returning home from a movie with two friends, an event I subsequently wrote about in the July 14 issue of the *Bay Area Reporter*. In that article I expressed my determination to prosecute one of my assailants: the one who, after he ran down the street, was cornered by witnesses in a grocery store and held until the police arrived. I wanted to do this for two reasons. Even though I knew that conviction was by no means certain, I wanted him "to suffer the time, expense, and trouble of judicial proceedings," as I said at the time. Furthermore, I wanted him to learn that he couldn't go around beating up on faggots without bearing the consequences—which I hoped would be as severe as possible.

Reactions to my original article from the gay community were swift and overwhelming. Most of the letters and calls I received at the paper and at home were tremendously supportive. Obviously I had touched a collective nerve. "Congratulations for fighting back," said one. "You did the right thing. Your attackers deserve to have their asses kicked. Gay people are not going to put up with *crap* from assholes like that." "I want to thank you for sharing what must have been a harrowing experience," wrote another. "It felt very powerful to be able to read about a gay brother, confronted with violence, who was able to take action." Some of the reactions, however, were excessive. One man wrote, "I suggest that as soon as a few fag bashers are shot and killed by citizens exercising their right to self-defense, antigay violence will end." And others got carried away in another direction. One man wrote, "Mr. Hippler, you have my 'respect' and my ass anytime you want it." Another asked, "Mike, how about a date? I'll be at your side, if need be, fighting."

Although I was touched by most of these letters, I felt that some of the authors had missed the point. I thought I had made it quite clear in my article that I was not sure that fighting back on the spot was the correct thing to do. By fighting back I endangered myself and my friends. Mightn't it have been wiser to ignore the teenagers, whose first offense was merely that one of them bumped into me deliberately and called me a faggot, and to move on? There *was* the matter of pride, to be sure, but as my friend at work pointed out, "Your pride and self-respect can't possibly depend on what they think of you, can it?" I also thought I had made it clear that I did feel a certain measure of responsibility for escalating the incident. Had I not spoken back, perhaps nothing would have happened. Yet most of my "admirers" completely ignored that point, although some acknowledged and then dismissed it. They seemed determined to make me a hero—which was okay by me, except that it all seemed a little artificial and overblown. I felt they were admiring me for the wrong things—for my "courage," which might equally have been termed "stupidity," or for my picture in the paper, which was more embarrassing than anything else.

Not all the responses were positive. One man wrote a fairly nasty letter, beginning "Mike Hippler is a fool and that he writes for *B.A.R.* is no surprise." After calling me a "meek fellow" and criticizing my "convenient memory," he went on to say, "Having lost the fight—and it was a fight—mutual combat—as the cop said, he now demands justice. . . . The courts and the police have better things to do. No doubt he will drag CUAV [Community United Against Violence] down to the police station and complain to anyone who will listen about just about everything. . . . The D.A. has better things to do too." Yet this man, too, missed the point. Although I admitted my reservations about standing up to my assailants, it was always clear to me that this was no mutual combat. I was the one who was attacked and thrown through the window, after all, and I have never felt any guilt about that. Furthermore, I sincerely doubt that the police, courts, and D.A. have better things to do than to investigate assault cases. Granted, there are more serious crimes in the world—rape and murder, for instance—but if the responsibility of the police is not to protect and the duty of the courts is not to ensure justice, then what are their responsibilities and duties?

I was well aware when I wrote my article in July that I was not the only faggot ever to be attacked by hostile youths. "People get accosted every day, . . ." I wrote then, "and some get hurt a lot worse than I was." Two weeks after I wrote those words, in fact, I read an article by Dion Sanders in the *B.A.R.* that chronicled attacks against gay people in Seattle by "roving gangs of teenagers armed with clubs, chains, and baseball bats." During one of the assaults, a gay man and his companion were beaten and raped with crowbars by a group of about a dozen teenagers screaming, "Diseased faggots!" The results? "Smashed ligaments, welts and lacerations on their faces and bodies, and severe rectal damage that required surgery." I was horrified. But the attacks continue in cities across the nation, even in the very hearts of the "ghettos" that many of us consider havens of freedom, and it is a rare week indeed when one can read an entire issue of the *B.A.R.* without encountering at least one story of antigay violence.

Immediately after my own incident occurred, I contacted Randy Schell of CUAV, who referred me to Ron Huberman, an investigator in the district attorney's office. Ron promised to follow the case as closely as possible and to see that it was investigated thoroughly. "The problem that we have with these kinds of cases," he told me, "is that the victims are often unwilling to come forward and testify." In many instances, he explained, the victim is an older man who has been robbed or beaten by some kid he has picked up on Polk Street. After he has reported it to the police, he sometimes has second thoughts about carrying on with the case, for he doesn't want the publicity that might result. Perhaps he has a wife or a homophobic boss. "But because you are willing and eager to testify, and because you have witnesses, we should have a fairly good case," Ron concluded.

Ron did not promise a conviction; he could not. But he did believe that we could at least get the case to a pretrial hearing, where, in all likelihood, my attacker, whose only previous arrest had been for loitering with an open beverage, would be placed on probation. Probation, Ron continued, was a more serious situation than it sounded. For a certain period of this kid's future, his life would belong to his probation officer. He would have to report for periodic meetings, and he would have to keep away from trouble. In all respects he would have to lead an exemplary life—which would include leaving faggots alone—or else he would find himself faced with criminal proceedings again. Good, I thought. That's exactly what I want and what the kid needs: supervision that will, I hope, force him to get his life in order. And with any luck at all, according to Ron Huberman, that was often what probation did. Although the kids didn't appreciate this at the time, of course, often probation forced them to take a second look at the direction their lives were taking and caused them to make necessary changes. It was a second chance. At any rate, Ron told me to expect the kid, whose name was George, to be arraigned on August 10, at which time he would be formally charged and a date for the pretrial hearing would be set.

All of this, however, would not happen without aggressive action on my part.

As Ron explained, the district attorney's office received as many as forty to fifty cases a day, a far greater number than it could fully investigate or the courts could handle. What often happened, therefore, was that when the case was read by an investigator, although he or she was supposed to contact all parties concerned in order to determine whether to proceed with the case, he or she would often make only a half-hearted attempt to investigate and then throw the case out, with the excuse that he or she couldn't get in touch with the victim. In all fairness, many times the victim was legitimately unavailable: perhaps the victim had moved in the meantime or had no phone. If I didn't want this to happen with my case, therefore, I would have to contact the investigator myself and make myself available to him or her. I did this immediately, and within a week or two after the incident, I gave my statement concerning the attack to a Sergeant Malone over the telephone. Then I waited for the August 10 arraignment.

Soon after my article appeared in the *B.A.R.* I received a message on my answering machine from someone I assumed to be one of my three assailants. The voice on the tape stated simply in a strong Southern (working class?) accent, "My name is Eddie. Would you call me, please?" Because the caller sounded young, scared, and vulnerable, I was sure it was one of the two who had not been caught, that he had seen my article in the *B.A.R.* and found my number in the phone book. If it *was* one of the three, I wondered, what could he want? Perhaps he wanted to plead with me to drop the charges against his friend, assuring me that they were all sorry and would never do it again. Perhaps he wanted to threaten me instead. One of the letter writers to the *B.A.R.* had warned me of just such a possibility, in fact, and had cautioned me to be careful, for fear of reprisals. If it was a threat, I wasn't worried. I would not allow myself to be intimidated. If it was a plea for understanding, however, I feared I might play the sucker and succumb to the caller's sob story, if it was good enough. So I called both Randy Schell and Ron Huberman and related this latest development. They both encouraged me to be firm and to stand fast. "This is one of the tricks they pull," said Ron. "Just explain to him that the matter is out of your hands now. Say there is nothing you can do." Resolved to follow his advice, I called "Eddie" back—three times—but never reached him, so all my trauma was for naught.

On August 10 my assailant, George, was arraigned, but instead of requesting a date for a pretrial hearing, the district attorney's office moved to drop the case. I didn't find out about this for several weeks, for Ron Huberman, who had promised to keep me informed, was out of town on vacation. When Ron returned, he was as surprised and disappointed as I was that the charges against my assailant had been dropped. "What happened?" I asked. "I don't know," he replied. "It was my understanding when I left that we were going ahead with your case." He called Sergeant Malone, who had taken my statement over the phone, and Malone said that he didn't know what had happened either. He had sent my case "upstairs" to the charging deputies, who were to make the decision whether there was sufficient evidence to prosecute, and he didn't know why they had moved to drop it. "It looked like a pretty clear case of assault to me," Malone told me later. Ron then suggested I pay a visit to the Hall of Justice in order to give my statement to Sergeant Malone a second time, this time in person. "Although the case has been discharged, it is possible to reopen it," he explained. "I'll also show the deputies your article, and maybe together we can convince them to reconsider the situation." In mid-August, therefore, I drove down to the Hall of Justice to tell my story for the umpteenth time, and soon thereafter the charging deputies agreed to reopen the case.

One of the concerns I wrote about in my July 14 article was what I would do if I was confronted with a similar situation in the future. Would I fight back, as I did the first time? Or would I ignore all provocation? On September 15, while on the way home from a trip to the Russian River with my friend Steve, I had the opportunity to discover exactly what I would do in such a case. Steve and I were driving along winding River Road an hour before sunset, sunburned and feeling wonderful, when we noticed a car full of teenagers tailgating us. For miles they followed us, seemingly anxious to pass, but when I gave them the chance to do so, they never took it. In the rearview mirror I could see them drinking and I sensed trouble. Finally, when the road straightened, they pulled out, and as they passed they threw a giant-sized paper cup full of beer at us, gave us the finger, shouted, laughed, and sped ahead.

Because the top was down on the car, the beer drenched both Steve and me and sprayed the entire inside of the car. (It is amazing how much beer will fit into a Hardee's cup.) I was livid with rage and immediately pressed the gas pedal to the floor, determined to catch up with the teenagers and get my revenge somehow. After a few seconds, however, I thought, What in the hell am I doing? The last thing in the world I want to do is to catch up with those fellows. What would I do with them if I did? So I slowed down, pulled over, and Steve and I wiped the beer off our faces, dried our hair, and mopped the car. Steve was still furious and—what was far worse—humiliated. He had never before been the victim of that kind of aggression, and he couldn't understand it. "Why would they do such a thing?" he asked. "Perhaps because we are faggots," I answered, although in this case I had no clear evidence to support such an assumption, for those teenagers had not made antigay remarks as they passed. Perhaps they were just out joy riding and would have thrown beer at anyone. In any case, in trying to console Steve, I quickly overcame my own anger. And I learned that I could indeed respond nonviolently to violent provocation without losing my sense of dignity, even as beer dripped down my neck.

In late October, months after the original incident, I finally received another call from Ron Huberman. "I just wanted to let you know," he said, "that they've dropped the charges against George a second time, so that's it. It can't be reopened again."

"But why?" I begged, astonished. "What went wrong this time?"

"Basically, the charging deputy didn't think it was winnable," he replied. "On the original police report there were no witnesses listed, so the only thing they had to go on was your testimony. Naturally, your assailant would challenge that with his own version, and so the situation would become what we call a one on one: your word against his."

I protested that I had witnesses: my two friends, who were willing to testify. He countered that the court might consider them biased, and, in any case, George could come up with witnesses of his own: his two friends. Furthermore, George was only one of the three who had attacked me, and therefore did not bear the entire responsibility for the assault, especially because I did not remember whether he was the ringleader. Finally, I was not hurt badly enough. "Even though you *might* have suffered severe injury from the falling glass, you did not," said Ron, "and the deputies take that into consideration."

Ron continued, explaining to me the various other factors that the charging deputies considered when determining whether to proceed with a case. Assault cases such as mine they did indeed take seriously, far more seriously than cases of jaywalking, sleeping in the park, possession of marijuana, or prostitution, which were other types of cases they received. Cases involving bodily injury or loss of property they took even more seriously, and cases involving repeat offenders were almost sure to be tried. The one thing they did *not* care about was the sexuality of the victim, according to Ron Huberman. "This was not a case of gay discrimination," he assured me. "The district attorney's office has prosecuted several fag-bashing cases vigorously. It is unfortunate that we are not prosecuting yours." With a final suggestion to be sure in the future always to obtain unbiased witnesses in a situation such as this, Ron expressed his disappointment that the case was dead and suggested that I contact the charging deputy who had made the final decision to drop the case, Hugh Donahue, in order to learn more about his reasons.

Although I thought he might want to avoid me, I was able to reach Hugh Donahue on my second try. He assured me that he had investigated my case thoroughly and that there simply wasn't enough evidence to gain a conviction. "As I recall, we had our investigators go out and talk to five or six of the people involved," he stated.

"But they didn't contact *my* witnesses," I protested, "and I gave their names to Sergeant Malone."

"It wouldn't have mattered," Donahue continued. "The main thing is that we wouldn't have been able to establish the element of intent. We wouldn't have been able to prove that he *intended* to shove you through that window."

"But his friends *tackled* me!" I cried.

"And how would the court know that there was no provocation on your part?" Donahue asked. "He might say that he believed there was going to be a fight, and so he struck out in self-defense."

This was a bit much for me—the logic of this escaped me—but I understood that Donahue was trying to explain how the court might look at the incident, which dictated how the district attorney's office would proceed. Why waste time on hopeless cases? was Donahue's unvoiced reasoning. Just recently, in fact, Donahue had had a case very similar to mine, which he had felt he could win, yet the jury acquitted the assailant. "We've got a good record of *judges* screaming and yelling at suspects," said Donahue, "but when it comes to a jury, *they* don't do that. They follow the law and say we don't have enough evidence."

Before he hung up, Donahue added, "This really upsets me, believe me—this kind of conduct," referring to that of my assailants.

"Yeah, thanks," I answered. "It doesn't change things much, but I do understand. I don't agree with your decision, but I understand."

So. It's all over. I tried my best to follow through with this thing, but little has come of it: a good deal of publicity, some public indignation—that's about it. George and his two friends may have been temporarily frightened or inconvenienced, but they did not suffer the consequences of a sentence, a trial, or even a pretrial hearing, as I wanted. They are still at liberty to walk on Haight Street, and, for all I know, they may be beating up on faggots at this very moment.

I am not surprised at the way things have turned out. Neither am I disillusioned or embittered by the experience. I know that the American system of justice has a million flaws and that it hardly approximates the ideal. The thing to do is simply to learn the system and make it work for you, if you can. I tried. I just didn't try hard enough. What else could I have done? I could have rounded up those "unbiased" witnesses in the beginning, perhaps. I wanted to do it at the time, but they were fading from the scene fast, and I didn't want to bother them. All of this may seem like an awful lot of work for the victim of a crime, of course, but there is a principle involved here—that every person is entitled to freedom from assault—and it is a principle worth working for, even when the case is a "minor" one such as mine.

The thing that is the most disturbing to me about this affair is that by dropping the charges against George, the district attorney's office has sent a clear signal to my three assailants that it is perfectly okay to attack queers. Perhaps I will sound like a fascist when I say this, but if society fails to punish adequately those who break its rules, then it is, in effect, condoning such errant behavior—as in the Dan White case. Naturally Hugh Donahue disagrees with me and says that those who attacked me knew the case was discharged not because the district attorney's office didn't take it seriously enough, but because they didn't have enough evidence to convict them, and besides, the courts were too jammed anyway. Somehow I doubt that my attackers fully appreciated this reasoning. But Donahue persists: "I don't think they got away with it. We called every one of the guys in here to question them. The word went out. It put a pretty good scare in them to have to make a statement." Is he serious? I can just hear my assailants now, saying (à la Leo Gorcey), "Oooh, I'm scared. I had to make a *statement*." The word went out all right. Go ahead and get the pansies, was the word. Just don't get caught. But if you do, it won't matter much. They may ask you a few questions, but they usually let you go free.

I still go out at night, of course. I can't let one mugging in my four years in this city keep me off the streets of San Francisco. But whenever I return home after dark, I walk down the middle of the street rather than the sidewalk, and I am constantly on the lookout for suspicious-appearing groups of people. I also carry a whistle when feeling particularly paranoid, although I admit I ought to wear it all the time. Living like this is annoying, to be sure. I often feel as if I am living in a state of siege. But as long as attacks against gay people continue, we *are* living in a state of siege, and it is wise to remember it. It is also advisable to do something about it. We should not accept this state of affairs without fighting back. But I don't think that that fight should take place in the streets: take it from one who knows. Fight in the newspapers, in the churches, in the schools, or in the homes—even fight in the courts if you can—but keep it verbal and keep it off the streets. Windows get broken that way.

A Crime Against Nature

OCTOBER 1984

FORGIVE ME FOR writing so soon again about my friend Nikita, but he called the other day with distressing news.

"What's up?" I asked.

"What's the worst thing that could possibly happen to a faggot?" he responded. "What's every gay person's nightmare?"

"AIDS," I answered, but I knew that couldn't be it. He didn't sound at all frightened: quite the opposite, actually. He sounded as if he were about to let me in on some kind of private joke.

"I've been arrested," he confessed, "for crimes against nature."

"You're not serious," I said, aghast.

"I wish I weren't."

It had happened just a few days before, in the early hours of the morning. He had been drinking and partying on the boardwalk of the small beach town where he lived near the Outer Banks of North Carolina when he was approached by a young man, twenty-two, who offered sex in exchange for cash: twenty dollars' worth. Nikita, who swore that he had never paid for sex before, agreed, and off into the dunes the two of them went. "Money changed hands," he admitted, and afterward he trotted home to bed.

A few hours later, at 5:00 A.M., he was awakened by the police banging on his door. When he answered, they arrested him, hauled him down to the police station, and charged him with rape. "What!" he stammered, but that's what his partner of a few hours before claimed. For some reason—Nikita had no idea why—the kid had gone to the police. Perhaps he had some sort of blackmail scheme in mind, or he was feeling guilty or afraid, or maybe he was living at home and his parents had found out. Whatever the reason, he snitched, and Nikita suddenly found himself in a great deal of trouble.

Nikita, who was quite drunk when the police questioned him, defended himself by confessing all, and the police, after questioning the boy a second time, dropped the rape charge but added two more: aiding and abetting prostitution and crimes against nature. Seriously, that's what it was called: crimes against nature. In North Carolina homosexual acts are still a felony, unlike California, where consenting adults can do whatever they please (at least in private and as long as no money is involved). The kid was also charged—with soliciting—so as far as I'm concerned, he got what he deserved for running to the police and making a false accusation. But still, that didn't help Nikita any.

After being fingerprinted and photographed, Nikita was released on $1000 bond. He then had to retain a lawyer, which set him back another $2500. He does not know exactly when his case will go to trial, but when it does he will be tried in Superior Court. The judge, he hopes, will be lenient. I hope so too, for he faces up to *ten years* in jail.

"So," I sighed, when Nikita had finished with his tale, "I guess this means we won't be going to Greece this fall."

Realistically, Nikita does not think he will end up in jail. He can't believe that the state still sends gay people to jail for having sex, even if they do pay for it. (The state does, of course—and it does worse things than that.) The main thing Nikita fears, besides the expense, is the possible loss of his job. On Tuesday a three-inch article about his arrest appeared on page 14 of the local paper, so everyone at work now knows about it. Luckily, they already knew he was gay, so that didn't come as a big shock to them. They hadn't, however, expected him to get arrested for it. But then, neither had he.

So far, the board of the exclusive country club where he works as head chef has been quite good to him by "doing everything they can" for him, even helping him to find his lawyer. But if the extremely conservative members of the club (and that is 90 percent of the club, at least) get upset and demand his resignation, Nikita believes that the board will be forced to ask for it. If they do, "I won't fight it," he says. "It's just one of those things."

I don't know that I agree with his attitude in this particular matter. The militant in me wishes he would fight. But if I were in his position, I might do the same as he is doing. On the one hand, it is ungrateful to bite the hand that has fed you. On the other hand, just as it is no damn business of the government how Nikita chooses to use his genitals, it is no damn business of his employers when he gets arrested for using them.

Luckily, Nikita has retained a sense of humor about all this so far. When I asked him exactly what he *had* done in the bushes—had he fucked the boy, after all, which would have allowed the kid to cry rape?—he replied, "Are you serious? I mean, let's be realistic. It's too sandy to do that at the beach." He is also aware how lucky he is that the kid is twenty-two. What if he were a minor, after all? (Because this is Nikita, it is not unthinkable.) That would definitely land him in jail, especially in North Carolina. He is *not* amused, however, at the irony of getting arrested for aiding and abetting on his very first outing as a john. Sometimes life is too cruel.

My reaction to all this is confused. I do see the black humor in the situation, and I laugh with Nikita at the same time that I worry for him. Most of all, though, I am angry. How dare he be branded a criminal for having sex with another man, even if he did pay for it? This is the thing that made us gay activists the maddest when we were first coming out as a group, the thing we shouted about the loudest back in the early days of gay liberation. "We are *not* criminals!" we screamed. "We are not sinners! And we are not sick!" And, yes, this was one of our worst fears: that someday we would be arrested simply for being who and what we were.

So now that this has happened to one of my best friends, what do I do about it? Do I shout and scream and write articles for the paper as well as letters to the governor and to every petty official in North Carolina? Do I fly to Nikita's side and lead protest demonstrations on the Outer Banks?

Or do I shrug it off and say, "Well, those are the breaks. He knew the chances he was taking, not only by paying for it and by doing it in the bushes, but also by choosing to live an openly gay life in a backwoods, backward town." It is sometimes difficult, after all, to feel a great deal of sympathy for one who deliberately walks a dangerous path.

Do I mean that? No, I couldn't possibly, for those who walk dangerous paths, as long as they do it for the right reasons, are the true heroes, the true radicals. And what are those right reasons? Oh, I don't know: to advance the cause of personal liberty and homosexual freedom, certainly. To advance the right to get your rocks off? Maybe. At any rate, it is never difficult to feel sympathy for Nikita—he is my friend—or for any faggot who breaks idiotic, antiquated laws, however he comes to do it.

I suppose that what Nikita must do now, in spite of what I just said, is to play by the rules. It would do him no good to destroy himself in a fight he cannot possibly win. He must stand up for himself and feel no shame, of course. Yet, if in the long run, after spending the money and arguing his case, he must declare himself guilty in order to get off lightly, he should do so. It would be silly to serve jail time because of a vain attempt to convince a Neanderthal judge that it is okay to give a blow job to a male prostitute. The judge would never believe it.

Emma Goldman would be ashamed of me.

Anatomy of a Murder Trial

FEBRUARY 1987

FOR MEMBERS OF San Francisco's gay community, it was the fag-bashing case of the decade. On Sunday evening, July 29, 1984, two gay men, John O'Connell and Andy Woodward, were attacked at the intersection of California and Polk streets by a group of young white men. Woodward, thirty-seven, escaped relatively unharmed, but O'Connell, forty-two, was beaten and knocked to the ground, where he struck his head on the pavement and suffered severe head injuries. Lapsing into a coma, O'Connell was taken to San Francisco General Hospital, where he died early Wednesday morning without regaining consciousness.

Less than two weeks later, acting on information received from a young woman named Kathy Kilgore, police arrested five young men in connection with the case: Tim White, twenty-two, David Rogers, nineteen, Donny Clanton, nineteen, Doug Barr, nineteen, and Jay Reyes, twenty. Like Kilgore, Donny Clanton's girlfriend at the time, all were residents of the city of Vallejo, a town of eighty thousand people located thirty miles northeast of San Francisco. Four of the five were eventually charged with second-degree murder. The fifth young man, Jay Reyes, was initially charged as an accessory to murder, but the charges were later dropped. Bail was set at one million dollars apiece, and for more than a year, the four languished in jail in San Francisco while the case against them was being prepared.

The O'Connell incident was not the only fag bashing of 1984—or since. According to Randy Schell and Diane Christensen, the codirectors of Community United Against Violence (CUAV), a local, nonprofit organization founded in 1979 specifically to deal with the problem of violence against gay people, more than forty assaults a month are reported directly to the organization—and the number is increasing. For the nine-month period ending September 30, 1985, assaults were 32 percent greater than they had been during the same period the year before, the year of the O'Connell assault—an increase Christensen attributes to the public's growing awareness and fear of AIDS. "Very few" of these attacks, however, result in arrest, even fewer come to trial, and as far as convictions are concerned, "the numbers are so miniscule we don't bother to take statistics," says Christensen.

The reason for this is not a lack of willingness to prosecute on the part of the district attorney's office, continues Christensen. "A lot of it has to do with how assaults happen. These are usually hit-and-run incidents by a group of kids. Because things happen so fast, there are few good, solid, reliable witnesses. So even if the kids are caught, the D.A.'s office has little to go on. It's the victim's word against the kids'. And that never stands up in court."

Even when there are witnesses, it's often not enough. "A year ago my lover was assaulted by a man who beat her with a trash can lid and called her a fucking dyke," reports Christensen. "There were three lesbian witnesses to that attack, but they refused to make statements. After we pressured them, one finally agreed, but the D.A.'s office decided not to prosecute. Not enough to go on."

At a preliminary hearing in January 1985, Judge Alex Salamando decided that there was certainly enough to go on in the O'Connell case, and a trial date was set for July 1985. Due to scheduling conflicts, however, jury selection did not begin until October, and when it did, all hell broke loose in a community already emotionally traumatized by the assaults. The reason for the uproar was that the defense attorneys for the Vallejo youths, who earlier had asked for a change of venue because they claimed their clients could not get a fair trial in a city with such a large and powerful gay population, moved to bar gay people from the jury. They did this by asking prospective jurors if they had gay family members or belonged to gay organizations. The attorneys did not question them directly, however, about their sexual orientation.

Many gay community leaders were stunned and outraged. "I can see what's coming down from a million miles away," wrote Brian Jones in an editorial in the *Bay Area Reporter*, San Francisco's leading gay newspaper. "The Public Defender will stack the jury with Good Family types. Then the gay community—not the four defendants—will be put on trial." After predicting that the jury would convict O'Connell's attackers on reduced charges, Jones continued, "There's a message here. If gays can be systematically excluded from A Jury of Your Peers, then we're not really peers. We're not equal citizens under the law. That's what is happening at the Bastille on Bryant Street. . . . The thugs are getting the message. . . . It's not as big a deal to kill a fag as anyone else."

The sentiments of Brian Jones struck a responsive chord among those embittered by the lenient sentence given convicted "manslaughterer" Dan White six years earlier: a mere five years for the execution-style killings of the city's mayor and its gay supervisor. But not all shared his views. The following week gay attorney Tom Horn stated, "I don't fault the Public Defender for inquiring about the sexual preferences of the prospective jurors. I would do it also. The emotional feeling regarding 'fag bashing' in general is going to make any defense lawyer question whether a gay juror can be fair in a case where fag bashing is charged. It is an obvious, possible preconceived prejudice, and a defense lawyer who did not seek to eliminate jurors who had preconceived prejudices would not be doing his or her job."

Continued Horn, "A jury of your peers does not mean a jury that is mad as hell because of the condition of things generally and thus willing to string the bastards up by the balls in this specific case." Calling the Dan White case "the obvious exception to the rule," Horn concluded, "I firmly believe that in 99 percent of the cases . . . the jury will reach the right verdict."

While this furor raged in the gay press, a jury was eventually empaneled, a process that took three weeks. Presumably a jury with no gay members, the twelve men and women did represent an otherwise fairly broad cross-section of San Francisco's populace: two white men, one black man, three Asian women, and six white women. Sworn in by Superior Court Judge Edward Sterne, the jury promised to consider only the evidence presented in court, to form no judgments until the last piece of evidence was presented in court, to discuss the case with no one, and to avoid all mention of the case on TV or in the press. At last, on November 25, 1985, opening arguments began.

Representing the people of San Francisco in the case, Assistant District Attorney Bill Fazio told the jury what he believed had happened on the evening of July 29, 1984. According to Fazio, the six Vallejo youths—the five young men plus Clanton's girlfriend, Kathy Kilgore—had decided to go to San Francisco at the instigation of David "Stretch" Rogers, who suggested the trip in order "to beat up some faggots." Driving to the city in two cars, Kilgore's Volkswagen and Reyes's truck, they met at the intersection of Polk and California streets, outside a small shopping mall called Chelsea Square. There they sat, passing around a bottle of Yukon Jack, when two men, John O'Connell and Andy Woodward, walked by on their way from Kimo's bar on Polk Street to a Versateller machine on California.

Solely because the two were perceived as gay, continued Fazio, one of the youths, Donny Clanton, said, "Somebody get that dude," and then, "If you guys aren't going to do anything, then I am." Clanton then chased after O'Connell and Woodward, followed by White, Rogers, and Barr, while Jay Reyes and Kathy Kilgore remained at a distance. As someone yelled "mother-fucking faggot queers"—the last words O'Connell heard, according to Fazio—White and Rogers struck O'Connell in the face, unleashing a "fury of homophobic rage and hate." Returning to Kilgore's car, the defendants regrouped and bragged about what they had done. There they parted company, Reyes returning to Vallejo, the others remaining in San Francisco.

After Fazio concluded his opening statement, the four defense attorneys presented their versions of the attacks. White's attorney, Harvey Goldfine, offered no alternate version of the facts as Fazio had presented them, admitting that his client had struck O'Connell. "I'm sorry to tell you that, but he did it," Goldfine said. "I can offer no reason for my client following those men except for the fact that they were gay." He did, however, offer a different interpretation of those facts, suggesting that facial damage to O'Connell was so slight that it was impossible that death had been caused by the blows to the face. Rather, it had been caused by the injury to the back of the head, for which his client may not have been responsible.

The attorney for Rogers, Michael Burt from the public defender's office, concurred with Goldfine and added that O'Connell had been drinking that night and had an alcohol blood level of 2.9. It was this that had caused him to trip, not the blows from White or Rogers, suggested Burt. Furthermore, the witnesses for the prosecution, he added, hadn't seen enough of what was going on to be able to ascertain the truth of that night. Burt concluded by asking the jury to convict his client of involuntary manslaughter rather than second-degree murder.

Clanton's attorney, Michael Gaines, suggested that the case against his client would fall apart when the prosecution failed to prove exactly what it was that

Danny Clanton had said that night. And as the charges against Clanton were based solely upon his allegedly inciting others to action, exactly what Clanton had said was of extreme importance, according to Gaines. Finally, Barr's attorney, Martin Lurie, predicted that his client would be acquitted because he had done nothing at all that night. In fact, said Lurie, he had been returning from a pizza parlor on Polk Street when the incident occurred.

While the prosecution and the defense set the stage, others besides the jury listened carefully to their arguments. One one side of the courtroom, behind the defendants, sat family and friends of the young men from Vallejo. On the other, behind an imposing array of television cameras and journalists, sat interested members of the gay community. One particular individual was more interested than most: Ron Rod, O'Connell's lover. During a break on the first day of the trial, he talked about his reaction to the death of his lover, the man he had met the day before Christmas 1983 and called his Christmas present.

"I didn't find out until I got back from lunch the next day," Rod recalled. "He hadn't come home the night before, and someone from San Francisco General had to track me down. I immediately went to the hospital, where he was in a coma, having undergone six hours of brain surgery the night before. I was there until he died two days later.

"The toughest part of the whole thing was telling John's mother," continued Rod. "It was one of the roughest phone calls I have ever made. Then later, when his two brothers came out from Phoenix, they were extremely angry. They didn't realize that everything was already under control, that I had taken care of everything, including funeral arrangements at Grace Cathedral. When they found that John was part of a community, a very caring community, their whole attitude changed."

Rod admitted to mixed feelings about the trial. "I hate to see young people's lives destroyed," he said, "but on the other hand, I have lost somebody very close to me, so they have affected my life very heavily. My biggest concern is that I don't want this to happen to anybody else, straight or gay. I have a sneaking suspicion, however, that the mentality of these people is such that it won't do any good. 'They're such good boys,' their friends and relatives will say. 'They didn't mean to hurt anybody.' Bullshit. If they are such good boys, why did they come to San Francisco to beat up gay people in the first place? You know, we hear all the time about fag bashings. But when was the last time a gay person went to Vallejo to beat up straight people?"

Rod noted that the death of his lover was not the first time he has been affected by violence. Not long ago another friend of his was raped and robbed by high school–aged youths in an alley off Geary Street in San Francisco. O'Connell's death, however, was the most direct intrusion of violence into his life, and it has prompted him to do something about the situation. Soon after retiring from his job of twenty-three years as a data processor, he began working at CUAV on a volunteer basis as a computer programmer helping to keep track of statistics. It was the only way he knew to make his lover's death mean something.

Before Rod returned to the courtroom to hear the testimony of the first witness in the trial, he was greeted by Randy Schell of CUAV, who said, "I've just returned from the coroner's office downstairs. More bad news: last night a man's body was discovered in Natoma Alley. The body had multiple stab wounds and a slashed throat, and it had been castrated. They thought I might be able to help identify the victim, but I couldn't tell them anything." Because Natoma Alley was a popular nighttime cruising spot for some gay men, it was assumed that the victim might be gay. But whether this was a specifically antigay assault, a sex killing, or some other kind of murder, Schell did not know. Whatever the motive for the crime, however, Schell was not unaware of the irony of a gay murder being committed the night before the opening of a gay murder trial. "It's a short walk from the courtroom down to the coroner's office," he said, "one I hadn't expected to take today."

The first witness for the people of San Francisco was Jay Reyes, who, along with Kathy Kilgore, had accompanied the four defendants to San Francisco that night. Reyes began his testimony by pinpointing Rogers as saying in a parking lot in Vallejo, "Let's go to San Francisco to beat up some faggots." He then claimed that Donny Clanton had made the statement that instigated the attack: "Somebody get that dude." According to Reyes, a dark-haired, self-assured young man, he did not join in the attack, nor did he see his friends actually hit O'Connell. He was following in a corridor in the shopping mall at the time and arrived only in time to see O'Connell fall, "straight as a board." He later added, "like a tree." Returning the way he had come, he told Kilgore, who had not followed, "They really laid that dude out. You don't want to have anything to do with this, and neither do I." Disturbed by the attitude of his friends, who were acting "proud" of themselves, Reyes then got in his truck and returned to Vallejo. When Fazio asked him why, he replied, "I didn't like what I saw, and I didn't want to be a part of it."

Reyes added that shortly after the attack he left the Bay Area with Barr and White—but not because of the incident, he said, although he "figured" the police would be looking for him. He was arrested with Barr on August 8 in Yonkalla, Washington. Although the charges against him were later dropped, he had not made a deal with the district attorney, he testified. In fact, he had never even spoken to the prosecutor before his appearance at the preliminary hearings in January—an appearance he did not wish. As he told attorney Goldfine on cross-examination, Tim White had been his best friend before the incident, and Reyes wished him no harm now. "I don't consider him my enemy," Reyes stated. "I feel bad having to sit up here and testify against him."

Defense attorneys tried to discredit Reyes by concentrating on statements that he had made to the police when he was arrested, statements that conflicted with his testimony in court. According to those statements, Reyes hadn't remembered much of what the defendants did or said. But, as Reyes pointed out, he was lying to the police in order to protect his friends, and he repeated that he had no desire to get anyone in trouble.

Kathy Kilgore, the prosecution's second witness, was not nearly as self-assured or as calm as Reyes on the stand. At the preliminary hearings she had broken into tears several times, and at the trial she delivered her testimony in a soft, sometimes quavering voice. Often confused by the intricate rules governing that testimony and by the legal thrusts and parries of counsel, she seemed relieved to retreat into the arms of her current boyfriend at the end of each period of questioning.

Like Reyes, Kilgore stated that she didn't want to get anyone in trouble, and that she didn't want to be in court, but had been subpoenaed. The only reason that she had talked to the police in the first place, she said, was not for the reward offered, but because her father had convinced her that she must. Besides, she added, "I was scared."

According to Kilgore, O'Connell and Woodward had been "minding their own business" when they passed the group from Vallejo on Polk Street. It was Clanton who said, "If you guys aren't going to do anything, then I am." But it was all four who were laughing about the attack when they returned from chasing O'Connell and Woodward on California Street. Later that night, back in Vallejo at a drive-in dairy, David Rogers bragged that he had punched the man who died. Tim White admitted hitting him as well. When asked if she knew why they did it, Kilgore replied, "Because they thought he was gay." This answer, however, was stricken from the record as hearsay.

Andy Woodward was the third witness for the prosecution. He testified that he had been only "slightly intoxicated" and that O'Connell, although drunker, had not been "stumbling drunk" when the two walked toward the Versateller on California Street. He said he had no verbal contact with anyone on the street and was not even aware of anyone else until he heard someone call O'Connell and himself "mother-fucking faggot queers." Then the two were attacked. Woodward said he did not know who attacked him or how many there were. All he heard was a whack and then a thud—two separate, distinct sounds—before he looked up and saw O'Connell lying on the ground. Like Reyes and Kilgore, he did not actually see O'Connell being struck. "I was hysterical at the time," he explained.

Later Woodward testified that there was an interval of between five and ten seconds between the whack and the thud. He was sure about that, he said several times. In addition, he said that he did not recognize the four defendants as his attackers, although he had identified them at the preliminary hearing. Woodward created a minor sensation in court when he offered this testimony, and the media pounced on it, but it proved to be insignificant, as the testimony of the previous witnesses had placed the defendants at the scene of the crime that night.

Two other witnesses for the prosecution offered little evidence that was compelling. One was the police inspector who had handled the arrests of the defendants. The other was a man who had been on his way home from the movies the night of the attack and had witnessed the commotion following the incident. The testimony given by the last witness for the prosecution, however, was crucial. This testimony was given by Dr. Boyd G. Stephens, medical examiner and coroner for the city of San Francisco since 1971.

After establishing his credentials (numerous degrees, as well as four thousand cases and two thousand autopsies a year), Dr. Stephens described the injuries O'Connell had received, as well as the surgical procedures undertaken in an attempt to save his life. The facial injuries O'Connell received, most likely as a result of being struck, were slight, Stephens stated. There was, however, a twenty-five-centimeter-long fracture across the back of the skull. In addition, direct injury to the brain had occurred when O'Connell's head hit the pavement. After six hours of surgery at San Francisco General Trauma Center, O'Connell died at 3:25 A.M. on August 1, 1984. The cause of death, Stephens testified, was cranial-cerebral trauma resulting from the blow to the back of the head.

Stephens continued that it takes at least four hundred to six hundred pounds per square inch to fracture the skull, and that in an injury of this severity and type, greater force must be applied. Therefore, Stephens concluded, "In my opinion, this is an accelerated injury," adding that the force of the blows to the face was enough to cause O'Connell to fall hard enough to sustain the injury to the back of the head that caused his death.

Later Stephens testified that O'Connell had an alcohol blood level of 2.9 before surgery, or the equivalent of fifteen drinks at one ounce per drink for a person of his size. By any definition, O'Connell was intoxicated, Stephens said; for a person with no tolerance, an alcohol blood level of 2.9 would be enough to cause death. Scar tissue and fatty deposits in O'Connell's liver, however, showed that he was a heavy drinker.

It was this testimony the defense attorneys used to suggest that O'Connell did not fall as a result of the blows to his face, but as a result of tripping on the curb. Stephens answered that this was possible but unlikely, as O'Connell fell from the sidewalk to the street and not vice versa. Furthermore, he added, the amount of force in this case was greater than that which would be seen in a typical fall. Defense attorneys then focused on Woodward's testimony concerning the alleged five-to-ten-second delay between the whack and the thud, and asked Stephens if it would be possible for an accelerated fall to result from a blow to the face after a ten-second delay. Stephens admitted that it would be impossible for this to occur.

Following testimony from Stephens, prosecutor Fazio offered the following statement, given by Tim White to an FBI agent in Vancouver, where he was arrested: "I hit Mr. O'Connell once with the back of my hand. I heard that he subsequently died." After this was admitted into evidence, Fazio rested his case on the fifth day of the trial.

In the absence of the jury, Martin Lurie immediately moved that the charges against his client, Doug Barr, be dropped, for his name had rarely come up during testimony. "He does not act, he doesn't say anything," stated Lurie. "Merely being present at the scene of a crime without assisting it does not amount to aiding and abetting. Neither does knowledge of the crime or failure to prevent it." Gaines and Burt then made the same motion on behalf of their clients, although on different grounds.

In response, Fazio spoke of the "totality of circumstances" and countered that the four had acted as a unit, shared in intent: they came to San Francisco together, they laughed afterward together. Admitting that the evidence was certainly stronger against the other three than against Barr, Fazio argued that surely it was a question that should be presented to the jury.

Siding with the prosecution, Judge Sterne agreed that there had been a community of interest in this case, to which Barr had responded. Comparing the situation to that of a lynch mob, Sterne said, "It doesn't really matter who provides the rope. They all acted as incentive to each other." He then denied the motions to drop the charges.

The defense attorneys called no witnesses of their own, and the four defendants, who had betrayed almost no sign of emotion throughout the trial thus far, never took the stand in their own behalf. At the end of the fifth day, the court adjourned to consider the closing arguments.

In Vallejo, California, residents followed closely the San Francisco trial of the hometown boys charged with murder. Particularly interested were shopkeepers and residents along Springs Road, a typical suburban stretch of gas stations, pizza parlors, auto supply stores, minimarkets, and the like, for this was the area where several of the defendants lived and where they had gathered before driving to San Francisco the night of the O'Connell attack.

According to a seventeen-year-old employee of the local Winchell's, a student at Hogan High, "Everybody at school is talking about the trial, especially one of the teachers, who knows everything about it. We all feel that they should get what's coming to them. They're definitely guilty."

Agreed the fifty-year-old cashier at the liquor store down the street, "Those boys are no good. They were just looking for trouble. The consensus here is that it was stupid to go down there and do something like that." Even a group of preteens playing video games at Rico's pizza parlor shared this opinion, and added, "What they did was wrong. Just because the guys who were attacked were gay doesn't make any difference."

In the parking lot of Springstowne Shopping Center, a gathering spot for area youths, however, opinion concerning the case was sharply divided among the twenty or thirty teenagers sitting in cars, riding bikes, listening to music, sharing cigarettes, and playing ball. Unlike the adults in the area, who referred to the victims of the attack as gay, these teenagers called them fags. Some knew the defendants personally.

"Those guys on trial are guilty as hell," offered one young man.

"No way," another interrupted. "Nobody saw nuthin'. They said on TV that the fag that was with the other fag couldn't even identify Donny and the others."

A third said, "I don't want to say nuthin'. I don't want to get involved. Don't want to get in trouble with the wrong people around here, you know?"

When asked if any of them might ever go to San Francisco to beat up "fags," they replied that they had never really thought about it. They'd be more likely to go to Berkeley to cruise around, pick up women, buy dope, or just hang out. "Hell, we take off every chance we get," said one young man, turning up his radio. "There sure isn't anything to do around here."

On Monday, December 9, the jury reconvened to hear closing arguments. Calling this a case of "unprovoked random street violence" and using words such as "sinister" and "dread," District Attorney Fazio opened his argument by dwelling on fears of city dwellers everywhere. He then appealed to the jurors' sense of fair play for minorities, comparing the victims to Jews and blacks and their persecutors to Nazis and racists.

Fazio next attempted to shore up the testimony of his witnesses and to denigrate the actions of the defendants. Woodward's testimony, he said, showed the effects of the assault; he was like "a wounded bird on the stand." His attackers, on the other hand, were cowards. Referring to the yellow pin used to represent the whereabouts of Donny Clanton on a map of Polk and California streets, Fazio stated, "I think that color is significant." Fazio discounted part of the testimony Woodward gave, however, such as the five-to-ten-second interval statement, attributing the statement to Woodward's faulty sense of timing. He called the defense theories about tripping and falling "perverted hypothetical nonsense."

Fazio also spoke a great deal about implied malice. The defendants had a "conscious disregard" for the welfare of John O'Connell and knew that their actions involved a high degree of probability of death, especially because O'Connell was drunk and therefore unusually vulnerable, Fazio argued. Consequently, the jury had no choice but to find the defendants guilty as charged of second-degree murder.

White's attorney, Goldfine, denied this assumption and argued that there was no malice aforethought. Punching someone in the face is not necessarily a life-threatening act. Goldfine also spoke of "reasonable doubt" and "moral certainty" and concluded by asking for an involuntary manslaughter conviction. Burt's arguments closely paralleled Goldfine's, but Burt also took pains to discredit the prosecution's witnesses. He concentrated especially on Reyes, who lied to the police only in order to protect himself, he suggested. "You might not believe a word he says," said Burt.

Attorneys Lurie and Gaines took a different approach. Lurie repeated the argument that he had made to the judge when he asked for dismissal of charges. His client, Barr, simply had not been involved, he said. Gaines, on the other hand, concentrated on casting doubt in the minds of the jurors concerning the statement Donny Clanton had made, a statement that was the basis for the charges brought against him. Lurie asked the jury to consider three things: were they sure what Donny Clanton had said, were they sure what he had meant, and had he had a specific knowledge what the others were going to do as a result? "I hope you don't get caught up in the role of avenging angels," he concluded.

In rebuttal, Fazio defended his earlier references to Jews, Nazis, blacks, and racists. Then, taking his cue from Judge Sterne, Fazio suggested the lynch mob metaphor and said, "You don't have to bring the rope to be guilty of a lynching." Finally he reiterated that "implied malice is the real guts of this case" and reminded the jury why the defendants had come to San Francisco in the first place: "They didn't come here to have crab *cioppino* at Fisherman's Wharf."

Following instructions by Judge Sterne, the jury retired to consider a verdict. For two and a half days the jurors deliberated. Then, on Friday afternoon, December 13, the twelve women and men reached a unanimous decision. White, Rogers, and Clanton were all found guilty of second-degree murder. Barr, however, was acquitted.

Both the prosecutor and the gay community were elated with the guilty verdicts. Said Fazio to the *Bay Area Reporter*, "I didn't want this to be another Dan White situation," adding that he was only sorry that he couldn't have asked for a first-degree murder conviction. Added investigator Ron Huberman, who had worked closely with Fazio on the case, "At one time beating up gays was laughed at. This sends a message to the punks—we are not fair game anymore."

Diane Christensen of CUAV said she was ecstatic about the verdict. But it wouldn't change one thing: John O'Connell was still dead. Nevertheless, concluded the editor of the *Bay Area Reporter,* "The conviction of three men from Vallejo . . . is one more signal that justice is possible for gay victims of brutal assaults."

On Thursday, January 9, 1986, more than seventeen months after the assault on O'Connell, Judge Sterne sentenced White, Rogers, and Clanton to fifteen years to life in prison. The three also pleaded guilty to three other assaults that had followed the attack on O'Connell—assaults that had never been mentioned in the trial and that came as a complete surprise to many in the gay community who had followed the case. For these assaults, the three youths received prison terms of thirteen years each, to be served concurrently with the fifteen-years-to-life sentences.

Despite his acquittal in the O'Connell case, even Doug Barr did not escape prison. He too pleaded guilty to another assault that night and was sentenced to seven years in prison. Unlike his companions, who will not be eligible for parole until 1995, Barr will be eligible in 1991. The attorneys for all four plan to appeal.

Ironically, just as the three convicted fag bashers were dsentenced to prison, news of another brutal San Francisco fag bashing was being investigated. Two weeks earlier, on December 21, two gay men had been assaulted and beaten in the parking lot of Petrini's Supermarket at Fulton and Masonic streets by a group of thugs wielding chains and skateboards. Unlike the O'Connell case, this time the attackers did not call the victims mother-fucking faggot queers, but merely faggots. Unlike the O'Connell case, no one died, although one of the victims was taken to the hospital to have his jaw wired. And, unlike the O'Connell case, no one has been charged, tried, or convicted.

Yet.

POLITICS: PROTEST

The Vigil: A Profile in Gay Courage

APRIL 1986

IT IS A COLD, wet day in San Francisco. For three days it has been raining incessantly. It is expected to do so for at least three more. It is a miserable day to spend outside. Nevertheless, on a small plot of grass in front of the old Federal Office Building on the United Nations Plaza, a group of weary, damp protestors huddles under a makeshift awning next to a circle of ten weather-beaten tents. Nearby, under sheets of plastic, two more protestors lie chained to two beds that block the doors of the Federal Building. No one who passes asks the protestors what they are doing, for the group is a common sight on the UN Plaza. For nearly five months they have been conducting an illegal yet officially undisturbed occupation: a vigil to call attention to the needs of people with AIDS or ARC (AIDS-related complex).

Evan Durant is one of these protestors. A former nurse at convalescent hospitals in Eureka and Ukiah who was diagnosed with AIDS, Evan moved to San Francisco in August 1984 because there was no adequate treatment for people with AIDS in those small Northern California towns. In San Francisco he found treatment at San Francisco General Hospital, and it was during a hospital stay one day last October when he heard about the AIDS/ARC vigil at the UN Plaza. As Evan says, "I decided to check it out on the recommendation of my social worker at the AIDS Foundation. He thought it would boost my morale."

The vigil proved to be a godsend for Evan, who, after learning of his AIDS diagnosis, had tried to commit suicide several times. "At the very least, it's kept me busy," he says. "Otherwise I would have been staying in my room and climbing the walls. You see, I've been unemployed and living on General Assistance since I moved here. But it's more than that. The vigil has given me something to live for." Although he does not like to think about it, it may also give him something to die for. Evan's health is not good, and spending nights outdoors in the rain in cold weather does not help. "But what can I do?" he asks. "If I don't do this, who will? Somebody has to call attention to the needs of people with AIDS or ARC, and this is the best way I know how to do it."

The vigil began on the night of Sunday, October 24, 1985, when nine individuals, after attending a demonstration and rally sponsored by Mobilization Against AIDS, an AIDS support group based in San Francisco, spontaneously decided to spend the night in front of the old Federal Office Building. Two of the protestors, Frank Bert and Steve Russell (both persons with ARC), chained themselves to the doors of the building and refused to leave until certain demands were met. These were that the federal government allocate five hundred million dollars in funds (equivalent to one hour of federal spending—more than twice what the government proposed to spend) for AIDS/ARC research and that the government extend to people with ARC the same benefits that people with AIDS presently receive (including Social Security and medical benefits). As Frank Bert recalls, "We didn't really expect to have our demands met that night. What we expected was to be arrested and to call attention to our demands. But instead the police and the security of the Federal Building left us alone. So our one-night protest turned into a long-term vigil."

During the next few days the number of protestors grew, and a third demand was added: that the Food and Drug Administration approve the use of drugs being used to treat AIDS and ARC in other countries, such as France and Mexico. According to Gene Ewans, a person with ARC who joined the vigil at the same time as Evan Durant, a week after it began, "We added this demand for several reasons. I know a lot of people who depend on these drugs, but who have to go to Mexico to get them. Why should that be so? If there's a chance of helping just one person, why shouldn't that person's doctor be able to prescribe them? If there are risks, those risks can be explained to the person. It ought to be our choice. But the government doesn't want to give us that choice."

As news of the vigil spread, members of the community lent their support. One of the first was the pastor of the Golden Gate Metropolitan Community Church, Reverend James Sandmire, whose son, Dean, was one of those chained to the door. But not everyone in San Francisco approved. In the early morning hours of Sunday, November 3, the protestors were attacked by a group of men shouting antigay epithets. The vigilers defended themselves, but three (including two straight supporters) received serious injuries, which required hospitalization. Recalls Wes North, thirty-one, another of the original protestors who was there that night, "It was terrible. They called us faggots and queers, all that stuff. Then they came at us. I was lying on the bed at the time, and because I was chained, I couldn't get away, but luckily Fred McClure, one of our group, intervened—and ended up in the hospital as a result." Two of the attackers, San Francisco men aged twenty-two and thirty-one, were later arrested. But Wes North is still afraid that others like them will return. "Some people just want to hurt us," he says. "I guess they're afraid too." One result of the attack was that the vigilers established their own security force. Another was that the president of the San Francisco board of supervisors, John Molinari, demanded police protection for the group—the first official show of support the group received.

Vigilers were further harassed when they were hosed by city workers several nights in a row during the second week of November, one of the coldest Novembers on record. The health of several vigilers consequently deteriorated, but they vowed to carry on. A short time later members of the group were given a much-appreciated boost in morale when supervisor Harry Britt, the only gay member of the board of supervisors, visited the site and introduced a resolution demonstrating the board's support. The resolution passed unanimously and resulted in the achievement in December of one of the vigil's goals, at least locally: the extension of AIDS benefits and services to people with ARC. According to Gene Ewans, "This was our first concrete victory, something we could really be proud of, for it was a direct result of vigil action. We knew we couldn't accomplish everything we wanted overnight, but at least this was a step in the right direction."

Throughout November support from the community continued to grow. Bars, theaters, and hotels offered free food, showers, blankets, clothing, and shelter. The Bay Area Physicians for Human Rights offered medical assistance, and several of the area's influential gay political clubs offered financial assistance. KRON television station provided a TV so that the vigilers could watch the showing of "An Early Frost," and Bay Area Rapid Transit allowed the use of one of its station's electrical power. Finally, near the end of the month, the vigilers heard from their congressional representatives, Sala Burton and Barbara Boxer, both of whom promised to visit the site. There was no word, however, from Senator Pete Wilson, whose aides said that the vigilers were "not really a concern."

Community support ran especially high at Thanksgiving, when the vigilers were inundated with food. The night before, the vigil site was the focus and destination of demonstrators participating in the annual candlelight march commemorating the assassinations of Harvey Milk and Mayor George Moscone. These demonstrators rallied to the vigilers' cause, taping the names of more than seven hundred persons with AIDS and ARC to the side of the Federal Building. "In many ways," states Wes North, "that was the highlight of the vigil for me. It was beautiful. On Thanksgiving we had so much food here, it was pitiful. I figure there were seventy-five or one hundred supporters, gay and straight, down here celebrating with us. And the candlelight march was wonderful, really great. When all those names went up, covering the building from end to end, I cried. I really cried."

Feeling continued to run high throughout the Christmas holidays. A tree was erected, carolers visited the site, and an outdoor mass was held. And this symbolic goodwill was reinforced by concrete action. In mid-December, thanks to the fact that more than one thousand dollars had been raised at the New Belle

Saloon on Polk Street, more than thirty vigil participants were able to travel to Los Angeles to testify at AIDS/ARC hearings held by the California Senate Committee on Health and Human Services.

But although the community was rallying to the cause of the vigilers, interpersonal interactions between vigilers was beginning to deteriorate. The group, which now numbered more than one hundred people, was experiencing dissension and in-fighting. Some of the original protestors left the site, claiming the goals of the vigil—to draw attention to their concerns—had been met. Others began lobbying efforts and actions of their own, not approved by the entire group. Vigilers accused one another of grandstanding or of taking advantage of the group for political or personal purposes. On top of it all, numbers of street people moved in to take advantage of the free food and shelter. Finally, in early February, one of the original vigilers, Steven Russell, set up his own protest by chaining himself to another door of the Federal Building, but was persuaded to leave when federal marshals threatened to eject all the protestors if he did not. Complicating matters was the fact that the vigilers had no organized structure and no designated leaders to deal with these problems. Few had any experience in resolving internal conflict of this kind.

Despite all this (and perhaps unaware of it), politicians continued to jump on the bandwagon. In January letters of support were received from Mayor Dianne Feinstein, Senator Alan Cranston, Congressperson Ron Dellums, State Senator Milton Marks, and, at last, Senator Pete Wilson. Perhaps Mayor Feinstein best summed up the feelings of this eclectic group of politicians when she wrote, "You have suffered many cold nights in your tents, warmed only by friendships. I look forward to a time when you can return to your homes." Returning to their homes, however, was the last thing on the minds of most of the vigilers. Determined to overcome their problems, vigilers organized, labeled themselves a family, and vowed to return to the original spirit of the group: a spirit of love, not jealousy. "We had to get back to the basics," explains Gene Ewans. "Love is what kept me going all that time. Love is what will continue to see me through." A fourth demand—now termed a moral appeal—was added to the previous three. This was a request that President Reagan issue a statement denouncing discrimination against people with AIDS or ARC.

At the end of January, plans were made to send a group to Washington, D.C., to lobby for acceptance of their goals, and the use of Senator Cranston's offices there was secured. Although two of the intended representatives later became too sick to go, in early February vigil participants Esther Oppenheimer and Michael Pritchard left for Washington to lobby members of Congress as well as federal bureaucracies such as the Food and Drug Administration and Health and Human Services. They also planned to open communication with and seek ties with other AIDS/ARC activists and organizations. But their visit was cut short when vigiler Jay Young died back in San Francisco—the first of the group to succumb to his disease. Young's death only made the remaining vigilers more determined than ever to carry on. As Bonnie McDonald, a straight member of the vigil family, explains, "Jay was one of the many friends we're going to lose. But that just makes me want to fight harder. He believed in us and loved us all so much, I think he'd be glad to know that the rest of us will stay here until we get what we want."

The group's determination was sorely tested by a huge storm in February that flooded parts of Northern California and nearly wiped out the vigil site as well. Rains continued unabated for days, and winds tore down more than half the tents at the site. Grimaces Wes North, "It was a bitch. Most people left the site and retreated indoors for a few days—for reasons of health, mostly—but a few of us stuck it out. True, some people resigned, but those who did were replaced by others. Individual people come and go, but the vigil goes on."

In the midst of the storm, the group was honored by the board of directors of the locally based Cable Car Awards at the organization's annual ceremony in downtown San Francisco. More than one thousand people stood and cheered as three of the vigilers—Frank Bert, Steve Russell, and John Lorenzini—accepted the award on behalf of their fellow vigilers. According to various members of the audience, it was the highlight of the evening and an expression of goodwill and support from the community at large. Furthermore, it was a mandate to the vigilers to continue their fight to draw attention to the needs of people with AIDS or ARC. Concludes Frank Bert, "Awards are nice and all, but the important thing is the four moral appeals. That's what we want—and that's what we'll get."

The rain continues. Despite the steady downpour, the small tent city outside the Federal Building has a festive air about it. At one corner flies a brightly colored rainbow flag. At another, above the mailbox marked 50½ UN Plaza, flies a Colonial serpent flag emblazoned with the words, Don't Tread On Me. A large billboard in front proclaims the four moral appeals of the vigil, and another celebrates the life of Jay Young, who died "fighting bigotry and fear." Piles of wet blankets and sleeping bags are stacked neatly near the main information desk, where cups of steaming hot coffee are offered, along with brochures, newspapers, and ribbons. The ribbons are emblems of support. They are colored green to represent the money needed to combat AIDS and ARC. There are chains attached to the ribbons; they represent not only the chains holding two of the vigilers to the doors of the Federal Building, but also the "links of life" that sustain them.

The revitalized look of the vigil is largely the work of the committees that were formed to take care of daily tasks, explains Frank Bert, one of the original protestors. There are several such committees, and each committee member wears a name tag indicating his or her position. The name tags are color coded: green for security, yellow for community service team, and so on. Although everyone who supports the vigil is welcome there, vigil family membership is restricted to those who contribute ten hours of work a week to the group—and to those who can show a valid ID and verifiable local street address. (This is to discourage uninterested street people.) All vigil family members have an equal say in the running of things, and outside interference is rejected. As one family member says, "We encourage support from everyone, as long as they don't come down here to tell us what to do."

As Frank willingly explains to passersby, no individual spends every night and every day at the vigil site. On any given night there may be as few as three or four and as many as ten or fifteen people sleeping in the tents—and two more on the beds, of course. Family members rotate vigils in order to allow one another to take care of tasks at home. Meals are taken either at home, at the site, or at one of the eateries in the area. Local businesses, such as the Starlite Room and the National Hotel, have been especially helpful in assisting with the daily needs of the vigilers—by offering the use of the bathrooms, for instance.

Keeping things functioning and the site orderly is important to Frank, for he realizes that although getting the federal government to act on the four moral appeals is the main goal of the group, spreading the word on a person-to-person basis to people who drop by is an equally valuable goal. Frank is not discouraged when a person asks an idiotic question, such as, "Are these tents for sale?" or when a crazy walks past shouting, "I know how to end AIDS: give it to Reagan! The day he gets the disease is the day we find a cure!" Instead Frank is rejuvenated by people who express a genuine interest in the aims of the group and in the personal concerns of vigil family members. Those who stop to ask questions quickly learn that the story of the vigil is as much a story of the individuals involved as it is a story of political and medical issues.

Wes North was not present that night in October when Frank Bert and Steve Russell chained themselves to the door of the Federal Building, but he visited the vigil the very next day, joined the third day, and has been a vigil family member ever since. A native of Henderson, Texas, Wes moved to San Francisco two years ago "for the gay lifestyle" and was diagnosed with AIDS in June 1985. As soon as he told his lover, his lover kicked him out of the house. He also lost most of his friends. With no one else to depend on, Wes turned to drugs, and when that didn't work, he didn't know what to do. Luckily, he then discovered the vigil.

Although he has a room at the Arlington Hotel in the Tenderloin (he would like an apartment but can't afford it), Wes spends most of his nights in a tent at the vigil site—against his doctors' wishes. Wes knows that he is very sick—he has been hospitalized twice and taken to the emergency room seven or eight times since the vigil began—and he understands his doctors' concerns, but he says that the best cure for him is the love he receives from fellow vigil family members. "There's so much love out here. That's what's keeping me going right now."

The support he receives is one of the main reasons Wes is taking part in the vigil, he admits, but he is not just fighting for his own life. "We are fighting for other people's lives too." He works as tirelessly as he can to help spread the message of the vigil—he has lobbied before the board of supervisors and spoken at benefits—but for Wes, the vigil means more than just achieving its four moral appeals. For him it means the chance to offer to others in his situation the same kind of support he has received. "Lots of people who have AIDS or ARC and don't know how to handle it have come down here to talk about it," he says. "That's one way I can help." Another is by remaining as independent as possible. Although he cannot work and collects only six hundred dollars a month through SSDI, Wes will not use money available from the San Francisco AIDS Fund. He prefers to leave that for "other people who need it more than I do."

Although sometimes he feels so weak he starts crying, and other times he hurts so much he feels like giving up completely, Wes vows he will be here "as long as it takes to have our moral appeals met." And although he does worry about dying, he is more worried, he says, that Congress won't respond to the vigil family's moral appeals or that by the time it does, nobody in the family will be left to find out about it.

Unlike Wes, Esther Oppenheimer is not gay, nor does she have AIDS or ARC. She *is* a devoted member of the vigil family, however, and, like Wes, she works tirelessly on its behalf. In her green pants suit and her straw bonnet bedecked with ribbons, she cuts quite a figure. Perhaps this is also because, at age sixty-plus, she is a good thirty or forty years older than many of the other members of the family.

Esther is a native San Franciscan, a former employee of Macy's and shop steward of her union (United Food and Commercial Workers, Local 1100), who has a long history of community activism. She has fought for the causes of Jewish, labor, American Indian, and gay rights organizations, and she has received numerous awards and certificates for the volunteer work she has done for groups such as KQED (the local public television station) and the Northern California Pharmaceutical Auxiliary. "I've had my finger in one hundred pies," she says. The metaphor is appropriate, for she has made more than fifteen thousand miniature cupcakes, each one decorated, for the members of the various organizations she supports.

Esther sees her role in the vigil family largely as a maternal one. "This is strictly a family," she says. "Most of the real families of these men have forgotten them. They have turned their backs because they don't understand. So I have tried to bring a little bit of home here. I cook turkeys and I bake. I wish I could give every one of them a home." The others in the group, however, see her as a valuable political activist as well, and that's one of the reasons she was selected to represent the group in Washington, D.C.

Although she is a nonstop talker who tends to ramble and is lovingly described as "crazy as a bedbug" by one of her admirers, Esther has certain skills that make her an effective spokesperson. "I concentrate on the human touch," she says. "I go to churches, to labor groups. I talk to people. And I don't give up. Furthermore, I never make appointments. I walk in, ask for five minutes of their time, and start talking. They can't escape, for I know where to find them." And although Esther believes in the importance of talking with politicians and influential community members to further the acceptance of the four moral appeals, she says that nothing takes the place of letter writing. "I know that if you bombard Washington through the post office, they'll hear the message loud and clear. If people would do that, we'd get what we want."

Bill Paul is another vigil family member. Bill is a member of Mobilization Against AIDS, the organization that sponsored the rally preceding the vigil (although not the vigil itself), and, like Esther Oppenheimer, he is a long-time community activist. He became involved in a group called Gay Rap in 1969 and later served as a block captain for Gays for McGovern. He was formerly a member of the United States Olympic judo team, and he is presently employed as an educational psychologist at San Francisco State University.

Although Bill has been involved with the vigil from the very first night—he was the one who bought the chains, he says—he is quick to concede that the vigilers have had many problems. For one thing, there has been little sense of accountability. There has also been a good deal of drug use and even theft. (The night of the candlelight march, more than four thousand dollars in contributions disappeared.) Another problem has been the undesirable presence of freeloading street people, who have no interest in the political or social goals of the group. And in the group, a number of people became drunk with power and infatuated with their roles as media stars. But the worst problem, according to Bill, has been the coverage of the vigil by certain members of the gay press, coverage that Bill calls "bitchy, venomous, and oppressive."

In spite of these problems, Bill feels that the vigil has served a very worthwhile purpose. "It has enabled ordinary people to do something concrete and practical," he says. "They may not be able to find a cure for AIDS or ARC, but they *can* hug somebody or put a warm coat on him. There has been a spontaneous community show of support for the vigilers, and in this way the vigil is very much like the 1960s. There's a lot of love here."

The 1960s comparison is an apt one. The vigil is a happening, an event that was born of civil disobedience and social unrest. The unique thing about the vigil, as opposed to other gay political events, Bill continues, is that most of the people involved with it are not from the entrenched middle-class power structure that has long dominated the local gay political scene. Rather, they are, for the most part, working-class newcomers who, out of a sense of anger and desperation, felt compelled to act. Like their predecessors, they have had to learn quickly a great deal about the politics of change.

More than anything else, Bill would like the world to know that "there are a lot of wonderful, wonderful people here"—people such as Fred McClure, the person in charge of security, who, the day after Christmas, put himself in the way of an attack on other vigilers and sustained a severe back injury as a result; and people such as Tim Byron, who was fired from his job when his boss saw him on television at the vigil site. Bill also admires people such as John Belkus, another of the original nine, who has spent a great deal of time and money lobbying in New York and Washington on behalf of the vigil; and people such as Bonnie McDonald and her husband, who spend up to sixteen hours a day answering questions at the information table, standing security shifts, coordinating and organizing food donations, doing laundry, and overseeing financial contributions.

Finally Bill points to Grannie, an old woman with heart trouble who is confined to a wheelchair and who became a member of the vigil family "because they were so nice to me to take me out of the rain." Grannie, who gave up her bed at the Episcopal Sanctuary to join the vigilers and who spent her seventieth birthday at the vigil site, now spends her days soliciting donations for the vigil on Market Street with the sign, Please Help Me To Help Others. As Grannie explains, "These people really need help. I'll stay with them as long as I can." It is this diverse group, concludes Bill, that best sums up the spirit of the vigil.

At last the rain stops. Frank Bert shakes the water off the plastic sheets covering his bed as Wes North emerges from a tent. At the main information desk, Bonnie McDonald rearranges pamphlets and admits, "Sure, it's a strain. It burns you out being here all the time. But we'll be here until we get what we want." Bonnie's dream is the establishment of a vigil in every major city across the nation. "The worst thing about this crisis," she explains, "is the ignorance, the lack of information. And the vigil is the best way I know to get the point across—that this is not just a gay disease. It's everybody's concern." Frank and Wes nod in agreement and then excuse themselves to go about their business. Another day at the vigil site begins.

Out and Outrageous: An Experiment in Civil Disobedience

OCTOBER 1987

WHEN THE SUPREME COURT upheld the constitutionality of Georgia's sodomy law in the *Hardwick* case last year, I was as disappointed as I have ever been in the American system of justice. Later, after the Gay "Olympics" decision, my frustration turned to rage, and I wanted to throw rocks at the Federal Building downtown. Luckily, I found a better way to express myself. I flew to Washington to participate in Out and Outraged, last week's nonviolent civil disobedience at the Supreme Court.

Doing this was extremely important to me. I had always counted on the Supreme Court as the court of last resort, and when it failed to recognize our rights, I felt we had no place left to turn. Like Thoreau, Gandhi, and Martin Luther King, Jr., before me, I took matters into my own hands and rebelled. I refused to accept an unjust situation.

Early on the morning of October 13, therefore, I rode the D.C. subway with two dykes from Los Angeles wearing Screw the U.S. Supreme Court sweatshirts to the park across the street from the Supreme Court building. There thousands of demonstrators were assembling. I soon spotted my friend Jim, who had agreed to act as my support person and to keep track of my whereabouts from the outside throughout the day.

At an information table I tried to sign up with one of the organized affinity groups, groups of people with shared goals who planned to be arrested together. When I admitted that I had undergone no civil disobedience training, however, I was asked not to participate.

"But I've counted on this for months," I protested. "I've talked with people who've had the training, and I know what to expect. Don't make me disobey the civil disobedians."

Fortunately, Jim and I located a friend of his, Reid, who was the support person for an affinity group from San Francisco called A More Perfect Union. Even though they had all undergone training and had previously agreed to be a closed group, they allowed me to join. The ten of us linked arms in solidarity.

At a nine o'clock rally, speakers stated our purpose and proclaimed, "Today we are sitting in at the lunch counters of the gay and lesbian civil rights movement." Then the first wave of protestors surged across the street to the cheers and cries of thousands.

In the press of hundreds of spectators, photographers, and fellow protestors, only half our group managed to cross the police barricades on the steps of the court. The others were held back by the crowd.

Retracing our steps, we reunited and sat down just outside the barricades. There we chanted the words chiseled in stone above us—Equal Rights Under Law—and sang the songs "We Shall Overcome," "America the Beautiful," and "We Are a Gentle, Loving People." Some protestors threw pink triangles like confetti into the air. Others waved banners reading Civil Rights or Civil War and The Whole World Is Watching.

For hours we sat, waiting our turn to pass through the opening to the other side of the barricades. Meanwhile, in the crowd we spotted Michael Hardwick, the man whose court battle was largely responsible for this demonstration. His presence was inspirational.

Nevertheless, the wait was tedious and the steps were cold. Finally, frustrated and tired, we followed a group called the United Fruit Company of Boston and marched around the building to the poorly defended north entrance to the court. Shouting "No violence!" and "Don't run!" to other protestors, we made our way to the steps and sat down.

Immediately the police arrived and told us to move. "We had an agreement with you people that you'd be arrested on the front steps," they said. We replied that this was an act of civil disobedience, not a tea party, and refused to budge.

The Fruit Company waved yellow gloves and matching purses, mimicking the police, who wore similar gloves to protect themselves from infection. Finally, after warning us twice to disperse, the police arrested us. Some of us chose to walk to the processing area. Others practiced passive resistance and were carried or dragged.

After being handcuffed (with plastic straps), photographed (by amateurs), and tagged (my number was 509651), we were led onto a nearby city transit bus, commandeered for the occasion. Six of our group were placed on this bus.

We lost track of the others, who were placed elsewhere. Once inside, I couldn't help noticing a sign above the door, ordinarily intended for pickpockets and muggers: This Bus is Under Police Surveillance. I was not the only one to appreciate the irony.

Because the city's holding facility, Cell Block B, was by this time full, the police had no idea where to take us. For more than two hours we sat on the bus. At first we were a rowdy and boisterous bunch. Some of us protested that our handcuffs were too tight. "But you're prisoners," said the police, implying that we should act like it.

Others objected to the handling of two passengers who were taken off the bus following two dramatic incidents. One person fell and inadvertently broke a window. Another, a deaf lesbian, fainted. Many on the bus insisted on viewing the police as the enemy and suspected every move. Others argued that this was not Chile, and that the vast majority of police had behaved in a manner above reproach so far.

At about two o'clock our bus departed, the first of a convoy headed toward the Police Academy (*not* the movie) across the river in Southwest D.C. There temporary facilities were prepared to house and process us in the academy gymnasium. As we pulled away behind a motorcycle escort, we heard cheers from the crowd still assembled in the park. One of our group threw a note to a spectator. "Find our support person!" we shouted. "Tell him where we're going!"

At the academy we were kept on the bus for another two hours. Fortunately, the police took pity on us and removed our handcuffs. They also led us, in groups of four, into the building for bathroom breaks. In the gym we saw hundreds of other protestors, including the rest of our affinity group. They cheered each group of potty people. "Really, there's no need to applaud," I answered. "I've used the bathroom before."

On the bus the mood of the protestors mellowed. Some of us, punchy for lack of food and rest, passed the time by making animal noises, playing condom toss, holding pull-up contests, giving massages, and exchanging recipes. Others took it upon themselves to educate our police guards by holding seminars in AIDS transmission and safe sex practices.

By the time we were taken inside, various officials had explained the charges against us—"refusal to obey police orders and crossing police lines," both misdemeanors. We had also been told that we had three choices at the processing: to offer and forfeit one hundred dollars collateral; to post bail and agree to reappear at a later date; or to wait for arraignment within twenty-four hours. The first two choices would result in our release. The consequences of the third choice were unclear.

Most of our group decided to plead guilty at arraignment rather than to pay into the system by forfeiting collateral. Some also refused to give their true names, in order to disrupt the system as much as possible. Many men called themselves Harvey Milk or Michael Hardwick. Many women took the name Sharon Kowalski, after a disabled lesbian whose parents have refused her lover visitation rights.

With one other member of the group, I chose to forfeit the collateral. I would rather have stayed with my friends and pleaded guilty, for I wanted to see this thing through to the end. But my sisters, who hadn't wanted me to participate in the first place, were worried about me. Besides, I had only a limited amount of time to spend with my family in D.C.

Fortunately, my excuses were unnecessary, for the other members of the group supported each individual decision. Gratefully, I promised to keep track of them when I was released early in the evening. Outside the gates of the academy, support people offered food and supplied a ride to the nearest Metro station. After providing what information I could about the people still inside, I stumbled into bed, exhausted, at ten.

In all, 840 protestors were arrested, the largest number of people ever arrested at the Supreme Court. Although the Superior Court stayed open until 2:30 A.M. in order to arraign those who had not paid collateral or posted bail, 111 people still had to spend the night in jail, including several of my friends. Eventually, most of those who pleaded guilty were fined fifty dollars plus ten dollars in court costs. Others elected to serve jail time instead. Still others pleaded not guilty.

Many who appeared before the judge at Superior Court made brief statements before being sentenced. One man told the judge he was tired and hungry. When the judge said he could well understand it, the man replied, "I'm tired of being beaten on the streets and hungry for equal justice under the law." This time no one cheered, for this would have resulted in his or her expulsion from the court. But more than a few smiling faces expressed great pride.

I returned to San Francisco two days later with a pair of plastic handcuffs and a pink collateral receipt as souvenirs. I also returned with a sense of accomplishment and satisfaction. When friends at home questioned the demonstration's effectiveness, I replied that sometimes we have to do what we feel is right regardless of the consequences. In this case our efforts had been successful. Media coverage was extensive and, for the most part, positive. Besides, I continued, this was only one of the methods we chose to promote our goals in Washington. We also lobbied, marched—and quilted. With the civil disobedience, we covered all bases.

I have no illusions that the arrest of more than eight hundred people on October 13 will bring about immediate change. But it might alert some people to our passion and commitment. And my own particular arrest, by confirming my belief in nonviolent resistance, might prevent me from throwing rocks at government buildings in the near future. For that, my sisters, the police, and even I, are all grateful.

AIDS

Don't Fuck with Me, Mary

APRIL 1983

I HAVE JUST returned from my weekly visit to my doctor at the University of California Medical Center Dermatology Clinic, and he told me that there were several good reasons why my skin looked so bad. "You have pseudomonas," he said, "a bacterial infection related to staph that's fairly uncommon, but we're seeing it in more and more gay people these days. You also have folliculitis [an inflammation of the follicles], an aggravated case of acne, candida [a yeast infection], and athlete's foot. Furthermore, your glands are swollen and your spleen is enlarged. Obviously your immune system isn't working properly. That's why you're coming down with all these minor infections. But cheer up. You don't have AIDS."

"Thanks a lot, Doc," I replied. "Some consolation."

All my doctor really meant when he said I didn't have AIDS was that I didn't have Kaposi's sarcoma (KS) or pneumocystis—yet. But if my immune system isn't working properly, then it's probably the next step, unless I am either very careful or very lucky—or both. I can't allow myself to worry about that, but I do think about it and I am prepared for it. My friends call that pessimistic and negative. I call it realistic and sensible.

How did I ever come to such a state: *moi,* who was always such a healthy little boy? The answer is simple. From my home in secluded, backwoods Virginia I moved to LA and discovered the joys of Boys' Town—West Hollywood—the first gay ghetto I ever came to know intimately—perhaps too intimately. I moved to LA in late 1976. In 1977 the trouble began. For those of you who discourage easily, don't read the next few paragraphs. For those of you with stamina, read on.

June 1977: I came down with gonorrhea for the first time in my life, the first of many times to come. A few months later I discovered what it was like to get crabs. I hated them. They, unfortunately, were attracted to me, and, like the clap, they returned periodically during the next few years. In October 1978, living in New York City a block from Christopher Street, I learned what nonspecific urethritis meant—through personal experience, of course. In January 1979 I was treated for venereal warts—four treatments, lasting two and a half months.

In the summer of 1979 I moved to San Francisco, and in January 1980 I hit the jackpot: hepatitis B plus two cases of internal parasites, ghiardia and shigella. In July 1980 I had a hepatitis relapse. This time my eyes turned yellow and I was in bed a month. Oh yes, the shigella returned as well. In October

1980 I played host to another parasite, camphylobacter, and in April 1981 the venereal warts returned.

In September 1981 I discovered the recurring joys of herpes. In December 1981 I got amoebas. The year 1982 was a good one. I suffered from only three or four herpes attacks and the clap (once), although I do have to confess to numerous inexplicable aches and pains. Then in February 1983, thinking there was little else to catch, I began this latest series of visits to the doctor for dermatological problems that have just this morning been identified. I've already tried three or four drugs to keep these infections under control, but nothing seems to work. Today I begin another.

No wonder my friends call me Typhoid Mary.

For years I've taken a good deal of ribbing from friends, who, because of my health record consider me a disease queen—"What *has* she got now?" they ask each other on a weekly basis—and I have always taken it in stride. But when they try to make me feel guilty for my troubles, I balk. Responsible, yes; guilty, never: for what did I ever do wrong? I fucked—that's all—and I've never felt guilty for that.

I admit that at times in my life I've fucked indiscriminately. Like many others, I've gone through my trashy slut phase. In New York I discovered the Anvil, and in San Francisco, Buena Vista Park. But even if I had never visited these places, I couldn't have avoided some degree of promiscuity, and I fully believe that I would have been nearly as susceptible to hepatitis or warts at the baths, in the bars, or even at private parties as I was at the more notorious places. Besides, at the time I was not aware of all the consequences involved. Five years ago, who among us had heard of AIDS? At any rate, the phase didn't last long, and if it is any justification (which it is not), there were thousands who were (and still are) trashier than I.

Even though I've "reformed" since then—I lead a more circumspect sex life through necessity, not choice—I still suffer from actions—not "sins"—of the past. Many of these diseases, once contracted, never go away. Even if I never fucked again, I still might have a herpes outbreak, for example. Consequently, when I get sick and my friends say, "You look horrible. Why *don't* you take care of yourself, Mike?" as if I am to blame for being ill, it is doubly frustrating. "But I *do* take care of myself," I respond. "I haven't been to the baths in more than a year. I rarely even trick anymore. I go to the gym five times a week, I eat well, I get plenty of sleep, and I almost never do drugs anymore. What more do you want?"

The worst critics are the ones who never get sick themselves and are therefore smug to the point of self-righteousness. I can't stand people who fuck three or four different men a week and brag about never getting the clap, as if they were in any way responsible for their immunity. Some of them may take especially good care of themselves, but for most it is simply a matter of chemistry: hardy genes or God knows what. They and I could fuck the same person, and I'd probably get sick while they stayed well. (A friend of mine who is more like me once told me, "Honey, whenever I come I just roll over and call the doctor, 'cause I know I'm gonna come down with something.")

There are others who say, "You've got the clap *again?* But, my dear, *who* have you been sleeping with?" Their reaction always reminds me of my first experience with gonorrhea and my father's reaction when I told him about it. I wasn't at all embarrassed or ashamed, but he was shocked. As far as he was concerned, only people who slept with Mexican prostitutes got the clap. Decent people just didn't come down with that sort of thing.

In one way I don't mind having had so many diseases. At least, having had them, I have learned a great deal and now know what to expect. Ignorance and fear of a disease is often worse than the disease itself. I used to think I would die if I ever got venereal warts on my asshole, for God's sake. Well, I've had 'em, and although they were a royal pain in the ass, so to speak, I learned to deal with them. I'm sure it's the same with AIDS. We're all scared to death, and although the consequences are far worse than anything I've yet experienced, I'm sure that even if I get KS I'll learn to deal with that too.

The worst part about the fear of disease is the misunderstanding and the mistrust it engenders. When people at the gym see the marks of a skin infection on my arms and legs, they shy away from me as they would from the plague. Admittedly, the marks do look a lot like KS bruises, but they aren't—and I shudder to think how my gym friends would react if I did have KS. A week ago on TV I saw part of *Ben Hur,* the part about the Valley of the Lepers, and as Ben Hur's mother and sister hobbled around trying to avoid the stone throwers, I said, "Girls! I know just how you feel." Now, in order to avoid the accusatory glances at the gym, I wear sweatpants and long-sleeved T-shirts.

I am fully aware that publicizing my health troubles may not be the wisest thing in the world for me to do. After all, after reading this, who in his right mind will ever again want to fuck me? Perhaps subconsciously, then, I am doing this partly as a means of self-preservation. I may want to scare people away. But I don't think so. I think there is a larger purpose here. I want people to understand and to sympathize with me. I want them to stop blaming me—or themselves—for something over which they have only a limited amount of control. Besides, I can do all the scaring away I need to do on my own without resorting to newspaper articles. Just a few days ago one of my all-time favorite boyfriends came over after a year's absence and wanted to fuck. "I can't—or I shouldn't," I said, and then I showed him my arms. He fled in terror, and I returned to the typewriter. That was incredibly frustrating for me, but I'll do it again if I have to. If a temporary abstinence from sex is what is required, I'll do it.

The most discouraging thing about disease—about AIDS in particular—is not the inconvenience, the discomfort, or even the potentially disastrous consequences: it's the way we seem to be affected by it. Too often these days I hear gay people say that there is not only something wrong with our bodies, there is something wrong with our souls as well. Such hogwash is disheartening. These people are confusing issues of health with those of morality. It may not be wise to go to the baths and fuck a dozen men, but there's nothing morally wrong with it. (And heaven help those gay people who think there is.) Granted, some changes may be in order here, but we don't have to stop being gay in order to protect ourselves.

Unfortunately, that is exactly what some people are doing. The other day I went to the hospital to visit a friend with pneumocystis, and I took him a copy of *Gay Comix Number Two* to cheer him up. He didn't want it, however, for it reminded him of the society he blames for his illness. Unlike my friend, I've never blamed my own health troubles on being gay, even though those troubles date from the year I discovered Boys' Town. As far as AIDS is concerned, I regard it as I would have regarded polio or smallpox years ago: as a matter of health. We can't afford to view this as anything more—as God's answer to homosexuality, for instance. There are too many others around us who will be glad to do that for us.

Visit to an AIDS Ward

OCTOBER–DECEMBER 1983

STEVE CORPUZ was the first friend of mine to come down with AIDS. I say "friend," but I hardly knew him, really. We worked together at Badlands restaurant in San Francisco for a few months in 1980. I waited tables. Steve washed dishes. He was an unusual dishwasher. Hell, he was an unusual person. First of all, he enjoyed his job, which to most people would have been intolerable. Second, he fit into no known categories within the rigidly structured gay subculture: butch or femme, top or bottom, clone or leatherman, attractive or un. I never even knew what race he was. I liked Steve, for he always seemed to be smiling. He was so outgoing and personable that in an instant he cut through the layers of attitude and posturing that plague most of us.

When Badlands closed, I lost touch with Steve. From time to time I would see him around the city, and we would exchange pleasantries for a few minutes before moving on. After a while, I heard more about Steve from my friend Randy, who had been a closer friend of his and who had moved to New Orleans in the meantime, than I did from Steve himself. It was Randy, in fact, who told me that Steve had AIDS. He had it pretty bad, Randy wrote, and was staying in San Francisco General Hospital. "Pray for him," Randy suggested, but I decided to do better than that. I decided to visit Steve at the hospital.

I don't know why I was so anxious to see Steve in the hospital when I had never bothered to see him at home. Partly I saw myself as Randy's proxy, paying the visit he would have made if he could have. Also, I viewed myself as an angel of mercy, I must confess. My mother used to make the rounds of the hospitals when I was a kid, bringing genuine goodwill and cheer to those whose names appeared in the church bulletin as down but not out, and to a degree I saw myself as valiantly carrying on the family tradition. Furthermore, I put myself in Steve's position and decided that if I were in the hospital, I would appreciate visits from any friend, no matter how minor or foul weather—anything to break up the dull hospital routine and to keep me from self-pity. But mostly, I realized, I wanted to see Steve out of a sense of curiosity and a desire to learn more about AIDS. No, that sounds too clinical, too detached, and perhaps a little morbid. I am not one of those who rushes to the scene of an accident for the fun of it. I just wanted to bring myself into closer personal contact with AIDS. After months and months of reading about it, hearing about it, talking about it, and dreading it, it still hadn't touched my life significantly. I knew no one with AIDS. It seemed about as real to me as the fighting in Lebanon and El Salvador thousands of miles away. But unlike those battles, in this case the enemy was all around. Even if I couldn't do anything about it, I at least wanted to know what the enemy was.

I went to see Steve in March. I didn't call to let him know I was coming. I was afraid he might not connect the name with the face after all this time, and that would have been awkward. Also, I think, I was embarrassed about my motives, and I was afraid that if I talked to him on the phone first, he might somehow divine that I was coming to see him more for my own sake than for his. I realized, of course, that by showing up at the hospital without calling first, I was decreasing my chances of seeing him, but even that would have been okay—an easy out. The situation *was* a little false, after all, and if Steve wouldn't see me, I could console myself by noting that at least I had made the gesture.

When I introduced myself to the nurse at the nurses' station, I was asked to wait a moment. "He hasn't been seeing people lately," she said. "It upsets him." Of all the things I'd expected, I hadn't expected that. "Tell him I'm here for

Randy Brooks," I suggested. "See if that makes a difference." Perhaps it did, for when she returned she handed me a mask and directed me to a door down the hall on the right. "He's in isolation," she informed me, "and we have to protect him from infection." Although Randy had already told me that Steve had pneumocystis, I hadn't understood what that would involve.

When I saw Steve, he didn't look so bad—a little tired, I suppose, but who wouldn't look that way after several weeks in the hospital? His hair was disheveled. Perhaps he had lost some weight. The major difference was that he spoke with difficulty, and every few moments he reached over for an oxygen mask. He was definitely very sick. We didn't talk much about his illness, though. I think he was trying to block it out. Instead we talked about Randy ("So what's he doing, anyway?") and about the television programs Steve spent his day watching. I tried to pretend that there was nothing unusual about our situation, that I often spoke with a mask on my face to friends in hospital beds. The mask, however, was hard to ignore. It kept slipping down over my nose.

The only truly uncomfortable moment came at the very beginning of the visit, when I handed Steve the copy of *Gay Comix Number Two* that I had brought as a present. He took one look at it and handed it back to me in disgust. "No, thanks, I don't want it," he said, and then, after a pause: "It's not that I don't appreciate it. It's just that that's not where my head is at right now." I had thought he would find it funny, but it was clear that the freewheeling, heady gay life that the comic book represented appalled Steve now. "That's what put me here," he explained, "and I don't want to have anything to do with it." I was amazed, not so much at the depth of Steve's bitterness, but at the focus of it. Obviously he blamed his illness on being gay. If he weren't gay, he implied, he would never have gotten pneumocystis. Suddenly I felt guilty—not just for being healthy, but also for being gay and still glad to be so. I knew he was wrong to feel the way he did, but as I sat by that hospital bed, I wondered if perhaps I would feel the same if I were the one reaching for the oxygen mask.

Later Steve spoke about the future and how he couldn't wait to leave the hospital, which he hated. "When I get out of here," he said, not once, but several times, and I don't remember the rest, for again and again my mind objected, But what if you don't get out of here, Steve? He wouldn't let himself think about that possibility, which was perhaps the wise and sensible approach, but hardly a realistic one. Death was by no means a certainty, but it hovered close by, a near neighbor.

When I rose to go, Steve reached out to shake hands. Again he surprised me, for once or twice during the visit he had shown great concern about his vulnerability to infection, and I hadn't thought he would want to take any risks, even through contact that casual. I immediately shook hands, but couldn't help worrying about my own vulnerability. I'm no hysteric. I know how stupid it is to worry that AIDS can be passed through the air or by a handshake. And yet my own health has been none too good this year, and I do worry, even about the stupidest things. "Good-bye, Steve," I said. He replied, "I'll call you when I get out."

Steve didn't call, and I didn't pay another visit to the hospital. The prospect was too unpleasant. I suppose I could have at least phoned to find out how he was, but I was afraid. Not until I ran into another friend from Badlands days some time later—was it a month? six weeks?—did I learn how Steve was doing. "Did you hear?" my friend asked me. "Steve Corpuz died this week. He had AIDS."

I heard.

I've spent a lot of time in hospitals, and I know what it's like, if not to have a serious illness, at least to live with someone who has. When I was twenty-four my mother had a stroke and spent the next four months in the hospital, first at Verdugo Hills Hospital and then at Glendale Memorial Hospital in LA. It was a terrible time. Everything that could go wrong did go wrong, and I watched my mother, who had been relatively young and healthy when the stroke hit her, rapidly fade away into a shriveled version of her former self. The doctors couldn't tell us why she had had the stroke or why she was beset by so many complications. They couldn't tell us when or if she would get better, and I don't think they had the foggiest notion what to do. They shaved her head and drained her skull. They took her pulse and gave her drugs—but nothing worked. She only got worse. At Christmastime, after three months spent watching Mom deteriorate, I prepared myself for the possibility of her death. The prospect terrified me, but I had to face it. I didn't think she would make it.

Throughout that period I spent my days working at a library in Pasadena and my nights at the hospital. I drove there directly from work just in time to meet Dad, who drove in from the opposite direction, from Burbank. Together we shared Mom's hospital dinner if she wasn't hungry or had one sent up for the two of us if she was. I don't remember exactly what we did all night. I do remember that we played a lot of bridge. Occasionally I read to her or watched TV while she slept. Dad and I stayed there every night until they kicked us out about ten o'clock, for we hated to leave her alone. We became hospital regulars and soon had the run of the place.

My sister Judy says that hospitals oppress her, and I can certainly understand that. They don't oppress me, however—not anymore. They remind me of Mom, and I appreciate those memories, even the painful ones. One particular memory still comes to mind whenever I enter a hospital corridor. I am standing at the end of the hallway outside Mom's room at Verdugo Hills Hospital about a week after the stroke, looking through a large plate glass window with a panoramic view of the San Gabriel Mountains. Against the mountains a lone figure stands out: the gleaming white statue of a prophet. He is facing the mountains, and his arms reach out to the sky. Having passed that statue, which stands on the front lawn of a church on Foothill Boulevard, many times, I know what is written at the base: "Unto these hills I will lift mine eyes." It is a stirring sight, and as I watch, I begin to cry. It isn't fair, I think. It just isn't fair. Things will never be the same. People pass in the hall, but they don't stop to inquire what is wrong. In the hospital people cry all the time.

San Francisco General Hospital doesn't look much like Verdugo Hills or Glendale Memorial, but inside it is much the same. Do all hospital corridors look alike? I went back there last week for the first time since Steve had died, and I couldn't even remember exactly where I had last seen him. Remembering the location of my friend's room, however, wasn't the purpose of this visit. I wanted to see the new AIDS ward that Steve had never had the chance to see. Why? Because visiting Steve had brought me no closer to AIDS than I had been before. I've seen my friends change their habits since then, and I've read about others dying—Patrick Cowley, James Howell, Michael Malone, Mark Feldman, James Moore—but I still don't understand. Who are the people with AIDS, and how are they dealing with it? Who takes care of these people, and how does this affect them? What is life like on a ward where no one fully understands the nature of the disease being treated, much less the treatment itself? How do any of them deal with the uncertainty, the ignorance, the fear? I hoped that at San Francisco General, I might find answers to some of these questions.

Cliff Morrison is the clinical coordinator of the AIDS ward, the big boss, the top banana. Although the idea for a separate facility for people with AIDS was not entirely his, setting it up *was* largely his responsibility. Since April he has been involved not only in planning and opening Ward 5B, officially known as the Medical Special Care Unit, but also in coordinating care for all persons with AIDS throughout the hospital. He is well qualified to do this. He finished nursing school at eighteen and worked his way through eight years of college, eventually attaining a bachelor's degree as well as a master's degree in hospital management. He has worked as an emergency room nurse and has served as a director of nursing. He has taught for many years and has worked as a psychotherapist for the criminally insane. He has been at San Francisco General for four years.

A year ago Morrison wasn't interested in a separate facility for people with

AIDS. It sounded like separatism, he thought: a way to remove gay people from contact with the rest of the hospital population. Later, however, he realized that the doctors at the hospital were treating the illness but not the "whole person." AIDS patients were kept in isolation rooms at the end of the hall, farthest from the nurses' station. Their rooms were rarely cleaned, their meals were served cold, and they were often ignored. "Because this is a city hospital, we *are* understaffed," Morrison explains. "There was a true sense of alienation, a true sense of isolation." Recognizing this, he went to the administration and presented his plans for a separate facility. The hospital management gave him free rein in setting it up, and with funding from the city and after four months of planning, the facility opened on July 25.

There are only twelve rooms and twelve beds on Ward 5B—one bed to a room. Before the ward opened, a lot of people thought that twelve was too many. Last winter there were as many as fifteen people in the hospital with AIDS, true, but that number had dwindled to between two and eight when the warmer weather arrived. Since the second day it opened, however, the ward has been full, and there is presently a waiting list. Morrison is the one who processes admissions. He takes the most acute cases first and sends the others to other units in the hospital and works with them there. Many more people with AIDS visit the hospital as outpatients. They are seen in Ward 86, the AIDS clinic. Morrison works closely with them too, meeting all the new patients and following up with those who are discharged from 5B to 86.

Approximately 50 percent of the people who have AIDS in the Bay Area are seen at San Francisco General, Morrison claims. The majority of these are from San Francisco. Others go to Davies Medical Center, the University of California Medical Center, the Pacific Medical Center, and a few other hospitals. In addition, there are more AIDS patients at San Francisco General than at any other hospital in the country. Although there are more people with AIDS in New York, they are scattered in a number of different hospitals and are not concentrated like they are here. "We do have a distinct advantage here," explains Morrison, "in that we have a larger gay population in a smaller city. That's probably why we've been able to do what we've done. The gay community has power here. Consequently, the city has been responsive. The federal government has done little for us. The state has done even less. If it weren't for the city, where would we be?" Morrison credits Mayor Feinstein for responding quickly to the crisis, and the Department of Health, he says, has been "marvelous."

Since July, about eighty-five people have been treated on Ward 5B. Seventy of these have been discharged and are being seen in the AIDS clinic. Two have died on the ward. Two or three others have died in the critical care unit next door, and two or three more have died at home. Mainly the patients on the AIDS ward are treated for pneumocystis, which is an acute medical emergency. Kaposi's sarcoma, which was once called gay cancer, is not acute but chronic, and people with KS are treated mostly in the clinic rather than on the ward. Unfortunately, many of those who are discharged from the ward return—70 percent of those who are there now have been there before—but this *can* be viewed as a kind of success, notes Morrison. "A year ago most people with pneumocystis died after their first infection. Over the past six to eight months, however, our treatment has gotten much better, and our success rate is improving. Now we have people who have had three or more infections and are surviving."

Who takes care of these patients? Morrison selected his staff of twelve from a group of thirty-five nurses who had volunteered for the assignment. (Morrison hates the term *volunteer nurses,* for it makes them sound like goodhearted amateurs rather than dedicated, experienced professionals, he says.) In addition, there are three Shanti counselors, one psychiatrist, one nutritionist, one medical social worker, and two secretaries working on Ward 5B. Approximately half the staff is gay, including Morrison himself. He cautions that he wasn't looking for a specifically gay staff, however, any more than he was looking for special care for gay people when he organized the ward. "I'm simply interested in quality health care," he states. Before the ward opened, there was extensive orientation for the staff, and Morrison continues to hold two support groups weekly for the staff, so that they can discuss problems that arise—specifically, their own emotional needs, as well as the needs of the patients.

Has Ward 5B become an isolation ward for diseased faggots, as some feared? "No," states Morrison emphatically, "not in any sense. All that I was told might happen has proved to be untrue. This is not a depressing place. It's a very optimistic place. There's a sense of camaraderie here." One of the reasons the ward is so positive a place, Morrison points out, is that his staff *has* volunteered for the assignment. Consequently, "we haven't had the kind of horror stories that other places have had, where health care workers have refused to deal with AIDS patients." Another reason is that Morrison has deliberately tried to involve patients in their own care. Patients decide, for instance, what visitors they'll see and when they'll see them: there are no set visiting hours. In some cases patients make decisions concerning their medication, their treatment, and even the length of their stay.

To a degree, Morrison hasn't had a choice in allowing patients this kind of responsibility. For the first time, he says, "We have a group of young, well-educated, middle-class consumers, who are saying we aren't going to be treated the way people have been in the past: 'We want to become involved in our own care.' These people are vocal. This is the first group that's been able to organize." This is all to the good, Morrison adds, and he concludes, "I've never in my life been so proud to be gay. Gay people have been stereotyped as being weak, but we're dealing with it. We're strong, we're handling it. We've had to struggle all our lives, and this is just another struggle."

Does Morrison really think it is possible, I question, for people to receive top-notch care at General? As a city hospital, isn't it simply a place to go for people who can't afford better care elsewhere? Morrison bristles. "I am a first-rate professional," he responds, "with an excellent clinical background. I do not work in second-rate institutions. There is no place in the country where you can receive the kind of care you can here. Patients request to come here from all over the country." He notes that because San Francisco General is a teaching campus of the University of California, UC's resources are available to them. He also mentions the capabilities of Paul Volberding and Connie Wofsy, who run the AIDS clinic and are attending physicians for Ward 5B. He concludes, "Our treatment here is in the forefront."

I press on. Even if I concede that the treatment at General is first rate, is a hospital really the best place for people with AIDS? These are people whose immune systems are barely working, after all. Mightn't they be exposed to all sorts of bizarre infections in the hospital that wouldn't confront them elsewhere? Morrison states that my question is based on erroneous notions about AIDS and hospitals. The infections that people with AIDS get, he points out, are unusual reactions to common elements in our environment. "There is no way to avoid exposure to this kind of infection," he continues. "At least here we can control it. The worst thing you can do if you are vulnerable to infections is to get on a city bus." Infection precautions at the hospital are specific and consistent, Morrison claims. Staff members wash their hands constantly. They wear gloves, and they wear masks only if the patient has an active or persistent cough. At the same time, they try to avoid unnecessary, potentially alienating precautions. "We are doing everything we can to try to demystify AIDS," Morrison adds.

Because Morrison spends the great majority of his waking hours working with AIDS patients, does he ever worry about getting the disease himself? Morrison sighs and tells me what he has probably told so many before me and what I have heard so many times before. "AIDS is not contracted casually. Yes, I am in a high risk group as a gay male, but no, I do not feel that health care workers are at any greater risk than that." What is much harder for Morrison to deal with than the fear of catching AIDS is the day-to-day stress that comes from working in a high-power, highly emotional environment. "It takes a lot out of me," he confesses, "and every day I have to cry a little. There are times when I'm so sick of AIDS, I just wish it would go away, but it won't. I don't know how long I'll be able to do this. I've made a year's commitment. Then I'll step back and see." In spite of these drawbacks, Morrison admits, "Professionally, this is the most fulfilling thing I've ever done. We feel that we really have made a difference. Sometimes I ask myself, How can I feel so good about something so bad? But you have to be optimistic. I think we'll find a cause. It's only a matter of time: perhaps a year or two down the road." In the meantime, he concludes, he wants to give as much support as he can to a group of people whose needs, he says, are overwhelming.

II

Unlike Cliff Morrison, I've never worked in a hospital or been responsible for the care of one patient after another, each with a serious illness. But I know what it's like to spend my nights in the hospital by the side of a person who has lost all movement on one side of her body, a person who may never come home again. Like Cliff Morrison, I know what it's like to cry a little every day. Life changed drastically for me the fall my mother was sick. Her troubles became my troubles, and when December turned into January with no improvement in her condition, my fear seemed a certainty: things would never be the same.

I remember driving down the freeway one evening on my way to the hospital and listening to a symphony by Mozart. It was a gorgeous piece, a work of genius, and yet all I could think was, How could he have cared enough to write it? Why did he even bother? Didn't death loom as heavily for him as it did for my mother? And if it did, what on Earth was the point? When I lost hope for her, I ceased to care about my own life. I lost all desire to create my own symphonies. If there was no guarantee that we would fulfill even the meager span seemingly allotted to us, then carrying on seemed meaningless, absurd.

Later, though, I learned to hope again. Perhaps it happened when Mom began to improve a little. First she learned to twitch her knee, and then her foot, and then her whole leg. Inexplicably the complications that had beset her ceased. The doctors decided to move her into the rehabilitation unit, and although she still had no use of her right arm, she slowly learned how to walk again, using a leg brace and a three-pronged cane. At the same time I decided to follow through with an old dream of mine and take dance classes, and as I struggled to force my body into awkward, unnatural positions—to balance, to turn out, to beat (never to pirouette)—Mom struggled merely to walk again. But we both struggled to control; we both worked toward mastery of our bodies. It was a wonderful time, however brief. Each night, when I stumbled exhausted into her hospital room after a hard hour or two at dance class, we compared notes. I showed her an entrechat quatre, and she showed me one of her trembling steps. Both of us were excited once again. Both of us were as proud as we could be of ourselves and of each other.

In February Mom came home again.

Patrick Walker, who is an AIDS patient at San Francisco General, reminded me a little of Mom the day I met him on Ward 5B, for as we talked, he was waiting for the results of a test that would determine whether he could go home that day or have to remain yet another two weeks in the hospital. He was just as anxious and as excited as she would have been about the prospect of going home. Mom thought that when she finally left the hospital all would suddenly be well. Somehow everything would work itself out, and life as it was before the stroke would miraculously resume. Does Patrick think that his disease will fade away entirely when he returns to his home and his lover? No, but then Patrick is more pragmatic than Mom was and has a clearer idea of what he has to face, even though his disease, AIDS, is a far bigger mystery than hers was.

Patrick (an assumed name: he prefers to remain anonymous so that his mother, who is in her eighties and is in poor health, doesn't find out about his disease) is forty-two years of age and had been unemployed and living off his savings for two years when he first discovered that he had pneumocystis in late August of this year. He came to the hospital because of a series of 105 degree temperatures and a persistent and unusual cough. "I would have come in much earlier," he assured me, "but there's not sufficient information about pneumocystis, and I didn't know enough about it." Nevertheless, he thought his troubles might be serious, and he wanted to know one way or the other. Because he checked into the hospital just before a weekend, however, he had to wait three days for the results of his tests, and when they arrived, his worst fears were confirmed.

Did Patrick fall completely apart when he learned he had AIDS? "No, I accepted it," he says. He and his lover of the past twelve years had discussed the possibility while they were waiting for the test results, and were prepared for it. "I'm with you whatever you have," his lover told him, and they both decided that if it was AIDS, there would be "no recriminations, no anger, no 'Why me?' That attitude has carried me through since then," continues Patrick. "I simply said, 'Okay, now I have to get well.' I try to be as positive about everything as I can. Actually, I am fortunate, for I'm not half as sick as some of the people here."

Patrick is convinced he knows why and how he got AIDS. Although he and his lover had been monogamous for quite some time, Patrick reached what he calls a "foolish point" about two years ago. "I felt I was getting old and unattractive," he explains. "I wanted to prove to myself that I wasn't as bad as I thought I was, so I began visiting the bars and the baths. My lover said, 'That's okay, just as long as you come home at night when it's over.' And that's when I contracted it." Although Patrick is not a drug user and was never as promiscuous as some of his friends ("I am fascinated by an older friend who has a different trick every night," he says), he is not bitter that he got AIDS when others did not. Instead, he merely comments upon the irony of life and concludes, "I was in the wrong place at the wrong time."

Unlike my friend Steve, Patrick does not blame his contracting AIDS on being gay. "I don't blame *anything* on being gay, certainly not my disease. Each person is responsible for himself or herself, and if you blame the gay lifestyle for contracting this disease, you might as well blame the straight lifestyle for the diseases they get: herpes, for instance." He does feel, however, that particular aspects of the gay way of life might be circumscribed—after all, according to Patrick, it was his period of promiscuity that resulted in his hospital stay—and he has little sympathy or understanding for people who still screw around, "who think that this won't happen to them." Happily, Patrick's lover has been true to his word and has not indulged in recriminations. He does not regret giving Patrick his freedom. Consequently, Patrick says, he is much happier now than when he was visiting the bars and baths. "I accept myself for what I am now. I find myself liked more. I've even let myself go gray."

Patrick's hospital visit has not been without pain, of course. His treatment has consisted of two major drugs. The first, Septra, is administered intravenously and caused him to have a terrible reaction. The second, pentamidine, is given by injections in the buttocks. He has also taken morphine for lung discomfort, and he has had to endure several bronchoscopies, which are hell for most patients. Surprisingly, Patrick didn't mind the bronchoscopy. "I have a large throat," he says slyly, "so the tube they stuck down my throat didn't hurt. The doctors were impressed."

In spite of the pain he endured, Patrick says that the care he has received at San Francisco General has been excellent. "I want everyone to know how fantastic and wonderful the care is here. People should know that this is a place where they will be healed. The staff does its best for you. They are remarkable, outgoing, caring. If anything has helped me to get better, it's been the support and affection they've given me. There is no reason to be afraid." Did he consider going anywhere else for treatment? "No, I had to come here because I had no insurance," he replies. "But I'm not worried financially. MediCal is taking care of this, and my lover is taking care of the rent."

This lover, who takes care of the rent and who thinks "the sun rises and sets with Patrick," has been a great support to him, visiting every other night and all day on the weekends. He also receives visits from a few friends, two of whom work at the hospital. He doesn't receive as many visits as he might, however, for he has told only five people that he has AIDS. "I don't want to distress them," he confesses. "There are so many unknowns. People are frightened by this. Why subject them and us to that? It's easier to keep it simple." Doesn't he feel a little bit guilty for withholding that kind of information from them? "No," he replies. "It's a personal and private thing. It's my business. I've investigated and there's no way I am a threat to them, for there is no exchange of blood products and no sex between my friends and myself. I see no point in broadcasting what could be a detriment: people might have to drop us. Besides, I admit to being lazy. I don't want to spend the better part of the next few years explaining what is happening to me."

Not only does Patrick see relatively few friends from outside the hospital, but he sees few of the other patients either. "Most are on oxygen or are confined to their rooms because they are so sick," he explains. "But I'm not afraid to meet them." He is not a member of any support group, although the Shanti people have come to visit and have done counseling as well as massage. "Basically my lover and I are loners," he adds.

Patrick talks a lot about his lover, I've noticed. Obviously he cares for him a great deal. He seems to need him a great deal too, especially now. Doesn't he worry, though, that things won't be the same when he gets out, I ask? It may sound petty, but what of their sex life? "When you're as sick as I am," answers Patrick, "that's the least of your worries. I have absolutely no sexual interest at all." He and his lover have made plans, however, to change their sex life so that they won't jeopardize each other's health. Specifically, they plan to cut out exchange of fluids. "It won't be hard," he muses. "After twelve years, it will be nice to try something new."

Suddenly I notice that as we talk of the future and of Patrick's future plans, we are assuming that he will indeed have one, despite the great possibility that he may not. Most people who have contracted pneumocystis have died, after all. Does Patrick ever think about dying? "When I first came here, I was afraid I might die," he admits, "so I paid all my bills." The next step is to have wills made, which he and his lover plan to do soon. "I think I am prepared now, far more prepared than someone who gets hit by a truck, for instance." Basically, however, Patrick wants to concentrate on continuing to live, not preparing to die. "I have to seriously watch my health, to exercise (which I never did—I was very sedentary), and to eat well (which I never did)." Does he think he will have AIDS forever? Will he always have to be so careful about his health? "Eventually

I think they'll find a cure, whether it is in ten months or ten years," he concludes. "They'd better. I have to think that, for it's horrible that people have to go through this."

It's horrible that people have to go through this. I know, I know. It's horrible that people have to face half the things that befall them. That Mom had a stroke at fifty-seven years of age was horrible. It was horrible too that she had to face being largely confined to a wheelchair or to the couch when she came home from the hospital that February. There was little in her experience to help her prepare for that situation. She knew no way to deal with it. And yet she either had to learn or to face a life of misery and self-pity, repeating to herself over and over, Why me? Why me?

Mom's last day was one of the more difficult ones. She had been at home about a month and was finding that life at home was in some ways more difficult than life in the hospital. She was learning to be a little more self-reliant, true, but still she had to endure our watching after her. She had to get up at six so that Dad could help her bathe and dress before leaving for work. She had to be ready to be placed on the couch at eight (within reach of the phone, the television, and her cigarettes and coffee, naturally), for at eight I left for work, and she would be alone until a day nurse came an hour later. When I came home and the nurse left, she had to bear my pulling up her underwear for her every time she went to the bathroom (and she had to endure a cracked rib the one time she tried to do it herself and fell). She even had to pretend to enjoy my cooking.

Often she did all this willingly, but some days it was too much for her, and her last day was one of these. I had left my library job and was substitute teaching at the time, and as I had not gotten a call to teach that day, I was free to spend it with Mom. We spent the morning sitting in the sun together, she in her wheelchair and I in a lawn chair next to her, and at one point, when I looked up from the book I was reading, I noticed that she was crying silently. I tried to ignore it at first. It sounds harsh, I know, but Dad and I believed that if we pampered Mom too much, she would never learn to take care of herself. If we showed her how sorry we felt for her, she would only feel sorrier for herself. Of course we loved her, and we showed her that time and time again, but still, we wanted her to be tough. We wanted her to concentrate on beating this thing. So I let her cry—but not for long. I couldn't take it, so I reached out and said, "What's wrong, Mom?"

"Everything," she replied. "You and your father don't have time for me. Nobody cares about me. I'd be better off dead."

"You know that's not true," I replied, trying to appease her, but she would not be comforted. And so I wheeled her back inside, where she spent the rest of the day gloomily watching TV and complaining about a headache.

That evening, after we had finished a game of bridge—Dad, Mom, my grandmother, and myself—I was getting ready for bed when I heard Dad scream from the bathroom, "Mike, get in here quick!" I ran to see what was the matter and found my mother leaning against the bathroom wall, rapidly losing consciousness. I helped Dad get her to bed and then held her hand as Dad called the doctor. The doctor wanted to know exactly what was wrong. Then he asked to speak to Mom. I didn't hear what he asked her, but her reply—the last thing I heard her say—was, "Sure, I can!"

Dad and I rushed Mom back down to Glendale Memorial in the back seat of the station wagon, and when we got to the hospital, the doctors told us what we already knew by then: Mom had suffered a second stroke. This one was severe, they explained, probably fatal. There was nothing to do but to wait, so we waited. Twelve hours later, as Dad and I watched the activity on the graph monitoring her vital functions fade away to nothing, Mom died.

Bill Nelson, Anne Steinlauf, and Alison Moed are three of the R.N.s who volunteered to work on the AIDS ward at San Francisco General and who have been working fourteen- and fifteen-hour days fifteen days a month since July, when the ward opened. I know waiters who work fourteen-hour days occasionally—I am one of them—but we didn't volunteer for our jobs, and we don't have life-and-death responsibilities. All we have to do is slam food down in front of people: we don't have to keep them alive. Furthermore, unlike the nurses on Ward 5B, we don't have to deal with a set of potentially terrifying unknowns. Instead we deal with simple things, such as coffee refills, dessert choices, and daily specials. And most of us do it just for the money. So why do *they* do it? What motivates these nurses to work long, hard hours in an emotionally exhausting environment?

Bill Nelson cites two reasons for volunteering to work on the AIDS ward, one professional and one personal. First he notes "the excitement of being involved on the front lines against a new disease." AIDS is to medical workers interested in research what a ride in a space shuttle is to scientist-astronauts: a chance to explore the unknown. But there is more: Bill volunteered because a number of his friends have contracted the disease, and he wanted to be of some help to them. Unlike Bill, Alison Moed had no friends with AIDS when she volunteered to work with AIDS patients. Nevertheless, she volunteered for similar personal reasons. "It was a way for me to hold back the waters," she explains. "If *I'm* fighting for it in some way, then I'm protecting the people that I love."

And it is no longer true that she has no friends with AIDS, for "once you work here," she notes, "they are all people you love." When Bill speaks of the sense of dedication that sustains him in his work, Alison adds, "We *are* a fantastic bunch. There's no one here who does not care. It's not an easy job, and the money isn't adequate compensation."

What of the hazards? Do they ever worry about catching AIDS themselves? True, there have been no cases of health care workers contracting AIDS, and it is fairly well accepted now that AIDS can be passed only through the exchange of bodily fluids, but don't nurses work with bodily fluids all the time, and isn't there always a first time for everything? "It doesn't bother me," says Alison. "I wash my hands and that's enough." Bill echoes Cliff Morrison when he says, "My risk is because I'm a gay man, not because I'm a nurse." And Anne Steinlauf admits, "I think you can't help but wonder about it. But I don't think I'll get it."

Every day there are stories in the paper about the discrimination that people with AIDS face because of ignorance and hysteria. But what of the people who work with AIDS patients? What do they face when their friends and family find out where they are working? "My friends *are* real curious about what's going on here," says Anne. "It's the first thing my mom asks about," adds Alison. "And a couple of my friends won't have me over for dinner anymore. But my parents do think I'm brave." All mention that their social lives have virtually disappeared since the AIDS ward opened, but this is mainly due to the long hours they keep rather than to adverse reactions on the part of their friends. "All you do is work and sleep," says Bill, "and dream of being here."

When Mom was sick, I noticed that some nurses tended to form close relationships with their patients while others maintained a distant, formal attitude. On the AIDS ward, says Bill, maintaining distance is impossible. "You do get close to them," he says. "Having this disease cuts through the bullshit, and you build relationships that are solid. Patients will share things with us that they won't share with others. But it hurts." Bill and the other nurses also have formed close relationships with each other. "We have to stay in touch with each other," says Alison. "We need each other. It's real important to keep talking about it a lot." The nurses work in teams of four and meet in support groups twice a week, and this reinforces the bonds between them. The meetings also give them a chance to talk about the things they see as well as the way they react to those things.

The main thing they see, of course, is how the patients cope with their disease. "You do see negativism, cynicism, and self-pity," Alison confesses. "If people didn't go through these things, they wouldn't be human. They'd be robots. But that's rarely what you see. You also see humor: wonderful, sweet humor." I am immediately reminded of Patrick, the self-described Marguerite Gautier of Ward 5B. After a brief coughing spell during our interview, he turned to a friend who was present and said, "I suffer so, don't I?" "And so well!" the friend replied.

Unfortunately, the nurses on the AIDS ward also confront death as a part of their daily routine. "I've seen lots of people die," admits Bill, "because I've worked in ICU. Since being here, I've seen four die. Some you are glad to see die, for then their suffering is over. But you never get used to it." Adds Alison, "I don't like to see people die alone. I want someone to be with them. People greet death in different ways—some are ready for it, and some fight it up to the very last minute—and part of what we can do is to help them find acceptance." Sometimes, in addition to acceptance, patients discover something greater: inner reserves of strength and courage they did not know they had. Concludes Bill, "What is brought out in these people is often the highest part of them, and that brings out the highest in you."

Perhaps the hardest part of the nurses' job is the feeling that despite the advances made and the victories won inside Ward 5B, these advances and victories won't make a great deal of difference on the outside. "There's still a lot of naïveté out there," says Bill. "It surprises me. People still insist on leading the lifestyle of a few years ago. They're still taking drugs, indulging in heavy sex, and going to the baths three or four times a week. We're putting all this time and energy into helping and educating people, and there are a lot of people not listening." Alison agrees that this is frustrating. "We hope every day that the dying won't be the dying anymore." Yet Ward 5B is full, and at the rate things are going, it will be full for some time to come.

III

The dying. I try not to focus excessively on death. Like Patrick, who has the disease I write of, I try to concentrate on survival instead and to remember that AIDS and death are not synonymous. Ward 5B is not a terminal ward, after all. But the subject is hard to avoid: the mortality rate for people with AIDS is so awfully high. Even the nurses who take care of the people with AIDS often refer to them as the dying, and every week, it seems, there is an article in the newspaper about someone else who has died. We are forced to think about it.

I've always been curious about death. When I was a child I used to burn stuffed animals at the stake and throw moths into spider webs to watch them struggle against the inevitable. I constructed elaborate graveyards in the backyard for all our household pets, including dogs, parakeets, guinea pigs, and rabbits, as well as a few stray squirrels and songbirds. I even cherished childhood fantasies of my own death and spent countless hours planning my funeral and contemplating life in heaven. I liked to imagine myself on a cloud high above that funeral, enjoying the spectacle immensely. "He was such a good boy. Why did he have to die so young?" everyone would weep. "I *knew* they'd be sorry," I would exult. "Let 'em suffer."

Later I progressed beyond romanticizing death and learned to joke about it. My family and I used to kid Mom by telling her that when she died, we were going to set her up in her casket at the funeral parlor, install a Chatty Cathy voice box, and instruct mourners to pull the string. Mom would then still be able to entertain her guests as she had in the past by repeating her favorite phrases over and over: "Michael, bring me my cigarettes." "Get 'em, Gators!" "First mistake I ever made." My family believed strongly that laughter helped to ease the pain of dying, and we even joked on the way to the hospital when my grandfather died during my senior year in high school. His death was the first I had to experience, his lifeless body was the first I saw, except for that of my other grandfather, who died when I was too young to care a great deal.

Grandma died a year before Mom did. Losing her to cancer was one of the hardest things Mom ever had to bear and may have helped to bring about her stroke. We all met in Atlanta for the funeral and drove to nearby Rockmart, Georgia, for the burial services. I don't remember much about either, except that I know I played some of Grandma's favorite hymns on the piano. Oh yes, and later, at a neighboring grave, I saw written in glitter under a blue plastic telephone in the middle of a floral wreath the words, Jesus Called and He Answered. I could only hope that that family had a sense of humor too.

When Mom died in March 1977, I took it matter of factly. Although the second stroke was unexpected, her lengthy illness had given us time to prepare for the possibility of her death. So I wrote withdrawn, sterile letters to everyone and flew with Dad to Florida for the funeral, carrying her ashes in a cardboard box at the bottom of a cheap straw shopping bag from Mexico. We buried her under the Spanish moss, palm trees, and sandspurs of her childhood, and Dad placed her wedding ring amidst the ashes. The engagement ring I kept for myself. "I'm so sorry," everyone said, "but it's probably better this way, don't you think? She led such an active life. She wouldn't have been happy as an invalid." Perhaps she wouldn't have been, but I couldn't agree that it was better for my mother to have died.

Mom's death was gradual, slow. The end came quickly, but like most of the AIDS patients who die, the means did not. I have also seen death strike like a lightning bolt, without warning, without consideration. In September 1981, four and half years after Mom died, Dad died of a massive heart attack while on vacation in Germany. There was no pain, no suffering. He didn't even have time to recognize the blow, nor did I have time to prepare for it. I had spent a gorgeous, wonderful day at the beach when the call came from my sister, and I refused to believe it at first, for he too had been so young, so vibrant. I was angry and bitter, and I vowed revenge.

Shortly after Dad died and soon after my thirtieth birthday, I made my first will. I think the will was as much a result of one too many nights on acid as it was a consequence of anything else, but whatever the reason, I figured that the way luck was running in my family, I didn't have any time to waste. So I put Bic ballpoint pen to college-ruled notebook paper and wrote a few brief paragraphs leaving everything to my two sisters. Then I added a six-page coda detailing scores of items I wanted my sisters to be sure to save, including my journals, of course, a couple of unfinished novels, a signed copy of *The Mayor of Castro Street* (how could they live without it?), Mom's ring, Grandma's china, broken glass from Tintern Abbey, even a box of stuffed animals that I kept on the stairs (the ones I hadn't burned at the stake twenty years before). I'm not sure if the will could hold up in court, although I did get an ex-boyfriend to witness it (which was fairly brazen of me, because I didn't leave him anything). But even if it is not legal, at least now I feel that I have done my part to bring some order to my eventual end. I have tidied up my house.

I don't always joke about death, you must understand. It's just that having lost both parents, three grandparents, and a few friends and acquaintances, I feel I am used to death now. It does not hold the horror for me that it does for so many of my friends these days. Occasionally I still rage, rage against the dying of the light, but, more often than not, I shrug my shoulders and tell myself it's really not that big a deal. What difference does it make to Mom and Dad now, after all? Sure, the survivors hurt, but that pain fades eventually, and it is inevitable in any case. So what difference will it make to me *when* my time comes? And if my car sends me over a cliff someday, will I care that my apartment has no bay view or that I still haven't published in *Harper's?*

In some ways I even look forward to death as a rest, a release from care. It will be nice not to have to worry about the future anymore: about happiness and success, about ambition and fulfillment. It will be nice not to have to try so hard to find meaning in everything and to make every moment count. Toward the end of her life, I know my grandmother was ready to go, to lay down the "weary burden" of life. She couldn't wait to see heaven, where she believed she would be reunited with her husband. Unfortunately, I don't share her belief about heaven—that delightful fairyland where all will be just as we would like it to be—but that doesn't seem to matter a lot. The void doesn't frighten me. And there are times when I too am ready to go.

You might say, of course, that never having been in the position of someone who really was dying, I don't know what the hell I am talking about, and that it is an insult to people with AIDS to compare my thoughts about death to their struggle to live. I can only reply that you are probably right, but that I did find myself in that position for a few days this past spring, when the skin troubles that I was having got out of hand and my doctors biopsied a lesion on my arm for Kaposi's sarcoma. Although they assured me that the results would almost certainly be negative, still I managed to convince myself that they would be otherwise. Yes, yes, it was self-dramatizing, I know, but for a few short days, I fully expected to be told I had AIDS, and I immediately assumed I would die, even though I recognized that people with AIDS did not expire on the spot. The point is that rather than panic, I resigned myself and prayed, Just please let me live until my first magazine article is published. At the same time I called my friends John and Alex and instructed them that if the test was positive and I did die within the week, they were to come over and clear out my paltry porno collection. Call me a closet queen if you will, but I didn't want my sisters to inherit *that*.

Enough already. Enough about dying.

Reid Beitrusten, a former bartender at the Lion Pub and only thirty-four years old, first discovered that he had Kaposi's sarcoma in April of this year, when a private physician asked him about the six purple spots on his arm and ran tests on him. Although he hadn't even noticed the spots before the doctor did, for a few months before he did notice them he had known that something was wrong. He had had a series of minor diseases, such as empitigo, and a six-week herpes attack, and his health was so feeble that he could not work.

When KS was diagnosed, Reid's physician referred him to San Francisco General, and he began a grueling series of treatments for the disease. First he was treated with interferon as an outpatient for two months. Because he didn't respond to the interferon, he was switched to chemotherapy. With the chemotherapy he improved a great deal; unfortunately, in August he came down with pneumocystis and was forced to discontinue the treatments. Does Reid have any idea why his luck has been so bad, why one disease has followed another inexorably? "There's some feeling that chemotherapy reduces immunity," he says. "But I'd be hesitant to say that that's *why* I got pneumocystis."

Like Patrick Walker, his neighbor on Ward 5B, Reid was treated with both pentamidine and Septra for his pneumocystis, although in reverse order from Patrick. After thirteen days of pentamidine, there was a severe drop in his white blood count, so he was switched to Septra. The Septra caused severe nausea and a total loss of appetite—for two weeks he was fed intravenously—but at least his condition stabilized, and in mid-September he was sent home. There his parents, who had flown in from Miami—"It was the best thing I had going for me then"—cooked for him and tried to nurse him back to health, but after he had been home only a short time, he developed a 102 degree temperature for five days and had to go back to the hospital. When I spoke with Reid the day after his readmittance to the ward, the doctors were testing to see what was the matter this time. His face and arms were covered with purple spots, and his breathing was labored. He seemed to be very, very tired.

Reid's first reaction when he learned in April that he had KS was one of shock and dismay. "At first I was kind of shattered," he explains, "but then I changed my mind. I decided that it was silly to be shattered. At least I knew I had it. At least the frightening tension and the uncertainty were over." Since then Reid has had time to adjust to his situation and to resolve to make the best of it. "It's just one of those things," he continues. "I guess I was singled out by fate. I've decided that if I have less time to live, then the quality of life had better be great."

Like Patrick, Reid says that his sex life probably had a lot to do with his contracting AIDS. Reid, however, was rather more promiscuous than Patrick. From two or three tricks a week he cut down to one in January (and he stopped going to the baths altogether), when he finally realized that AIDS was a serious threat. For a while he became "extremely paranoid"; then he got it anyway. He hasn't had sex since his diagnosis, but it hasn't bothered him much, for, he says, "My drive is real low. It's the last thing on my mind."

Hadn't Patrick said exactly the same thing? Suddenly I am struck by the similar attitudes of the two men. Like Patrick, Reid does not blame his illness on being gay. "I've had a good time being gay," he says. "I erased the guilt when I was thirteen years old, and I have had no regrets since then." Nor can Reid believe that "there are still people who don't seem to realize that [promiscuity] is a danger. The things to be done are so simple. It amazes me to think that people don't pay attention to them."

Listening to Patrick and Reid, I begin to wonder if positivism tempered by reason and caution is the indoctrinaire party line of San Francisco General's AIDS ward. Are patients trained to think this way? No, I know better. These are simply two hopeful, cautious, and reasonable men who happen to find themselves in the same situation and know no other way to deal with their illness. No, wait, even that is wrong. Patrick and Reid know other ways to deal with their illness, I am sure. They simply have chosen to deal with it this way. But have I been set up, I wonder? Where is the bitterness, the sorrow? Have I been given the ward's two Pollyannas to interview? Perhaps. These were the only two of the twelve on the ward who agreed to speak to me, after all. Maybe the others are all locked in their rooms feeling sorry for themselves—but I doubt it.

Perhaps one reason that Reid's attitude is so positive is that his family and friends have been "extremely supportive," especially since he's been in the hospital. His parents flew in from Miami when he got pneumocystis and have been in San Francisco ever since. They have known for fifteen years that Reid is gay, which made it much easier for him to tell them about his illness in the first place and for them to cope with it. His friends (he prefers to call them his guests) visit every day, bring him presents, and have even thrown a surprise birthday party for him in the hospital. Only two people have backed away from him because of AIDS, Reid says. "I've heard all kinds of stories, but I haven't experienced them. Of course, my KS hasn't been as obvious as it is now. When I stopped chemotherapy, my face was all cleared up. But most of my friends realize it isn't easily communicable anyway."

As if to underscore this fact, one of his friends stops by to visit while we are talking. His parents are also in and out of the room during the interview. In addition, Reid is visited by the attending doctor, the woman who writes the menu, and clinical coordinator Cliff Morrison while I am there. With the constant interruptions, it is hard to see how Reid ever rests, but it is nice to know that he is no recluse, no isolated outcast. When a young man arrives to collect the garbage, however, he is wearing a mask: a reminder that some people still have fears of contamination.

Reid feels that the individual attention he has received on Ward 5B has been "wonderful," largely because the unit is "real personal." Every fifteen minutes someone stops in to look after him and to see if he needs anything. "Their response is really warm," he says. When asked if he is equally satisfied with the medical treatment he has received, he responds, "That's a harder question. It's been rough. And the food is horrible." When pressed for details, Reid responds vaguely. Clearly he would be happier with his treatment if it were working better. But would he find more successful treatment elsewhere? Reid doesn't know.

Since coming down with AIDS, Reid has met a great many others with the disease, although he was the first and only of his old friends to get it. Most of his friends now, in fact, are people who have AIDS, and most of these he has met through the clinic at San Francisco General. He is not, however, presently a member of any kind of support group. His reason is simple. When Reid first got AIDS he went to a Shanti meeting and spent his time "distributing boxes of Kleenexes." It was an unpleasant experience for him, and he said to himself, I don't really want to be a part of this. My life has been cut short. The last thing I want to do with my remaining time is to spend it lamenting and crying.

Which brings us to the main point. Twice Reid has mentioned that he has less time left to live than other people. He seems to accept that as fact, to take it for granted. Does he indeed think that he's dying, then? The other AIDS patient with whom I spoke, Patrick, talked about the future and counted on it. Does Reid think he even *has* a future? "I don't know," he candidly admits. "I have to be realistic. I have not been responding to treatment very well. And I *have* thought about dying. For a while, when I was first diagnosed with pneumocystis, I was terrified, and I thought that death was already here. I wasn't eating. I didn't have any will to live. But then a doctor told me, 'I see someone who really enjoys life being extinguished in the hospital. There are no guarantees that if you leave you'll get better, but because you've stabilized, you might consider it.' "

Reid acted upon the doctor's suggestion, and at home, with his parents' care, he changed his attitude about dying. He is no longer terrified of the possibility. Instead, he says, "Fear doesn't really seem to have any place in dealing with life." He has made no preparations for death, such as writing a will, but "It is something I definitely have to do," he notes. "The reason I'm avoiding it is laziness rather than denial, I think." I think so too. I have known Reid only an hour, but it seems obvious that this is someone who isn't denying anything. He knows what the future may hold. He only wants to make the best of what he has for as long as he has it.

Later that evening I had dinner with my friends John and Alex, and learned that Reid Beitrusten, although not a personal friend, was a friend of half the people I knew. "You interviewed Reid?" they asked. "How is he? We had heard he was getting worse." We talked about Reid for a while, and they told me that he was "real smart: a graduate of Yale. He reads books too," which is saying something, given the milieu in which we live. As we talked, I realized that this was someone people cared about, someone who played an important role in other people's lives, someone who would leave a void if he died. I had met his parents and one of his friends at the hospital, and, of course, I knew that to them Reid was a special person, but until I spoke with John and Alex, Reid Beitrusten had had no direct relationship to my own life. He was just a person with AIDS, someone to interview, someone I would feel interest in only as long as I wrote about him. Finding out that one of Reid's former co-workers was also an ex-boyfriend of mine changed that for me.

I also realized as my friends and I spoke that in some ways, despite the obvious KS spots or the giveaway cough of pneumocystis patients, AIDS is an invisible disease. I had thought I had no friends with AIDS other than Steve Corpuz, but was that true? There are hundreds of people I know by sight on the street, at the gym, in the grocery store, or at the movies. San Francisco is not such a large city, after all: we run into each other all the time. Sometimes these people drop from sight for a period of time, and I never know where they've gone. It may be months before I even realize that they *are* gone. Usually I assume that they have left town for New York, Los Angeles, or "back home," wherever that is. But how many of them are at San Francisco General or UC Medical Center or Davies Medical Center? How many of them have AIDS? Sometimes when I see a picture of someone who has died of AIDS in the local papers, I have a sense of déjà vu, and then I say, "Oh, *I* know *him!* I used to see him dancing at the Trocadero a few years ago." How many whom I have seen, I wonder, are dancing no longer?

I confess I have trouble using the present tense when writing of Reid and Patrick, particularly of Reid, for I don't know how long it will apply. I write this two weeks after my visit with them on the AIDS ward. God only knows how long it will be before you read it. What will happen to them in the meantime? Believe me, not for a moment have I forgotten the possibility that they may not be around to read this when it appears. I hope they will be. God, I hope they will be.

Regardless of what happens to Reid and Patrick, however, what of the rest of us? Will we get AIDS? That is what we really want to know, isn't it? I have told you how Reid and Patrick are reacting to their illness, but I have said nothing of those about me who may be future patients of Ward 5B. How are we coping with the possibility that we may also be people with AIDS someday? And how are we trying to prevent it?

Some of us ignore that possibility. Others are paralyzed by it. Some carry blithely on doing the things they have always done. Some cut out sex altogether in the hopes of preventing contagion. Most of us cut down, but not out, and those of us who would like to take reasonable precautions without bowing to extremes have a difficult road to travel. Patrick and Reid can't believe that people still exchange fluids when they have sex, for instance, but even as they expressed their concern, I knew that I was going home to have sex for the first time in months with a boyfriend I hadn't seen since February—and I wasn't going to follow their advice about what constituted safe sex. I knew I should, but I had been celibate for months because of my skin troubles, and I was tired of it. Besides, I just couldn't see my boyfriend as a threat to me, and I didn't want to forgo such fundamental pleasures as . . . well, you know what I mean. I may have been gambling, but it seemed like such a safe bet, considering the number of people with AIDS compared with the total number of gay people in this town—or in this country, for that matter. Yes, I have heard about the likelihood of a two-year incubation perod, but I can't help feeling that surely I must already have been exposed to the AIDS virus (if it is a virus) by now, and if I have, what difference does it make? Yet didn't Patrick and Reid think just the same things before they got AIDS?

I have said that I am not afraid to die, that I do not fear death as some of my friends do. Before visiting Ward 5B, neither was I afraid of catching AIDS. Oh, a little bit perhaps, but basically I saw it as a suitably symbolic way to go—if I had to go, that was. For someone who has been so very gay, who has let his homosexuality influence so much of his life, what better way to go than to die of what often has been called (if erroneously) a gay disease? I envisioned myself as a martyr of sorts, a sacrifice, but to what or for whom I had no idea. Since visiting Reid and Patrick, however, I no longer think that way. I am no longer unafraid of the disease. I have seen the pain, and I have heard from them of their suffering, both emotional and physical. I don't want to go through that. I don't want to endure a bronchoscopy, severe nausea, or a garbage collector wearing a paper mask. I don't want to lie in a hospital bed and think about dying.

Often, when I think of Mom and Dad, I think how lousy it is for them to have died so young. But think how much younger are the people who get AIDS. Perhaps that's the worst thing about the disease: by attacking the young, it upsets all our notions about what is right and fair. We ought to be able to live long and happy lives. We ought not to have to worry about dying, for God's sake. Instead, our worries should concern simple things: whether to buy Skippy or Jif, whether to join this gym or that one, whether to take him out to dinner or cook for him at home. Thanks to AIDS, our worries are no longer so simple. We no longer have as much control over what we are expected to deal with.

And that's another thing: AIDS shows us dramatically how little control we *do* have. I like to lead an orderly life. I like security. I like to know that when the first rolls around I will have enough money to pay rent, that when I come home at night my apartment will not be vandalized, and that my boyfriend—when I have one—is faithful to me (or at least tells me the truth when he is not). All of these things I have some control over. None can I control entirely. But my health: it is another matter altogether. It is an enigma. Theoretically I have as much control over this matter as I do over any of the others, but it never seems to work out that way. Perhaps it is because the unknowns are greater, both in number and in magnitude.

It would be nice, wouldn't it, to end this on an upbeat note. I wish I could do it. I wish I could report that Patrick and Reid are completely well again and are guaranteed to live full, rich, and lengthy lives. I wish I could report that Cliff, Bill, Anne, and Alison no longer work on Ward 5B, for Ward 5B no longer exists. I wish I could report that the AIDS crisis is over, for the cause and the cure have been discovered. But I can't. I am—we all are—forced to deal with things as they are and not as we would like them to be. And very little about AIDS is as we would like it to be.

The other day I received a letter from my sister Missy on the second anniversary of our father's death, and in it she summed up her feelings about his death, about Mom's, and about all sickness and loss in one word. "Robbed!" she wrote. "Robbed, robbed, robbed!"

I couldn't agree more.

A Belated Valentine for Dennis

MARCH 1985

I MET DENNIS at Land's End in October 1980 on one of those rare and wonderful days in San Francisco when the mercury soars to 90 degrees and everyone who can flees to the beach to bask in the sun. He was introduced to me by a mutual friend (and a boyfriend of mine at the time), Lionel, and as soon as I saw him in his skimpy bathing suit, or gym shorts, or was it nothing at all, I knew it wouldn't be long before Dennis would be a boyfriend too. Dark and wiry with luxuriant black hair, a scruffy, two-day beard, and gleaming, bottomless eyes, Dennis exuded an animal sensuality that drew me as surely as the sun had drawn me to the beach. In an instant it was obvious that the attraction was mutual, and, when I left the beach that day, it was Dennis, not Lionel, who sat by my side.

Within no time Dennis and I were "quite the item," according to Lionel's lover Jacques. We saw each other nearly every day, and we spent half our nights together. I quickly lost interest in all others I was dating, and whether Dennis did the same I have no idea, but he gave the impression of being equally as infatuated with me as I was with him. We had little in common other than an intense sexual bond, but that bond was so great that it overshadowed all other concerns. You see, like myself, Dennis was something of a slut at heart. We both had a healthy respect for lust, and, for a while at least, we directed that lust toward each other.

Oh, there were other things about Dennis I admired besides his considerable sexual appetite and skill. He was an accomplished fan dancer, for instance. Before I had ever met him, in fact, I had seen him perform once, at the Heat Wave Party the winter before, and he was sensational. Now I grant you, fan dancing may be a rather esoteric art, but Dennis was one of the best. On Friday and Saturday nights at the Trocadero, I used to love to watch the crowds part as Dennis, dressed only in Levi's or skin-tight black pants, worked those fans: two, four, as many as eight, at a time. When the fans caught the light just so, it was a sight to behold, especially when I was on LSD at four in the morning.

Nights at the Trocadero always ended in bed at home, at least for a while. Although the romance was intense, it didn't last very long. After only six weeks or so, Dennis told me that he didn't want to fuck anymore. He still wanted to be friends, of course, but he wanted to fuck with other people. He didn't say it just so, but I knew he was tired of me sexually, and I was crushed. For my part, I would have liked to continue fucking for—oh, for at least another month. But such was not to be, and although I was disappointed, I quickly adjusted to the situation. Instead of continuing to be boyfriends, therefore, Dennis and I became sisters—best girlfriends, like so many of my other ex-tricks and myself.

For a long time Dennis and I continued to party together, sometimes with Lionel and his best friend, Nick, sometimes with others. We always had a good time, Dennis and I, and only part of it was due to the acid, the MDA, the joints, and the ever-present bottle of ethyl chloride. (In any crowd we were easy to spot: we were the ones with rags in our mouths.) But after a few years we drifted apart, for I got tired of nights at the Trocadero, nights on LSD and ethyl, and nights searching for a trick or a parking space at five or six in the morning. Dennis never tired of life in the fast lane, though, so eventually we saw each other only occasionally at movies or inadvertently on Castro Street.

Over the next few years, Dennis's interest in pleasure turned professional, and, after a brief stint at Moby Dick Records, he entered the party-producing business with his friend Jerry. The first party he produced, Night Shift, in Los Angeles, was a great popular success, although hardly a financial *coup de foudre*, and two other parties in Southern California, Basic Energy and Dreams, had the same mixed results. I did not make it to any of these parties, as they were in LA and I had since lost my interest in disco parties anyway, but I was glad that Dennis had at last found something to work for and pleased that he was full of big plans and big dreams.

Unfortunately, late last summer Dennis was diagnosed with pneumocystis only a few weeks after his best friend, Nick, had also come down with AIDS. After several weeks on Ward 5B at San Francisco General, Dennis came home to Seventeenth Street to recuperate, and spent his days on the couch, watching soap operas, game shows, and trashy movies on TV. Because he couldn't work and had little money, he had a great deal of time on his hands. When I heard he was home, therefore, I went by to see him, and for the first time in several years we saw each other regularly again. We went to a movie together, cruised handsome young men (Dennis never tired of cruising handsome young men, the younger the better), and discussed plans to waterski as soon as he got better.

Of all my friends with AIDS—and there have been seven or eight now—

Dennis in some ways had the most realistic attitude. He alone talked of the possibility of dying. He alone took extraordinary precautions to protect himself. (He would not allow me to visit, for instance, when I had a cold and certainly not when I came down with a relapse of hepatitis.) At the same time, though, he was probably the most optimistic of my friends. "I'm sick," he told me, "and I've got to get better. I just have to be careful, that's all." Dennis never lost hope that he *would* get better, and, as far as I know, he never succumbed to feelings of despair or surrender, even when his friend, Nick, died in December. Later, when he was hospitalized a second and a third time, he continued to hope, and he never stopped planning his next party. This next one, he assured me, would star Tina Turner and would be the greatest party ever. He was moving to LA this summer to arrange it, and he wanted to buy my old convertible, the Jaynemobile, so he could cruise the freeways of Southern California in style. How he was to do all this with poor health and no money I didn't know, but I never expressed my doubts or fears to Dennis.

I last saw Dennis on Saturday, February 2, in the hospital. He was on several different drugs, as well as oxygen for another pneumocystis attack then, and he looked terrible. He looked so bad, in fact, that I did not see how he could possibly survive this latest onslaught. Because I didn't want to tire him, I didn't stay long, and I promised to come again soon when I left.

I really meant to keep that promise, but I got caught up in planning for my thirty-third birthday party, an upcoming trip to Reno, and a number of other things—you know how it is. I thought about Dennis, of course, and I did call once or twice, but the next I heard of him was a call from my friend John. "You heard about Dennis, didn't you? He died on Saturday." I was shocked. I had known he would probably die soon, but not *that* soon, and I was devastated that for one too many days I had neglected him. John also told me that his friends—friends I didn't know—were holding a memorial service for him the next night. I wanted to go, but unfortunately I was scheduled to be in Reno with another friend that night, and although I might have canceled the trip, I didn't. I have a hundred excuses why I didn't, none of which matter very much, and, in any case, I doubt that Dennis would have minded that while his memorial service was being held in San Francisco, I was gambling in Reno. He even might have appreciated the irony. Life does go on, after all. Nevertheless, I feel guilty for not helping to wish Dennis a formal farewell.

I do miss Dennis a great deal already. I don't think this is hypocritical of me, even though we were not particularly close these past few years, for I have found that once a sister, always a sister. Even if I didn't see Dennis often, I depended on him to be a part of my life always, and it hurts that all I have left of him now is the past—memories. For his sake too, as well as for my own, I am sorry. Dennis deserved more from life than a few years of happiness and then death at twenty-seven. It has been said many times before, and always it has made me angry when someone else has said it (for it is so banal), but Dennis was too young to die. It just isn't fair.

Lately I have been obsessed with Dennis's death, with death in general, and I can't help thinking that if death *is* inevitable, then surely there is no point: all is meaningless and absurd. But then I'll see a sunset or I'll have dinner with friends, and once again all will seem right with the world. I am happy and content. I fluctuate daily between these extremes and can't decide what it is I truly believe, but perhaps that is as it should be. Perhaps we are meant to wonder.

One thing I seldom think about, however, is how or why Dennis died. There are those who will blame his death on the life he led before his illness—the promiscuity, the drugs, whatever—but to me all that is irrelevant. When he did those things, Dennis did not know what might happen, and even if he had, what does it matter? We cannot avoid death; we can only try to postpone it, and the thing to do is to lead as significant and as satisfying a life as we can while we can. Some may choose to continue the party; others may choose the opposite course, a hermit's life, but whatever choices are made, we must not cast blame or make accusations. We must simply learn what we can about our options and make our own decisions concerning how to greet the future.

In the same issue of the *Bay Area Reporter* in which Dennis's obituary appeared, February 14—Valentine's Day—I read a letter from a Roger Buchanan, who wrote, "AIDS, AIDS, AIDS, AIDS, AIDS!!!!! That is all you people have to write about. . . . Why is it that you people have to continue filling our lives with gloom, doom, and depression?" Mr. Buchanan is tired of hearing "this shit about the negative side of AIDS" and would prefer that we write about "the joys of being in love instead." I can only respond that I *was* in love—infatuated, at least—with a man named Dennis once, and he died of AIDS. Even if people such as Mr. Buchanan don't care to hear about it, AIDS continues to strike people such as Dennis, who continue to die. Perhaps Mr. Buchanan can ignore this, but I can't, and I will not. We write about AIDS because we must.

I cried when I read Dennis's obituary, by the way. It was so brief and so sweet; and it wasn't enough. A few short paragraphs and a washed-out photo: is that all that is left of Dennis? His house on Seventeenth Street is empty now or soon will be, the parties he produced have long since ended, and even his Trocadero membership has expired. True, his friends have their memories and a picture or two, but even those will fade with time. Someday there will be nothing left of Dennis but a decaying headstone somewhere in Massachusetts. So it goes, of course, and there is little I can do about it—except to dedicate this belated Valentine to my friend in the hope that it will help somehow. Perhaps those who didn't know him and who otherwise would not have cared will feel some regret that a life has been lost. And perhaps someday in the future, someone will find a yellowed copy of this paper somewhere and be reminded that once there lived a man who brought joy into the lives of those he knew, a man who was missed by his grieving friends. Having missed Dennis's memorial service, it is the least I can do.

Scanning the Obituaries

JUNE 1986

IN THE OLD DAYS, like everyone else in town, I read the *Bay Area Reporter* from back to front. First came the classifieds (to see which of my friends were "modeling" this week), and then came John Karr's "Porn Corner," and finally came the latest dish from Mr. Marcus. Much, however, has changed since then. Karr and Mr. Marcus are still around, but many who once read their columns are not. Our community has been devastated by a virus from God knows where, and, as a result, when we open the paper these days, we turn not to the X-rated section in the back, but to the obituaries in the middle. We think not sleaze, but Please don't let me read the names of old friends today.

A few statistics first. During the month of March, 68 people died of AIDS-related diseases in San Francisco; 75 new cases were reported. (This brought the total number of local AIDS cases since July 1981 to 1870 and the number of deaths to 1023.) Only thirty obituaries appeared in the *B.A.R.*, however, and three of these were not AIDS related. (One man died of a heart attack, and two were murdered.) All the deceased who had obituaries in the *B.A.R.* were male. Of the eighteen whose ages were listed, the oldest was 59, the youngest 28. The average age was 37.5.

These men included a stockbroker, a jeweler, a bar owner, a floral designer, a pastor, a writer, a freelance photographer, an advertising art director, a lawyer, a tax accountant, a restaurant manager, three state bureaucrats, two transportation company executives, an artist, a student, an urban planner, a landscape architect, and a cinematographer. Occupations for nine of the men were not listed.

Hometowns for nearly half the men were not mentioned, but at least four were native Californians and four came from Massachusetts. Two were from Oregon, and there was one each from Florida, Texas, Arkansas, Maine, Wisconsin, Ohio, and Belgium. For quite a few their date of arrival in San Francisco was noted, as if this was an event of no small importance in their lives.

At least eight of the men whose obituaries appeared in the *B.A.R.* had some kind of higher education. Three or more were United States veterans. Their interests included music, sports, gardening, baking, and ship restoring, among others. Many of them belonged to or worked for such groups as the Tavern Guild, the Closet Ball, the Gay Games, the Gay Tennis Federation, the Larkin Street Youth Center, the Metropolitan Community Church, the Stonewall Gay Democratic Club, and, naturally enough, a variety of AIDS organizations and support groups.

At least eight of these men had lovers or long-term companions whose relationships with the deceased were cited as a source of strength and support for one or both of the parties involved. Other survivors included family, friends, and even pets. The lover of one man points out that his friend died with "our kitty by his side." Another man will be missed by "his constant canine companions Noodle and Zipper." A third man was surrounded when he died by "his favorite stuffed animals, his penguin collection, and most of his effects of home."

Nearly all had funeral services of some sort. One man made an "adamant" request for a traditional Catholic ceremony. Another wanted his friends to celebrate his life at an open house held in his home following his death. The friends of one man gathered at a picnic; the friends of another held an art show featuring his work. One man's ashes were scattered along the Pacific coastline; another's were dispersed near Angel Island. Furthermore, seventeen men (or their survivors) requested that contributions be made to Shanti, the San Francisco Hospice, the San Francisco AIDS Foundation, or other groups on their behalf or in their memory.

None of the obituaries commemorating these men was, to the best of my knowledge, written by a professional writer. Each was submitted instead by a friend of the deceased. Consequently, the obituaries vary greatly in style and substance. In many, information is sketchy and incomplete; others are more thorough. Some are touching, quite poetic. A few are dolorous, mournful, even lugubrious. And a surprising number are to some degree humorous—deliberately so. A friend of Mark Powers warns, for instance, that he "threatened dire punishment if anyone made an attempt to canonize him after his death." And a friend of Mark O'Brien notes that "he can also be remembered for his portrayal of Beauregard Jackson Pickett Burnside in the 1980 all-male version of *Mame*."

The friends who wrote these obituaries were affected in various ways by the deaths of their loved ones. Many were simply grateful, as were the friends of Scott Elliot, for the time they had shared with the deceased. Others were inspired by the examples set by the dying. Says a friend of Collin B. Kratz, "His kindness and courage in difficult times shall serve as an inspiration to all those who knew him." And one man, an atheist, was even persuaded to believe in God by his lover's faith and spirit.

Nearly all the men who died are eulogized by a friend for some particular quality or qualities. One is praised for his "great generosity of spirit," another for his "breadth of knowledge, depth of kindness, exquisite cooking, and the beauty [he] brought to all [he] touched." One is admired for his "very special energy and will," another for "his awesome courage, mordant wit, outrageous iconoclasm, genuine loving kindness, and, not least, the best Boston accent and Irish good looks this side of Somerville."

Yet despite all this information, despite the facts, the figures, the statistics—even the love and the sorrow—I feel as if I know very little about most of these men. How do you sum up a life in such a short space, after all? How can you possibly say all that ought to be said? I think that the friend who wrote Bruce Armitage's obituary did it best. He does not say how old Bruce was when he died or what he did for a living. He does not tell us about his educational background or professional affiliations. He does, however, tell us this: "[Bruce] was a little guy with big blue eyes who did such things as helped a stranger on a bus and then made best friends with her; grew beautiful begonias and corn in the hills of Massachusetts with rows of Mary Jane in between; liked the spontaneous quality of life and would suddenly decide to make nutmeg doughnuts at 2:30 A.M.; made adventures out of his life; made friends out of his acquaintances; made friends decide to love him." Who, reading this, could not love Bruce as well?

I knew none of the thirty whose obituaries were printed in this paper in March, but I knew some whose names appeared both before and since. It is painful to find those names in the space marked "Death"; it is painful to find *any* names there. Yet despite the hurt, I will continue to read the obituaries, for I want to be assured that if we—you, me, the people around us—must die, we will not die unnoticed. What is said may be incomplete, awkward, or inadequate, but it must be said. Even if the official notices of our deaths evoke no more than a relieved sigh from those who did not know us, we must not simply disappear.

I hope, however, that our obituaries will do more. I hope that the few paragraphs allotted will give our friends the chance to say, as a friend says to John Ryan, "Love ya, cowboy," or to conclude, as a friend does for Bruce Armitage, "How can we say he's gone—when he's so much an indelible part of us." I never knew Gerd Wagener, but in some way I can agree with his friend: "[He] will remain in our hearts forever."

A Time To Give Thanks

NOVEMBER 1987

WHEN I WAS a kid, before the family sat down to the annual Thanksgiving dinner of turkey, mashed potatoes, and canned green beans, my parents made each of us state at least one reason to be thankful. It was an awkward, forced ritual, and we kids hated it, for none of us ever came up with anything but trite, conventional, and predictable responses. Nevertheless the ritual has survived, even though my parents have not. It is part of a family tradition that those of us who carry on are loath to abandon.

This year I had to search hard for reasons to be thankful, for recent developments have been grim. In October, shortly before leaving for the march on Washington, my doctor told me that my T-cell count was low and getting lower. "Normal is 500 to 1500," he said. "Less than 200 is serious. You're at 145." He recommended that I take the HIV antibody test to pinpoint the reason for the decline. No longer able to rely on ignorance as my talisman, I followed his advice. When I returned from Washington, I learned the result. It was, in the twisted language that doctors use, "positive."

This didn't upset me as much as it might have, for I have assumed I was antibody positive for years—and have acted accordingly. But the next words my doctor spoke *were* disturbing: "Unless you do something about this, statistically you can expect an AIDS diagnosis within a year, two at most." I felt like Bette Davis in the movie *Dark Victory,* when she learns the truth about her condition: "Prognosis negative." As I wrote to a friend from high school, "I may make it to the class of 1970's twentieth reunion, but I wouldn't count on attending my fortieth birthday bash if I were you."

For a day or two I assumed the worst. I nursed melodramatic fantasies, updated my will, and planned my funeral. But I got over it quickly enough. If a survivor's instinct had prevented an AIDS diagnosis for this long, I reasoned, it might continue to serve me well. Besides, if I went on AZT, the doctor had said, I could expect to see my T-cell count improve significantly. He also had recommended nebulized pentamidine treatments once a month to prevent pneumocystis.

"With any luck at all," he said, "we'll get you through the winter without a diagnosis, and by next spring, who knows? By then we expect to have a battery of more effective, less toxic drugs than the ones we have now."

As a result I am now one of the legions of gay men in this city walking around with pillbox timers in their pockets, beeping every four hours around the clock. I am not a PWA—not yet, anyway—yet I share their concerns, fears, and hopes.

I realize that my future may indeed be a limited one, but whose is not? So instead I concentrate on the present. As long as it is satisfactory, I am content.

Ironically, at the same time future prospects dimmed, present prospects brightened with the start of a new relationship. On the steps of the Supreme Court building in Washington in October, I met someone from San Francisco who made me feel alive and whole again. We hit it off immediately, and I gave myself over, perhaps too rapidly, to infatuation. We saw each other regularly, and for the first time in years, I willingly spent hours on the phone.

Since then things have calmed down a bit. Because I still have at least one or two toes on the ground, I recognize that this relationship may develop in unforeseen ways. It may not even last. As my friend has taken great pains to point out, we do not seem to share the same level of interest in one another. But we are still close, and whatever happens, I will be eternally grateful to have met this man.

I've thought a lot about why this relationship blossomed when it did, and I think it was because only when I felt I had nothing left to lose did I allow myself to open up to the possibilities it represented. Two months ago I might have said, "He's too tall" or "He's too young" and left it at that, but now things have changed. It has become painfully evident that I don't have forever to search for perfection.

But it's more than that. Another reason I found support and intimacy with this man is that I needed to find it. My friend has given me a way to escape fear and self-pity. As Mother Superior tells Maria in *The Sound of Music* (and God forbid I should ever use *this* reference again), "When God closes one door, he always opens another." Over the past few years, I have seen AIDS bring out the best in many of my friends. Perhaps being this close to AIDS will bring out the best in me too, by helping me to grow emotionally.

There are still many doors open to me this Thanksgiving, of course, and a thousand reasons to be grateful. Whatever the state of my health, I'm not dead yet. Whatever the state of my heart, I'm not alone. Besides my Supreme Court friend, there are many others to offer love and encouragement. Backing them up is an entire network of AIDS support groups in this city. We really do live in a wonderful time in a phenomenal place, and I don't need an AIDS diagnosis or a special holiday to teach me that. If Mom and Dad were still alive, that's what I'd tell them at the dinner table this year.

A Cry of Despair

JULY 1988

I'M DEPRESSED—mainly because my boyfriend left for Chicago this morning after a brief visit, and I don't know when I'm going to see him again or what I'm going to do about this long-distance relationship. But I can't write about this now. I don't think my boyfriend likes the publicity, despite his assurances that I can write about whatever I please.

Besides, regardless of how he feels, I promised myself that I would not write about my personal life as much as I have in the past. I realize I have gotten away with murder for years, but readers can take only so much before they tune out and cease to identify.

In any case there are other reasons for my depression. When I arrived at the restaurant where I worked today, only a few hours after taking my boyfriend to the airport, I found out that the head chef had died the night before. Although he was not a close friend, he was a good man and a hard worker. I respected him a great deal and will miss his steady guidance and fair dealing. His death put my own paltry concerns into proper perspective, of course—but it sure didn't make me feel any better about the present or the future.

It seems as if I am surrounded by dissolution and death these days. This past week I saw in the obituary section of the *Bay Area Reporter* the name of someone I had met at the Gay Games in 1986. The week before that, Leonard Matlovich's obituary had appeared, as well as that of someone I had admired who had been a Barbary Coast Clogger. Earlier in the month I had found the picture of a gym friend in the space reserved for "Deaths," as well as that of another co-worker at the restaurant. I had hoped that after years of obituaries, the grim toll would lessen. But the numbers continue to climb, as relentless and ruthless as ever.

In the mail this past week I received a package that brought all this even closer to home. A reader sent me a T-shirt that had belonged to a mutual friend of ours who had died of AIDS in 1985. The reader's lover had also died of AIDS recently, and the reader was in the process of cleaning out his things and reorganizing his life. He sent me the T-shirt because he thought I would appreciate it.

I was touched but saddened by the gift. This mutual friend and I had been part of a tight-knit circle of friends who partied together our first few years in San Francisco. All are dead now except myself. I remember when my doctor at the University of California Medical Center suggested five years ago that within a few years every gay man of my generation in San Francisco *could* very well succumb to the disease. At the time I considered the prediction alarmist and extreme. I think so no longer.

What else *am* I to think when, one by one, my friends develop health problems, test positive, sicken, and die? This past week yet another friend told me that his T-cell count has sunk to less than 100 and his doctors have suggested AZT and pentamidine as countermeasures. I have heard this sort of news so often lately that I hardly react to it anymore. As Andrew Holleran says, "The more you live through this, the less august it seems." Yet it is still horrible, and from time to time I cry out in despair, unable to bear the situation any longer.

Sometimes I wonder why, of all my friends, I am one of the few who has survived. But then I look at my own T-cell count, and I wonder no longer. As I wrote to the reader who sent me the T-shirt, "It is probably only a matter of time before I get AIDS as well." I do not know if I really believe this. What I do know is that I have felt a hell of a lot better in my life than I do now—and this is beginning to make me awfully nervous.

I also know that on the wall of my bathroom there hangs a picture of a group of my friends rafting down the American River. Five of the eight people in the picture are gay. The two in the front left of the picture are now dead. When I look at that picture, I draw mental Xs over the faces of the deceased, and I wonder which of the three of us will be the next to go. It is a modern parlor game version of Agatha Christie's *Ten Little Indians*—but no fun to play.

I probably shouldn't be writing all this. I know no one wants to hear it. Most people in the community have already heard too much of AIDS. If I must write about the plague, they tell me, at least I should be upbeat and optimistic. Well, I try. And usually I succeed. I am well aware that the image I most often project (one that I deliberately cultivate) is that of a naive Pollyanna who is determined to view the world through rose-colored lenses. But sometimes I just can't pretend any longer that all is as it should be. Today, for instance, life seems a dismal affair at best, and I'm depressed.

The question is, What is to be done about it? Sometimes I just want to escape: quit my job and travel. But that's hardly a realistic option. Instead I should follow my boyfriend's advice to think about it as little as possible and to get through each day as painlessly and as graciously as I can. In time this too will pass, he says. A few days down the road, all will seem right again—or at least bearable. And even if my friends don't stop dying of AIDS, at least my boyfriend may come back to me—which would give me a reason for optimism.

GREAT TRANSITIONS

Entering Middle Age

APRIL 1986

LIKE MANY WRITERS, I claim to be an advocate of truth, but sometimes I have to be dragged, kicking and screaming, to face it. A few weeks ago, for instance, a friend at work, Rick, asked if I had seen the latest gay TV movie, this one about the relationship between a young man and his older lover.

"No," I replied. "How old was the old fart?"

"About our age," Rick answered. "Midthirties."

"Impossible!" I cried. "I'm sorry, but there's no way I could be anybody's older lover."

Rick snorted. "Get over yourself, hon. You're almost old enough to be that boy's father. Next time you see a mirror, take a good look at yourself."

Several days later I was in San Diego visiting an old heartthrob, Paul. Because he keeps an early schedule, Paul suggested we go to bed at ten.

"But I can't do that," I protested. "'St. Elsewhere' comes on at ten."

"Suit yourself," he said. "You can always join me later."

Maybe so—but I knew that later Paul would be fast asleep, dead to the world, that this was our only night together, and that I hadn't had sex in more weeks than I cared to admit publicly. Nevertheless, I still chose to watch "St. Elsewhere." Five years ago such a decision would have been unthinkable.

"Face it," said my friend Tom when I returned to San Francisco and Told All on the phone. "You ain't no spring chicken anymore. Neither one of us is as young as we used to be."

Tell me. But if this is so, then why has it come as such a surprise? How has middle age—if such it is—snuck up on me, practically unnoticed?

I suppose I should have had an inkling that the years were doing to me what they eventually do to everyone when I underlined the following passage in Robert Ferro's *Family of Max Desir*: "He continually fought back an incipient softness in his muscles and flesh. . . . How dare they? . . . His body had changed slowly and gradually from one thing to another in about five years."

But no. I failed to note the obvious until Andrew Holleran (to whom I had sent a series of fan letters as well as a couple of columns) wrote to me, "I think both your columns are about something that I've realized I keep writing about too: it's middle age! Growing up! Finding the craziness evaporate." Specifically, Mr. Holleran was referring to my stated preference for early evenings over late ones (primarily due to the scarcity of parking spaces in my neighborhood late at night). Personally, I didn't think this constituted entry into middle age. But he did, and if Andrew Holleran thinks I'm middle-aged, it *must* be true.

Trouble is, I don't *feel* middle-aged. I am as athletic as I ever was—nay, more so—although I do seem more prone to injury than before. And, all modesty aside, I don't think I look so bad for my age. True, as the protagonist of Mr. Ferro's book discovers, my waistline does have a distressing tendency to thicken, despite frantic efforts on my part to prevent it, and my hairline is doing its best to recede. But if I have to, I can live with that. The important thing, as Granny (and a million other grandmas) used to say, is that you're only as young as you feel—and, honey, I feel like a million dollars.

Actually, in many ways what I feel like is an adolescent. Maybe it's because I still think of myself in that way. My image of myself hasn't changed all that much since high school days, after all. I still consider myself relatively carefree, innocent, and adventuresome. When I look at most straight guys my age, especially those who have kids and high-pressure jobs, I wonder if it is possible that we belong to the same generation. Thank God I haven't yet developed that arrogant, slightly perturbed look that they all seem to have. Thank God I haven't allowed myself to become burdened by the responsibilities that they have taken on.

On the other hand, I wonder, at my age is this something for which I should be grateful? There is a time to grow up, after all. There is a time to put away childish things (such as poppers, membership at the Trocadero, and old address books). We gay people are often accused of being willing victims of arrested development, collective Dick Clarks, perversely refusing to grow old. But I don't want to be like that, any more than I want to be a jaded, tiresome, cynical straight man, drinking Maalox to keep the ulcers at bay. I have never had any desire to play Peter Pan.

Well, there is little chance of that. Even if I do not always recognize the changes in myself that denote middle age, others recognize them in me. ("But cha are, Blanche," I keep hearing. "But cha are!") The vast majority of letters I receive from readers, for instance, come from men in their late thirties and forties, and they tell me that one of the reasons they enjoy my articles (*when* they enjoy them) is that I write what they feel. I am a spokesperson for their (my?) generation. This came as quite a shock to me at first, I'll admit. But then it began to explain a few things. "So *that's* why the sweet young things at the Stud pay so little attention to me," I realized. "To them I am a relic, a reminder of another era."

Ah, me, if it's true, it's true. I suppose I can deal with this also. Oh, hell, I can deal with anything. The physical changes, the increasing responsibilities, the decline of giddy pleasures and the rise of subtler ones: none of this really bothers me. The one thing that does bother me, however, is that the older I get, the fewer options I seem to have. Oh, for the most part I can still go wherever I want to go and do whatever I want to do (*love* that sixties beat), but some freedoms *are* tempered by time. Some things are beyond my control. If I want to be an integral part of my nephews' lives, for instance, I'd better move to Washington, D.C., now. If I want to share a fiftieth anniversary with someone someday, I'd better fall in love now. Unfortunately, entering middle age necessarily entails making choices that I had wanted to postpone indefinitely—or had hoped to avoid entirely.

The other day in the comic strip *Bloom County*, Binkley—a child of ten or so—announces to no one in particular, "I'd like everyone to know that I'm looking for new directions in my life! I'm doubting my old values and reassessing my few accomplishments . . . and frankly, I'm getting a little depressed about things!!" Concludes his rabbit friend, "Middle age has come a wee early for Mr. Binkley."

I think middle age has come a wee early for me too. But unlike Binkley, I'm not depressed about things—not really. Oh, I know I kvetch a lot, sometimes simply for the sake of kvetching. (A cousin told me once that I thought too much, and it is certainly true in the case of my kvetching.) But I do it only because it keeps me alert. Actually, despite the concerns I voice, I am remarkably pleased with my life at present. And the older I get, the more content I am. The more experience I gain, the wiser I feel. I do not regret a single one of my thirty-four years. (Well, maybe one or two.) If I sometimes worry about middle age, well, at least I have a middle age about which to worry. In these times—in any times, perhaps—that ought to be enough.

The "Baths" at Eighth and Howard: Seeking Shelter from the Storm

JANUARY 1988

LET US BEGIN by giving credit where credit is due. The idea for this article was not mine, but that of Danny Williams, who, as a comedian, can get away with this sort of thing much better than I can.

"Don't you wonder sometimes," he asked, "whatever happened to the old Club Baths at Eighth and Howard? I know it's a shelter for the homeless now, but what I want to know is this: Is the dress code still enforced? What did they do with all the towels? Do the homeless leave their doors ajar to invite midnight company? And what night is buddy night, anyway?"

Scandalized but amused, I decided to check it out for myself. Although I never had been a great fan of the baths in their heyday, I was, I admit, not *entirely* unfamiliar with the establishment at Eighth and Howard, once one of the city's premier bathhouses. It was not a place where I had looked for love. It was, however, a place where I had attempted to fulfill a compelling need, especially during certain hours of the morning.

One of Danny's questions was answered as soon as I walked in the front door of the former bathhouse, now the Episcopal Sanctuary, a few days after our conversation. People wearing Lacoste shirts, designer sweaters, or perfume are not discouraged from entering the premises, as they were in "the old days." Neither are people wearing grocery boxes or newspapers on their heads, such as the woman who was standing in line next to me. At the new Eighth and Howard, all manner of dress and behavior, from bed sheets to chatting with invisible companions, are welcome. It is, in many ways, a far more democratic place than it used to be.

At the head of the line, facing the same bulletproof glass windows I had encountered years ago, but surrounded by newly placed job opportunity posters, I could have chosen to sign in and turn over my valuables in exchange for a room key, just like I had done eons ago. Instead I stated my business, filed through the same heavy security doors, and headed up the staircase to the second floor.

Father William B. Nern, an Episcopal priest who was the executive director of the shelter, welcomed me into his office, which is located along the wall where I once had watched porn movies (and performed an entirely natural act upon one Dan B., if the truth be told). I refrained, however, from mentioning this to the good father. Instead I commented on the light streaming in from the many open windows—windows I had never noticed when I was focusing on other things (and which, in any case, had been painted black to shut out the "real" world).

Father Nern soon turned me over to Stephen Suwalsky, the Episcopal Sanctuary's operations coordinator. Suwalsky explained that the shelter had opened in 1983 in the basement of Grace Cathedral, had moved six months later to the Canon–Kip Center on Eighth Street, and finally had opened on the site of the old bathhouse, following a year of construction and renovation, in October 1987.

The shelter, Suwalsky noted, existed primarily to serve three groups: the frail elderly, the disabled, and single young women. "Anyone who belongs to one of these groups can get in with no questions asked," he explained. "There are no requirements and no restrictions on the length of stay."

In addition, the Episcopal Sanctuary offered help to approximately thirty to forty client volunteers, young single men who did security, kitchen, and maintenance work four hours a day in exchange for food, shelter, counseling, and employment assistance. These men were accepted on a standby basis for a maximum stay of ninety days. If by some chance there was no room for them at the 250-bed facility, they could seek admittance to the Salvation Army or to one of the other shelters in town.

Suwalsky was quite enthusiastic about showing me the changes the shelter has undergone since the Episcopal Sanctuary has taken over. Women are housed in small singles or doubles on the first floor for security reasons. The male disabled are placed in nearby four-bed cubicles equipped for their special needs. Upstairs, compartments with one to four beds line the walls for other clients. These sleeping spaces are small, but they are sunny, light, and clean: a far cry from the cramped, Criscoed cubbyholes of days gone by.

Downstairs, a brand new kitchen gleams. The renovated bathrooms, with private stalls and showers (which used to be oh-so-public), are equally spotless. The old pool and sauna area upstairs is now a clothing, storage, and distribution area. Practically the only room in the entire place that hasn't changed is a room the bathhouse patrons never saw in the first place: the laundry room (where the towels were done, Mr. Williams).

In other rooms space is offered for several groups—a veterans' group, an ex-offenders' group, and a drug and alcohol abusers' group—who count the shelter's clients among their members, as well as for many of the Episcopal Sanctuary's twenty-six full-time staff members. A first-floor activity room contains couches and a TV. A chapel (!) provides a quiet place for meditation and worship; people still kneel, but not for the same reason they once did. (The orgy room, incidentally, has long since disappeared.)

Before ending the tour Suwalsky pointed out that "the Bishop blessed all these areas" before opening the shelter doors to the homeless. Perhaps because of that—or for more secular reasons—there never has been any stigma attached to the Episcopal Sanctuary, claimed Suwalsky, despite the building's checkered history. "We thought we might encounter some discomfort or AIDS-related hysteria," he admitted, "but we never have. Neither the officials nor our guests seemed to have minded—which is fortunate, because we thought it would be a very good use for the property, very compatible."

Of that there is no doubt. Thanks primarily to the efforts of men such as Suwalsky, Father Nern, and William H. Barcus, a canon to the AIDS ministry at Grace Cathedral who played a large part in establishing the Episcopal Sanctuary, there is now a safe, clean place where the homeless can recuperate. Because this was once a place where gay men could recreate, a home away from home for those seeking a different kind of refuge, some have viewed it as a loss to the community.

Having seen the place in both its incarnations, however, I cannot agree. We are all seeking shelter from the storm these days. Sure, the baths were fun, but "fun" isn't the point anymore. Survival is. Danny Williams, although he jokes about it, knows this. "I used to be homeless myself back in the early 1970s, when I first left home, so I know how important shelters are," he says. "They certainly saved my life."

Still, I wonder what Danny would make of the following sign, currently posted on one of the shelter walls: Ask in Clinic for Condoms and Bleach. I *know* what the condoms are for, but do the homeless really have time to do their hair? Maybe if the owners of the old Eighth and Howard had offered free henna treatments when rimming went out of style, the baths never would have closed in the first place. At least it's nice to think so.

EARLY LIFE

Camping the Boy Scout Way

NOVEMBER 1985

I DID MY DUTY. My dad, my uncles, and several of my cousins were all Boy Scouts. Not only that, but they were also Eagle Boy Scouts, Scouting's ultimate achievers. With such a pedigree, there was no escape for me. Although there were a million ways I would rather have spent my time—playing the piano, for instance, or drawing or organizing neighborhood theatrical events—I was fated to play toy soldier in an army for boys, doomed at a young and tender age.

I was hardly the kind of boy for whom the Boy Scouts was designed. I despised discipline and uniforms did nothing for me (although I had to admit that the merit badges were colorful and the neckerchiefs had a certain flair). Hiking gave me blisters and camping left me cold. Whenever Billy D. stretched his arms, beat his chest, inhaled, and sighed, "Ah, there's nothing like the great outdoors," I could only wonder, Can she be serious? And when his brother Bobby wolfed down some disgusting concoction of dirt and eggs and swore it was the best thing he had ever had, I could only fret, How am I ever going to get these filthy dishes clean?

And yet there was one thing the Scouts offered for which I will be eternally grateful, one aspect that thrilled me from the start: the chance for a homosexual education. Oh, I suppose I knew I was gay long before I joined the Scouts. I remember tying Jacky B. naked to a tree at age six, for instance, for ritual torture during one particularly vivid game of cowboys and Indians. But it was the Scouts that reconfirmed and reinforced my homosexuality. It was the Scouts that gave me the chance to act upon long-suppressed yet elemental desires. Ah, Scouting: a pedophiliac paradise.

Who was the first to set my heart afire? Ah, yes, Russell W., the senior patrol leader at my first summer camp. Russell was a great beauty, and I fell in love immediately, but the difference in our ages—he was sixteen and I was eleven—kept us apart. Still, I dreamed about Russell night after night, dreamed that I was in trouble and he rescued me, dreamed that we spent our lives together. Once, when the troop went swimming at Factory Shoals, I positioned myself so that I could watch Russell undress. What a body, and so mature! Russell had attributes that I could only hope to possess one day—if I couldn't possess Russell himself.

That same summer I learned what it was to masturbate when two of the older Scouts, Corky and Bob, put on a show for the entire troop while the Scoutmasters were away. Corky, who had the biggest one in camp, and Bob, who had the hairiest, placed themselves on a lower bunk in one of the three-sided cabins we occupied, and from that stage demonstrated acts I had never seen before and have never forgotten. Of course, Corky and Bob weren't queer. Nobody thought that. They were just kidding around. Boys will be boys, after all, and thank God for it.

I couldn't wait to practice at home what I had learned at camp. But then one day, while thumbing through the *Boy Scout Handbook,* I came across a few paragraphs under the heading "From Boy to Man," which described the physical changes a boy goes through when he grows older, including that marvelous event, the nocturnal emission, or, as the book would have it, the "wet dream." Of the few brief paragraphs I studied, these stood out like a flash of lightning:

> There are boys who do not let nature have its own way with them but cause emissions themselves. This may do no physical harm, but may cause them to worry.
>
> Any real boy knows that anything that causes him to worry should be avoided or overcome. If anything like this worries you, this is not unusual—just about all boys have the same problem. Seek the correct answer to any question which bothers you about your development from boy to man. But be sure to get your information from reliable sources—your parents, your physician, your spiritual adviser.

I must have read those paragraphs a thousand times. I especially liked the references in a preceding paragraph to hair around the sex organs and the sex organs' increase in size. But I didn't particularly care for the reference to worry in connection with masturbation, and I didn't like the book's solution: "Any real boy knows that anything that causes him to worry should be avoided or overcome." I didn't want to avoid or overcome masturbation. Did that mean I wasn't a *real* boy? No, I decided, the key word was "worry," and as long as I didn't worry about it, according to the book, then everything was okay. So I turned to the nearby picture on page 420 of a boy taking a shower and continued to masturbate.

I suppose it was a year or two after the Corky and Bob Show that Wayne S. asked me during one weekend campout, "Do you do it too?" and took me off into the woods to see for himself. Thus solitary masturbation led to mutual masturbation, and so began a monthly ritual that lasted for years. I actually learned to look forward to camping trips, for it was then that Wayne and I escaped to the woods together to discover the joys and delights of prolonged puberty. In the beginning, at least, we never worried that what we were doing was wrong. The *Boy Scout Handbook* said nothing about homosexuality, after all, and, if anything, we agreed with school counselors that this was probably a phase we were going through.

Of course, we weren't the only ones enjoying that phase. It was my great fortune to belong to a Boy Scout troop that was a hotbed of homosexual activity, an association of like-minded sybarites. True, Wayne was probably the most perverse of the bunch, for, among other things, he liked to steal other boys' jockstraps and to fantasize about the size of their balls. He also liked to catch them in the act, surprising them with his flashlight and the inevitable cry of triumph, "Aha, gotcha!" But there was also Butch, who did it with a plumber's helper in the latrine and who was the first to demonstrate the meaning of the verb *to cornhole*. There was Steve, who was addicted to games of grab ass, and Tommy B., who was fond of circle jerks. Then there was Tommy L., who confessed to . . . no, some things are simply too lurid to tell, and Tommy L., whom I still see from time to time, would never forgive me.

Although they aren't nearly as exciting, there *are* other gay-related memories besides sexual ones. While other boys were playing steal the bacon or capture the flag, I was collecting lavender flowers to decorate the campsite. While other boys were constructing small-scale Vietnamese villages and burning them to the ground, I was rearranging sleeping bags and planning dinner menus. And while other boys were giving each other orders and doing push-ups, I was writing skits to be presented at weekly meetings and monthly campfires. In fact, I was probably the only boy in the history of Scouting to narrate one such skit—about a pioneer family moving West, I think—in full drag and with a French accent, no less. God, the things I got away with—or didn't, for all I know.

In time the sexual activity lessened as, one by one, other boys grew out of the mutual masturbation phase. (I, of course, never did but eventually had no one with whom to do it.) In time, also, I learned to appreciate the butcher side of Scouting and added canoeing, lifesaving, and swimming merit badges to the ones I already had in music, art, and drama. By the time that I too progressed at last to Eagle, the homosexual phase of Scouting was largely a thing of the past, a phase after all. But it was not forgotten. Never forgotten. For as long as I'll remember Scouting, I'll remember the illicit pleasures it provided, for, as far as I was concerned, the two were always inextricably intertwined.

The national leaders of the Boy Scouts of America don't like to admit this, of course. They have even gone so far as to adopt a national policy stating that homosexuality and Scouting are "incompatible," that it is impossible to be both a homosexual and a Boy Scout at the same time. When a young man named Tim Curran, a Boy Scout from Berkeley, California, attempted to challenge this antiquated notion a few years ago, the national leadership did its best to bury Tim and the idea of gay rights for adolescents with him. But no matter what they say or do, they can't stop thousands of boys from getting the same kind of education that I got in Scouting, for as long as the Boy Scouts exists, some precocious little boys will be making excursions into the woods that Lord Baden-Powell could not have anticipated—but might have enjoyed.

Come to think of it, I wonder what stories my father could have told. . . .

First Love

FEBRUARY 1987

ALMOST EVERY GAY man can pinpoint the time when he first came out to himself, when he finally accepted that he was gay: when he was sixteen, when he graduated from school, when he moved to the city, whenever. Most gays realize that they are gay long before that, however, and some can pinpoint a time when, even if they didn't admit it to themselves yet, in retrospect they can say that they knew they were gay. Maybe it was the time a gay male first dressed in clothing of the opposite sex, or the time he spent an hour too long in the bathroom of the public library, reading the graffiti. Maybe it was the time he was born. For me, it was the time, at age twelve, when I fell in love with Tommy.

Oh, there were signs long before that. At six I carried Grandma's purses, asked for a Jenny doll for Christmas, and played with Jacky B. buck naked in the backyard. And at nine I began to avoid baseball at all costs. Yet only when I fell in love with Tommy was there no turning back. Even if I didn't have a word for it, I knew I was gay. I was hooked: by my sexuality and, no less, by Tommy.

Tommy and I met in the first grade, but I don't remember him making an impression on me until two years later, when we both had the same girlfriend, Beth. I had her first, as I recall, but I wasn't much good at heterosexual love and botched things up, naturally. Beth went on to Tommy after that, and they were together for quite some time. (Beth will probably deny this version of the facts, but to this day she challenges every memory I have, so I never pay attention anymore.) I never really blamed Beth for dumping me, for Tommy was by far the better catch.

Tommy and I were both smart. We were always at the head of the class, archrivals for the top grades and the teacher's affection. Whereas I was a little too pretty, however, Tommy was extremely good-looking in an all-American sort of way. Also, Tommy played sports, which is something I never did (if I could help it). From the third grade on, from Pop Warner to the high school ranks, he was the quarterback of the football team, and he excelled at other sports besides. Face it: in a one-on-one, best-all-round competition with Tommy, I never had a chance.

That never really bothered me, for Tommy was easy to like: outgoing, personable, genuine. Thank God he was so likable, for we were thrown together constantly. He lived right down the street and was always coming over to play. In addition, we belonged to about a trillion organizations together, among them Indian Y-Guys and the church choir. In the church choir we were both first sopranos, and even there we competed. Each of us tried to sing higher than the other on numbers such as "I Come to the Garden Alone." I don't remember who won.

The year we turned twelve, the year I fell in love with Tommy, sex reared its fateful head. We were studying math at my place together when suddenly the conversation began to drift. Soon we were sitting on the bed beside one another, promising, I'll show you mine if you show me yours.

If it is of any consequence, I won this competition, at least for the time being. I reached puberty before Tommy, and it showed. I doubt that this concerned Tommy, for he—and I—were interested in other things besides exhibitionism. Thus began a year and a half of unexpected bliss, as Tommy and I sought each other's company more often than ever. We met in our bedrooms, in our basements, in my backyard treehouse: wherever we could find a bit of privacy. Sometimes we took chances. There was the time we did it anyway, even though Tommy's mother was downstairs doing laundry. When she tried to put the laundry away, she discovered Tommy's door locked and nearly had a fit.

"What are you two doing in there?" she demanded as we struggled to pull our pants up. Later she handed Tommy a copy of some sex book for adolescents and warned against the danger of "other boys who will try to make you do things you know are wrong." My own mother, on the other hand, never suspected a thing and actually encouraged our get-togethers. Because of Tommy's many virtues, she thought he was a good influence on me.

This state of affairs continued until that black day, alas, when Tommy's parents announced they were moving to another city far away. I was absolutely distraught at losing my best friend—nay, my boyfriend—but Tommy didn't seem to mind. He was excited about the change, the cad. After he left I did find other sex partners, but it wasn't the same. For years I dreamed about him and wondered if he missed me as much as I missed him—or at all.

I didn't see Tommy again for four years, not until our high school choir traveled to his city on tour. He came to the concert and looked better than ever, but I felt like I hardly knew him anymore. I certainly didn't ask him if he remembered our escapades in the treehouse together. Neither did I ask him if he was as obsessed as I was by the continuing desire to do more of the same. We merely exchanged a few polite words of conversation and parted—forever.

For years afterward I wondered if Tommy was gay. He certainly enjoyed homosexuality at age twelve. Did it last? I found out later when our mutual childhood friend Beth, who attended college with him, kept me informed of the developments in his life. After college he went to medical school. At some point he got married. Later he got divorced. Aha! I said to myself. Does this mean something? It did not. I lost all hope when Beth herself had an affair with the man. It was too ironic. More than fifteen years before, Tommy had interfered with my relationship with Beth; now Beth was destroying my hopes for Tommy. Sometimes, I thought, life just ain't fair.

I still think about Tommy constantly. Sometimes I use his name when making reservations at a restaurant, for it is easier to spell his last name than my own. I even used it at the Haight-Ashbury Free Medical Clinic once, when I didn't want anyone to know that I might have intestinal parasites: an odd form of flattery, I admit. Although that might have offended Tommy, however, he could only be pleased that I also used his name as the main character of one of my unpublished novels. The name had to be special, and whenever I think of special, Tommy comes to mind.

That's one thing I hope never changes.

GENDER BENDING: DEFINING OURSELVES

From One Girl to Another

SEPTEMBER 1988

NOT LONG AGO I received the following letter in the mail:

> I've read your columns with interest off and on for a year or so. And you can be a damn good writer. At times you're downright inspired. . . . I beseech you, then, why is it you . . . resort to the anachronism of calling yourself and other guys girl? I've heard all the arguments over the years about gender bending, and why does it matter, etc., etc., etc. I've also heard black people call their black friends nigger, and I can buy the validity of doing that about as much as your calling yourself girl.
>
> Sure, words, gender words, are just a symbol, mere words. . . . And what power they have! You of all persons, being a writer, should know that. And the symbol in most persons' minds, gay and straight, of using the word *girl* to describe a guy is that of *Boys in the Band,* the old, stereotyped view of the gay male: weak, ineffectual, depressed, sad, effeminate, generally an unhappy mess.
>
> And how are bright, happy, natural, unpretentious young guys who are gay and . . . still looking for role models supposed to be affected by your choice of words? They read your column and what do they get? Regurgitated, recycled self-homophobia.
>
> Why? Where is your sense of male dignity? I didn't say "male pride" or "false pride," and I'm not talking about macho bullshit! But how about just a little calm, clear, down-to-earth sense of gay male dignity?

Well! My first reaction after reading this letter was to respond, "Aw, get over it, girl. It's a joke. I don't know why it's funny. It just is." But then, in the course of doing research for a book, I ran across an article entitled "Crossing Signals" from the September 8, 1975, issue of *Time* magazine (hardly the world's leading authority on homosexual matters, but so be it), which caused me to rethink the question. According to *Time:*

> Like most subcultures, the homosexual world has its own language. . . . Many gay terms for sexual styles and tastes are put-downs. Besides nellies, effeminate gay males are called twinkies, sissies or queens; they do their drinking in vanilla bars, swish joints or fluff parlors. . . . Butch women are sometimes called brothers; effeminate male homosexuals call each other sister. . . . Fag and faggot are acceptable terms among gays if no straights are present.
>
> Gay speech can be fresh and funny but also dirty and self-deprecating. Bruce Rodgers, who compiled more than 12,000 terms for his book *The*

Queens' Vernacular, acknowledges that many gay activists regard gay slang as "another link in the chain which holds the homosexual enslaved."

When I first came out, several years before this essay was published, I agreed entirely with the gay activists quoted by Rodgers. I'll never forget entering a gay bar that first summer and hearing the terms *Mary, sister,* and *girlfriend* bandied about. I was appalled, for I considered queens to be an embarrassing throwback to an earlier, darker era. The straight friends who had accompanied me to the bar were equally disgusted and confessed with a shudder, "You're okay, Mike, but these other guys make us sick. Thank God you're not like them."

Over the years, however, I grew less and less hostile to incidences of overt effeminate behavior, whether natural or affected, as I grew more comfortable with my sexuality. Rather than viewing such behavior as self-deprecating or homophobic, I saw it as liberating. No longer was I ashamed of effeminacy in general, or of having been a childhood sissy in particular; I was proud of the things that set me apart, that made me different. In time I too began to use some of the queens' vernacular—but always with a detached attitude.

Straight friends accused me of losing my critical perspective. I countered that I was actually gaining a new perspective. I was learning not only the dialectic of camp (it was *fun* to talk that way), but also the dynamics of radical, deliberate, confrontational politics. I understood that, like some of their enlightened predecessors, the queens of the 1970s were saying, This is who and what we are. Like it or not, we aren't apologizing or changing for anyone.

When other people claimed that by sanctioning this mode of speech I was institutionalizing oppression, I argued that the opposite was the case. By calling each other girlfriend or even faggot, my friends and I were turning the tables on our oppressors by transforming what they considered to be derogatory epithets into harmless endearments. For validation I turned to the example of Christopher Isherwood, who called himself and his friends queers. This shut my critics up; few had the courage to contradict Saint Christopher.

Of course I acknowledge that by using terms such as these we run the risk of confusing our opponents. They knew when we exchanged the words *pansy, fruit,* and *fairy* for the word *gay* that we were making a valiant, if obvious, attempt to change an age-old stereotype. It must be difficult for them to understand that the terms *faggot* and *queer* are no longer shameful.

My initial response to this problem is, Who cares what they think? But the answer is, I do. As much as I'd like to pretend otherwise, I want others to respect us—but I'm certainly not willing to gain that respect by playing by their rules—and I'm far more concerned that we respect ourselves.

So I still use the word *girl* occasionally—but only when kidding around, just as I always have. And I still use the word *faggot*—but never perjoratively. Obviously I still get flack for it from gay and straight people alike. But I honestly don't think it matters much what terms we use, as long as we know what we believe. Sure, words are powerful things, but ideas are still more powerful. And it is in ideas that I place my faith—as well as find my dignity.

Draggin' 'em into Finocchio's

JULY 1986

OUTSIDE ON Broadway the tour buses are lined up at the curb, and the stairs to the second-floor club are packed with middle-aged matrons and their husbands.

"You know, if we don't get in, we can always go to the male strip joint, the Casbah, across the street," I suggest to my friends, whom I have persuaded to join me here. "Or we can go to the Stone to cruise suburban punk rockers. I saw at least three blond, blue-eyed, eighteen-year-olds for whom I would have lain down and died."

But we do get in, past the doorman sporting a fancy green jacket with gold braid and the cashier collecting eight dollars a person in exchange for a ticket *and* a postcard of the joint. Not only do we get in, but we are ushered to seats in the very first row, where an elderly cocktail waiter takes our drink order. I settle back in my seat and smile, for I am here at last. For the first time in my life, I have entered the sacred precincts of Finocchio's, the "one-and-only, world-famous" female impersonator nightclub.

Finocchio's has been a San Francisco institution since 1936, when Joseph Finocchio, an Italian immigrant, opened his club on Broadway, on the same site it occupies now. According to an article in the *Chronicle* this past January, when Finocchio died at age eighty-eight, the founder was straight but "saw there was a tidy dollar to be made out of drag queens cracking bitchy jokes and flouncing about in bird-of-paradise costumes."

At first audiences flocked to the club to see what was regarded then as a perversion, but they eventually learned to "accept our show more as pure entertainment," according to Finocchio himself. Perhaps this was because it was "a clean show where all my fellas conduct themselves in a ladylike manner." Whatever the reason, the club has had its ups and downs over the past fifty years, but it is now one of the busiest spots on Broadway, consistently selling out three and four shows a night, five nights a week.

My friend Jay is not at all convinced that audiences today do not still regard the performers as perverse. He notes that the average age of the audience around us is about sixty or so, and that there are no other discernible gay people in the room besides our little group. "You realize, of course, that this is as close to the gay community as most of these people get," he says. "This is probably a very wicked thing for them to do—something to make Aunt Irma back in Kansas lose her bridgework.

"Uh-oh," Jay continues. "Looks like we've got a couple of live ones," as the seats behind us are taken by a couple of women with bouffant dos: New Yorkers, to judge by their accents.

"Can you see, Rita?" asks one. "Move over heah, then." They move to the seats to our right, turning their places over to two grateful Japanese business executives. While we wait for the show to start, the New Yorkers and I strike up a converstaion. Neither Rita nor her friend has ever been "heah" before, but the friend used to go to "woman impersonator" shows in the West Village back home. Yes, they are part of a tour group. Jefferson Tours, they think, is the name.

Our conversation is interrupted by a flourish from the band and the announcement, "Ladies and gentlemen, welcome to the one-and-only, world-famous Finocchio's!" To the strains of "Showtime on Broadway" and "Puttin' on the Ritz," the chorus line bursts onstage and struts its stuff. Dressed entirely in pink, the chorines flash sequins and ostrich feathers for days.

"Oh, my God!" gasps Rita, awestruck, while I mutter to my friends, "Tired." Jay adds, "Baryshnikov certainly has nothing to worry about," but Rita is more impressed. "What a lot of stamina they have," she sighs. Myself, I am surprised that the elderly blonde kicking up her heels onstage doesn't expire of a heart attack on the spot.

Following the opening number, Mistress of Ceremonies Sophia Petrakis makes her entrance. Sophia is simply too real to be believed. As she sings her heart out to "Last Dance," I suspect a Victor/Victoria scam. Is this really a woman pretending to be a man pretending to be a woman, I wonder? Whatever, she is certainly more believable than any drag queen I have ever seen in my life.

Sophia is followed by a queen in a gorilla suit doing a striptease. "Puh-leeze," I moan, but when the gorilla suit is discarded to reveal the elderly blonde in Carol Channing drag, I *am* impressed. This girl really works the stage, and there is no mistaking *her* for real. Now *this* is what we all came to see. Eventually the Carol Channing dress gives way to a scanty harem outfit, and the blonde (Rene de Carlo, we are to learn) pulls out a couple of lighted baby bottles, which she uses for nipples and then for a dick. The audience loves it, and even I appreciate the brief display of vulgarity.

Florenzia de la Santos, a regal Filipino in full evening wear, follows Rene. Florenzia circles the stage, making all the men in the front rows (including us) kiss her hand while she sings. The women in the audience scream to see their husbands kissing an actual *faggot's* hand, and I decide that this is borderline offensive. But Florenzia seems to think otherwise, and to ensure that this is all in good fun, she encourages the audience to thank the husbands for being good sports by clapping. Then, as a grand finale, she pulls out her falsies. After that, who could stay angry with Florenzia for long?

Someone does a Mexican fan dance, and then Rene teams up with a "real" man named Joselito for a bit of classical Spanish dancing, complete with castanets. Joselito is wearing the tightest pants in the world but still manages to sport no basket, not the least little bulge. That's the bad news. The good news is that at least Rene keeps her seams straight. And both work those castanets to death.

After this brief cultural interlude, a group of Asian harem girls storms the stage. Because I've always had a thing for harem girls, I love this number, and Jay and I decide that one of the girls, the one in purple, would actually be kind of cute, were it not for all the makeup. She is the least experienced of the chorines, however, and as she dances, she can't help moving her lips and counting, One, two, one, two, three, four.

The star of the show, Peter Collie, is the next to appear. Peter is an outrageous black dressed in gallons of glitter and tons of tulle who throws open her robes to expose a leopard jockstrap underneath—"for that Sheena-of-the-jungle effect," she says. After Peter belts out "Rollin' on a River," she remarks as she opens and closes her robe, "Ain't illusion glorious? You just create it and destroy it, create it and destroy it. It's one of those here-today-gone-tomorrow type of things." Later Peter sings "What I Did for Love" and describes herself thusly: "Hair by Donatelle, face by Max Factor, and body by Sara Lee." She brings down the house. Even tourists like sleaze, it seems.

The last act is "international star" Andre, who is the only one of the Finocchio impersonators to lip synch rather than to use her own voice. Dressed spectacularly in black, Andre is otherwise something of a disappointment until she relays what proves to be the show's only political statement, a statement of pride and personal courage: "No one has the right, you see, / to tell me what a man should be, / to say what makes a man a man." Perhaps it falls on deaf ears, but there are four in the audience, at least, who appreciate it.

The finale, a fiftieth anniversary tribute to Mr. Finocchio, is set to music from

La Cage Aux Folles and comes complete with a number of actual dance lifts. ("Risky, risky, very risky," says Jay.) Everyone is dressed all in gold, and I gaze longingly at the chorine who is my size. I'd *kill* for that dress. But it is unlikely that it will be given to me (I can't even get an interview with any of the performers). The show ends without answering the question that is burning in all our hearts: Is the mistress of ceremonies a real woman?

Rita from New York asks the doorman on her way out. "Oh, she's real all right: the first real woman we've ever had in the show," he assures her. Rita is pleased, but I'm unimpressed. It takes no talent to be a real woman; it takes a certain special something to be a female impersonator.

As we head back to the car, I ask Jay, "So what did you think?" He pauses for a moment and says, "Do you want the best or the worst?"

"The best."

"The audience was fun," he answers. "It's reassuring to know that the leisure suit isn't dead."

I decide to let the matter rest. Some people have no appreciation for art, no appreciation at all.

International Mr. Leather

JUNE 1988

MY BOYFRIEND, who recently moved to Chicago, refused to go to the finals of the International Mr. Leather Contest, even though he lived only a few blocks from the Clubland, the contest site. Compared with me, he has led a relatively tame sexual life, and he doesn't understand the leather scene. Neither do I, I tell him, but I've never let this get in my way. I enjoy it all the same.

My boyfriend, alas, finds it harder to suspend his analytical and critical powers, and the attraction for leather remains beyond his ken. I think an International Mr. Aesthete Contest is more in his line. Nevertheless, after hours of debate, he finally agreed to go, and laid out his usual tweed coat, button-down shirt, and paisley tie to wear. At the last minute, unfortunately, something else came up that required his attention. I was forced to go to the Clubland alone.

Which was actually fine with me. For years I had read about the contest in Mr. Marcus's column in the *Bay Area Reporter* and wanted to attend. Yet I had never been able to get away on Memorial Day weekend, and, frankly, I hadn't been sure that a trip to Chicago was worth the expense. This time, however, I was in Chicago anyway, which was particularly fortunate, because I suspected that I was witnessing the end of an era.

Although most leathermen and leatherwomen would doubtless disagree, the leather scene seems to be diminishing, perhaps dying out. Bars are closing left and right, primarily because of the AIDS crisis. Even Chicago's own Gold Coast, the granddaddy of them all, has not been able to survive. After more than twenty-five years in various locations around the North Side, the Gold Coast closed its doors for good in January 1988.

Oblivious to these darker issues, the crowd of gaping heterosexuals gathered at the entrance to the Clubland this past Memorial Day weekend could only snicker and sneer at the line of leathermen and leatherwomen waiting to get inside—which must have seemed a motley and bizarre crew. Even I was taken aback by some of the things I saw, such as the bones through the noses—although I was, of course, used to the bare asses, spiked collars, and studded gauntlets, harnesses, and jockstraps.

Had they entered the theater, the heterosexual observers would have been even more amazed at the spectacle inside. It was a veritable cornucopia of uniforms, whips, and chains: the stuff of fascist dreams. Yet despite the abundance of black, red, and yellow banners (the national colors of Germany, let me remind you), this was not Nuremberg, but the good old U.S.A. As proof, when the house lights dimmed, a police officer, a Marine, and two other members of the service (or facsimiles thereof) presented the colors of the United States while the boys and girls in black proudly rose to their feet and sang "The Star-Spangled Banner."

If this was a surprise, more was to follow. Challenging my own stereotypical notions concerning the leather community, the organizers of the event astonished me not only by arranging for gender parity onstage (by appointing male and female co-emcees) but also by providing a sign language interpreter. It was all too P.K. (politically korrect), even if one of the emcees, lesbian entertainer Lynn Lavner, described herself as short rather than vertically challenged. At least the other, porn star Al Parker, showed up in a tuxedo, for God's sake, instead of the skimpier attire he usually affected. My boyfriend himself would have approved.

After explaining the three judging categories (leather image, physical appearance, and attitude/personality), the emcees introduced last year's winner, Tom Karasch from Hamburg, West Germany, who took a "last walk" down the center of the stage (like Miss America without the tiara). Next, the judges, including our own Mr. Marcus (described as "the Brenda Starr of the *B.A.R.*" as well as "the future star of the TV show 'fifty-something' "), were introduced.

Finally, the forty-two contestants paraded onstage to the theme from *Star Wars*. Five were from San Francisco, and all five survived the prelims and entered the group of twenty finalists. Not so lucky was poor number nine, my own personal favorite, a very young man with shoulder-length hair and the smoothest of skin. Along with scores of other vocal protestors, I would gladly have consoled number nine backstage.

Instead, while country and western singer Deena Kay performed, I got the inside scoop on the finalists from a friend from San Francisco. One, I discovered, worked for Macy's, of all places, while another had "bought" his tan at the Muscle System. Equally insightful was *Ms.* International Leather, Shan Carr, who explained, "People always ask me why I wear leather. I answer, 'Because my mother told me to dress for success.'"

Demonstrating that advice, the twenty finalists strutted their stuff in the swimwear competition. One of the men from home wore a jock and hip boots. One of his competitors wore a giant dildo. Another wound himself in tattered rags. (Lazarus in bondage?) Still another, clearly the crowd favorite, sported a bone through his nose (as well as matching bones through his nipples). This was all well and good, but the highlight of the competition occurred when the snap on Brian Dawson's swimsuit broke. Brian was hardly nonplussed.

While the leathermen revealed themselves, Lavner (the lesbian Bert Parks) and Parker (a virile Vanna White) provided background information. The contestestants ranged in age from twenty-two to forty-four and in height from five-foot-six to six-foot-four. Their occupations included insurance salesperson, landscape architect, physical education teacher, respiratory therapist, building inspector, florist, attorney, and actor, among others. Hobbies included the obvious, such as leather, latex, weightlifting, and motorcycles. They also included more esoteric and unexpected pleasures, such as opera, gardening, house restoration, community work, and politics. Naturally, several contestants were interested in "collecting red hankies," "being a total pig," and, simply, "unmentionable."

After a volunteer for an AIDS hospice offered to have "any part" of his body shaved if the audience topped last year's contributions to the hospice fund, the contestants appeared once again for the attitude/personality section of the program. The majority of these tried in some fashion to explain their passion for leather. "When I entered a leather bar for the first time," said one, "I knew I had found a home." Noted another, "From the time my mother wrapped me in a greasy oil rag, I knew I liked the dirt, the grime, the look, feel, taste, and smell of leather."

According to Peter Morrison of Los Angeles, "Leather wasn't a choice. It was just the way I was. When I put on my older brother's jacket for the first time, I knew that my love of leather and my hard cock would point my way through life." Mitch Davis of Boston also had no choice. After describing a sexual experience involving a police officer, he said, "This is what leather means to me: a power, a strength, which holds me in its spell."

Others spoke of the "cohesive bond" of leather, the feeling of brotherhood. One traced his development through Catholic school ("my first uniform experience"), the Boy Scouts, and college fraternities to his involvement with the leather community. Another said that this involvement had taught him self-respect and pride. A third agreed and added, "It has also taught me that I need a bigger MasterCard."

While the judges made their final decisions, Al Parker begged his audience to register to vote and to establish penny drives for AIDS in their hometowns. "I feel like Jane Fonda," he noted. "I've gotten radical." The audience was more interested in Parker's body than his politics, however, and beseeched him to take off his clothes. "Oh, you've seen it all before," he said. "You've been seeing it forever."

Nevertheless, the audience was still interested—which was more than could be said of their attitude toward the evening's final performers, the Village People. The less said about the Village People, the better. Unlike Parker's performances, their act has not gotten better with the passing of (too many) years. "As you can see, nothing has changed," said the construction worker before breaking into the several thousandth rendition of "YMCA." Whispered my friend from San Francisco, "Nothing except the size of their waists. Have you ever seen such love handles?"

Well, sure. But not on the inevitable winner of the night's top award, Michael Pereyra of San Diego, the crowd's darling. Dark, hairy, masculine, confident, Pereyra was everything a leatherman should be and more: he actually looked like someone you could take home to Mama (once you removed the handcuffs). I'm sure I could have taken him home to my boyfriend, who never would have guessed his background. Without the drag, I mean.

But to hell with that idea. Despite my own dubious past, I remain a traditionalist at heart, at least where my boyfriend is concerned. I like him in his tweeds, and I don't need a man such as Mr. International Leather—no matter how cute—giving him ideas. So I don't mind that he didn't go with me to the contest, really I don't. Some things, perhaps, are best left unexplored, and Mr. International Leather—the man, if not the contest—is one of those.

JOCKS AND THEIR SUPPORTERS

A Kick in the Grass: The San Francisco Spikes

JUNE 1986

IT IS A PHENOMENALLY gorgeous Saturday morning in June, the first morning free of fog in weeks. At the polo fields in Golden Gate Park, several dozen rugby teams showing lots of grit, determination, and skin are crawling all over each other in piles, but it is not rugby players in whom I am interested—at least not this morning. I am seeking soccer players of a particular persuasion, and I think I see two of them at one end of the field. But neither glances at me with that unmistakable glimmer of recognition, and there are no other soccer players in sight. I am beginning to think that I have confused meeting time or place once again, or that I am losing the ability to spot a fellow faggot a mile away. Then I overhear a new arrival on the field say to his companion, "Gee, some of these rugby players are really cute." I smile and follow them to the far end of the field, where four, and then five, and soon fourteen other members of their team arrive: the Spikes, the official San Francisco soccer team of the 1986 Gay Games.

While the others warm up, twenty-one-year-old Josh Persky (who, along with teammate Mark Koval, usually runs practice for this officially leaderless and self-described anarchic group of people) talks a little about the history of the group. The team came together in the spring of 1982 for the first Gay Games, Josh explains, only to find that the competition at the games consisted of only one other team, a group of spirited but hopelessly overmatched players from Denver. San Francisco won the brief series, held in Kezar Stadium in September, 9–0, 8–0, and 3–2 (this last only after some members of the two teams switched sides).

After walking away with the gold, the team disbanded, but nine of the original players joined forces to form the nucleus of the 1986 team a year and a half ago. By no means an exclusive organization, the nine welcomed anyone who wanted to play to join them, regardless of age, race, gender, nationality, religion (or lack thereof), sexual persuasion (ditto), or level of experience. Eventually the group grew to eighteen, including people from every kind of category (even one straight man)—except for women. "If a woman wanted to join, she'd be welcome," explains Josh, "but they have a separate team, so most women would rather play with them."

About half the players, Josh estimates, played on high school teams once upon a time. Josh himself plays for San Francisco State at present. Some are quite good, including the Mexicans (some of whom are not here this morning because they are watching the World Cup matches on TV) and other immigrants who grew up with the sport. Others had no experience at all until they began attending the twice-weekly practices at the polo fields. "If they have no experience, they come out and learn," says Josh. "The experienced players teach the less experienced ones. That's what this is all about."

Indeed, in line with the official philosophy of the Gay Games, the emphasis of the soccer players is on participation, not competition. "The most important thing is the spirit," claims Josh, "and we've got that. Nevertheless, competition is a part of athletics, and it's inevitable that you become competitive at some level, either with yourself, another player, or another team. We still want to win. We still want the gold. But that doesn't mean that we'll forget what this is all about."

What this is all about is not just participation and enjoyment, of course, but gay pride and self-respect. "The main reason I joined the team was because I loved soccer," notes Josh. "But another reason was that I enjoyed spending time in the company of other gay men. I can be myself here. There is no fear of being condemned because of my sexuality, no need to prove my masculinity. This is a comfortable environment for me."

The sense of camaraderie that develops in this environment is something else that is important to Josh. "Whether we win or lose, it's a team effort," he notes, "and that's a far more satisfying feeling than doing something on an individual basis." Fortunately, that camaraderie lasts long after the season is over. Some of Josh's best friends are fellow teammates from the 1982 team; his roommate is also a former teammate.

Looking ahead to the 1986 games, Josh is pleased that this year four other teams instead of just one other will be competing: New York, Seattle, Phoenix, and Denver. The series will be held not at Kezar Stadium, but at the brand new fields behind St. Ignatius High School at Thirty-ninth and Quintara, and the first game is scheduled for August 12. Naturally Josh is hoping that attendance at the games will improve over the dismal showing at the 1982 soccer matches. It matters to him "because I want to know that the community supports us. Maybe we're not showing as much flesh as the bodybuilders, but still we should be supported." Josh, a bodybuilder himself who is employed at a local gay gym, believes that soccer isn't as popular a game as it might be because "the average gay man in San Francisco didn't grow up with the sport. He doesn't know the rules and hasn't developed an appreciation for it."

Actually, Josh hopes that the community will support *all* the athletes of the Gay Games, not just the soccer players, for reasons that he sees as vital. "We're all going through a hell of a lot right now with AIDS, and it's real easy to get caught up with negativity. Lots of us are depressed. But the games are a good way to focus on the positive again. They can give us a great feeling and prove that we're still surviving as a community, that we're still enjoying each other's company. Personally, I lost my best friend to AIDS this year—Earl Belk, the head medic for the last games—but even though I don't have him to share this with me this time, I'm still going to focus on who and what I do have for as long as I have it. The games are part of all that."

By this time the other players are getting restless, and Josh gets up to lead them in a few drills. The interview is complete, but I do not leave until I get a chance to see for myself what the games are all about, according to Josh and friends. "Can you join us?" asks Mark Koval. "We need a human obstacle for this drill." I agree, thinking that at least I am capable of that, and reflecting that with any luck at all perhaps I'll be tackled in the process, perhaps by the skinny young man with the curly hair in the white shorts.

This, however, does not happen, and when the drills are over, Mark and Josh suggest that I play with the team. Again I agree, although I have not kicked a soccer ball in more than ten years. I am assigned to play fullback (which is somewhat analogous to being an outfielder in baseball, or as far away from the action as you can get as long as your team is on the move). Kicking at a gopher hole instead of a soccer ball, I feel somewhat like one of the inept celebrity players on "$10,000 Pyramid," the one who always puts his teammates at a disadvantage because he plays so poorly. But my teammates in this case don't seem to care, so neither do I.

In fact, for the first fifteen minutes I have a blast. I especially enjoy the fellow in the pink bicycle cap, the team camp, who, after making a mistake, places his hands on his hips and pouts, "Tina made me do it!" I also enjoy the man who shouts, "Solo, Carlo, solo. Shoot, doll!" and the one who cheers, "Good play, Phil. We love you, Phil!" I have been here only an hour, but already I love this team.

I would continue to enjoy the game, but suddenly, with no warning, I hear a wrenching sound in my knee. My leg gives way under me, and I collapse in agony, writhing on the ground. Because there is no one anywhere near me, I cannot blame this on anyone except perhaps the industrious gopher I saw earlier. I am simply a thirty-four-year-old incompetent whose spirit is willing but whose flesh is weak. Yet no one laughs. No one makes fun of the asshole reporter doing the George Plimpton routine, and I hobble off the field with my honor and pride intact.

Despite my injury I hang around long enough to listen to the postpractice discussion about a team uniform. The team camp, naturally, insists on pearls and a mink collar, to complement his outfit. Before any decisions can be reached, however, another pesky gopher (or the same one) raises his or her nasty little head, and the team camp screeches, "Eek! My snatch!" The other players pelt the gopher with orange peels, and I decide it is time to leave, past the rugby players, who still look cute—but who are entirely too straight for me today.

City Bears: Fans or Fanatics?

DECEMBER 1987

ON MOST DAYS of the year, they look and act just like normal people. But on certain days in the fall, members of a group called City Bears dress in nothing but blue and gold, wave Go Bears pennants, and travel to Berkeley any way they can, all for the love of a certain college football team. The team, of course, is Cal, a school better known for its political activists than its football fans, and the City Bears is a predominantly gay group of sports enthusiasts whose compelling motive seems to be Any Excuse for a Party.

City Bears is, above all, the result of one man's love affair with Cal: a man named Hal Herkenhoff, who rates a paragraph or two of his own. Hal, a native of the Bay Area, attended his first Cal game in 1962, when his babysitter took the then-thirteen-year-old to the Big Game (Cal vs. Stanford, for the uninitiated), which Cal lost 30–13. Despite the defeat, Hal was hooked from the beginning.

"What a show," he recalls. "You wouldn't believe it: the women wearing their mums, the student pranks, the excitement. It was wonderful. After that I went back whenever I could get tickets—to seven of the next nine Big Games."

In 1967, following an impressive career as the Big Man on Campus at his high school, Hal turned down a full swimming scholarship to Stanford, the national champions at the time, to attend Berkeley on a full academic scholarship. At Berkeley he swam and played in the band. Through the band he was able to carry on his love affair with football. Of course, none of this was politically correct, but Hal, ever idiosyncratic, didn't mind.

Three weeks before he graduated in May 1971, Hal came out. "A blue-eyed swimmer from Hawaii did it," he remembers. "In the morning I was recruiting him for the team; in the afternoon we were in the sack." Two years after that he moved to LA. For a few years, therefore, Hal followed other interests besides Cal football games.

In 1977, however, Hal could stay away no longer, and bought season tickets to the games with his friend Jim Commander (aka Madge), a UCLA fan. The two commuted from LA for the games and decided to move to San Francisco permanently the following year, partly in order to follow the team more closely. Their seats were smack dab in the middle of the Old Blue alumni section. "But we were hardly your typical college grads," acknowledges Hal.

In 1980 two more friends joined them at the games. The next year eight bought season tickets, doubling the size of the group. All were gay except for one straight woman. None were Cal grads except Hal. "I dragged everyone along," he admits. "The draw was that I threw good theme parties, and they didn't care what the theme was. They were suckered into the games by a free cocktail—or two."

Since then City Bears has grown steadily. By 1984 the group was too large for everyone to sit together, so it branched out, creating satellite sections under different names. "That's when we started noticing other gay people and they started noticing us," states Hal. "Also, my involvement with the Gay Games [he was co-director of sports with Sara Lewenstein in 1986] helped, not to mention my T-shirt collection. I became a magnet for all these different gay people."

In 1985 straight people started attending City Bear parties, which were held at Hal's home, on the Cal campus, or on the train to Stanford (The Train to Nowhere) for the Big Game. Now, Hal claims, the football and party atmosphere "transcend the gay thing. Oh, we definitely provide a gay facade. We're obvious, flamboyant, some would even say blatant. But nobody cares, as long as we're rooting for Cal."

In fact, Hal continues, straight Cal fans may have actually learned something from City Bears. "We've taught them to overdo it in the gay way. But we've also broken the stereotypes that they may have had of us—of what gay people are interested in and what we do with our time. The nicknames may be a little much—Tricia Trojan, Lorna Longhorn, Brenda Buckeye—but most straight people see beyond that."

When asked if he is perhaps carrying all this a little far, Hal (whose own nickname is Buffy Bear) replies, "Well, I *have* been called a sports fanatic. But I think *fan* is enough. I like to think of myself, above all, as a sports sociologist. I know everything about the teams, followers, colors, etc.—all the social trappings. I'm not so interested in the statistics."

Whether a fan or a fanatic, Hal is well aware that his is an uncommon obsession in the gay community. Despite the community's growing interest in sports, few would willingly decorate their apartments with pom-poms, football posters, pictures of the Cal campus, and framed ticket stubs, as Hal has done. As Hal explains, "Outsiders have a hard time understanding what it's all about because it *is* a little unique. Away from a football setting, we would look a little ridiculous. But so what? We're having fun. Besides, seventy-five people dressed in blue and gold can't be all wrong. Tell *that* to the Stanford fans."

Behind the FrontRunners

FEBRUARY 1989

I REALLY DON'T know how I get myself into these things. All I know is that at a party I met an attractive man who started talking about his involvement with FrontRunners, the gay and lesbian running club. Soon I found myself promising to attend one of the group's Saturday morning runs at Stowe Lake. It must be true what they say: A penis has no brains.

The problem is that I don't run. Hell, I get exhausted chasing a bus for a block and a half, so it's not hard to imagine how I feel about a group of fanatics who rise at the crack of dawn and pound the pavement for pleasure. I do, however, enjoy other sports, such as tennis and skiing. "If I can do them," I reasoned, "then I can do this."

Checking the paper for confirmation, I saw nothing about a Saturday morning run at Stowe Lake, but I did see a notice for a Sunday run at Lake Merced. Thinking I must have gotten my days and lakes confused, I drove to Lake Merced and prepared to join the group. When I arrived, however, the lake looked huge—at least as big as the bay—and naturally, my friend from the party was nowhere in sight.

Prepared to use every excuse in the book—a bum knee, an ingrown toenail, AZT—I hesitantly joined the group of fifteen lean, athletic diehards gathered at the boathouse. They quickly and politely informed me that no excuses were necessary. When I told them I was no runner, they suggested that perhaps I would feel "more comfortable" at the shorter Stowe Lake run—which, indeed, did exist. Heaving a sigh of relief, I opened a book and read while the others easily negotiated the lake's five-mile perimeter.

When they returned, president Tim Cook told me a little about the organization. FrontRunners was founded in 1974 as a jogging club associated with Lavender U, although the name, which was taken from Patricia Nell Warren's best-selling novel, was not adopted until 1978. Currently the club has approximately 250 members. About 85 or 90 percent of those members are men.

The group welcomes runners of all abilities, whether beginning or experienced, recreational or competitive. Explains Cook, "Some of our members are weekend warriors with extensive cross-country backgrounds. Others are beginners who come along primarily for the social atmosphere. Overweight smokers are just as welcome as serious athletes."

The club meets three times a week to run: Thursday evenings at McLaren Lodge in Golden Gate Park, Saturday mornings at Stowe Lake, and Sunday mornings at varying locations around the Bay Area. These runs are noncompetitive. For those interested in racing, the club selects one local race a month to join. The Zoo Run in January, the Run for the Seals in March, and the Cherry Blossom Run in May are examples.

The club's major annual events include the Gay Run, its own 5/10K race with nearly 500 participants; the AIDS Pledge Run, a fund-raising event for AIDS charities; the Gay Sports Day, a festival on Angel Island with other sports clubs; the Bay to Breakers; and the San Francisco and Los Angeles marathons. The club also sponsors an ongoing array of social events, including camping trips to Yosemite and ski trips to Lake Tahoe.

Overwhelmed by the plethora of possibilities, I chose the following week's run at Stowe Lake as my official introduction to the group. This time, however, I asked my friend John to join me, so that there would be no chickening out. John, who was looking for an excuse to start running again after a two-year sabbatical, readily agreed.

After only four hours of sleep and one of nightmares the night before the run, I had second thoughts when I awoke Saturday morning. But I had promised, and I am nothing if not a man of my word. Besides, it was a beautiful morning, and the sun glimmering on the surface of the water convinced me that God was smiling on this enterprise, that this was meant to be.

I thought otherwise as soon as I took my first step. Of the fifty or sixty runners gathered at the lake, I was one of the few who chose the shortest of four possible courses: once around the lake. Even so, I almost died. My lungs hurt, my legs cramped. John wanted to carry on a conversation, but all I could do was nod. It was one of the few times in my life when I shut up long enough to enable another person to carry on a monologue.

To my credit, I made the mile without stopping. But I certainly didn't continue when John suggested another lap. If John weren't such a good friend, I might have been embarrassed. Because I had nothing to hide from him, however, a confession was in order. "I lift weights; I'm something of an athlete," I said. "Why can't I do this?"

It was the same cry I made to the group of twenty FrontRunners who gathered for brunch on Fillmore Street afterward. "Don't worry," they assured me. "It's like everything else. With time and practice, you get better." I suspect, however, that the time and practice will not be forthcoming. FrontRunners is a delightful group of people, and running is a commendable thing to do. But it's not *my* thing, and all the attractive men at all the parties in the world can't convince me otherwise.

Hard Hearts and Softballs

APRIL 1989

I HATE SOFTBALL. At least, I did when I was a kid. When it was my turn to bat, the other team moved closer, grinning like piranha moving in for the kill. When it was their turn, I did the opposite by isolating myself in the outfield as far from harm as possible. "It's yours, it's yours!" I screamed if the ball came my way. Fortunately, it rarely did.

Imagine my attitude, then, when my lover's sister, Marlene, called recently and asked me to participate in a "friendly neighborhood softball game." "I'd rather chew razor blades in hell," I replied, but Marlene was adamant. Eventually I agreed to take part, but only as a cheerleader. "I've got a bum knee," I said. "You can't expect me to risk reinjuring that."

On a scorching Saturday morning a few days after the opening of the season, therefore, I found myself in the midst of a ragtag group of friends, who were hardly more enthusiastic than myself, waiting for a field in Golden Gate Park. Occupying the field was a women's team from the Delancey Street Foundation, a drug rehab center.

Because there were no other fields available, Marlene spoke to the coach of the Delancey Street team about using theirs. Returning moments later, she informed us, "Okay, it's all set. Get ready. We play in ten minutes. I've challenged the other team to a game."

My teammates were terror-stricken. "Wait a minute," they balked. "You said this was going to be a friendly neighborhood game. These women look tough. Forget it, Marlene."

Marlene didn't listen. This was a woman, after all, who knew no fear. According to legend, Marlene was a fierce competitor and superb athlete, who once took a softball full in the face and played on, leading her team to victory despite the pain. She wasn't about to be intimidated by a group of underage Amazons, no matter how formidable.

For their part, the "Amazons" were equally as cautious as my own teammates. "Who are these people?" one of them asked a friend when the challenge was accepted. "If they're professional, I'm not playing."

Well, we were up first, and for a short time we looked good. Tim, the Dynamic Dane, fleet of feet and long of hair, scored first on Greg's double. Greg scored as well, and even Karen hit a single. But then Francis, muttering, "If this were soccer, I'd kick their asses, but I'm no good at softball," nearly struck out, and two of the women failed to deliver.

For Toni, it was a particularly excruciating experience. "I don't know how to hit," she whined to the coach of the opposing team, who generously offered advice. "I've never played this game before. I don't even know where to stand. *Now* can I smoke a cigarette?"

When the Delancey team took the plate, things deteriorated further. Marlene, our pitcher, struggled valiantly, but our lack of experience showed. Our fielding was abysmal. We committed one unforced error after another and watched helplessly as the enemy scored an enviable string of runs.

At 8–2 the team fell apart completely. Marlene relieved herself as pitcher and then got run over by a female behemoth who ploughed into her at third base. (It was probably the most exciting thing to happen to her all week.) The catcher begged for a lunch break. I begged for the score. Finally, at 10–2 ("We'll settle for 10, but we think it was more," said the Delancey coach), we got the third out, and the second inning began.

In the second inning we improved somewhat. Perhaps it was the presence of Tim's girlfriend, Lisbet, who joined me as a cheerleader. Lisbet had just placed third in the 10K Bonne Bell Run, and she had brought along her victory bell to inspire us. We scored three more runs. They scored only one. The score at the end of the inning: 11–5.

In the third inning Toni finally got a single, and the team went wild. Shouted Pam, "You run like a femme!" It was true. Toni was thrown out at second. But the rest of the team did okay. Even Donna got a piece of the ball for a change, and Francis improved so much that he threatened to handicap himself by using a cricket bat.

By the fourth inning we had all lost track of the score, but things had begun to even up. Then in the fifth all hell broke loose. Tim got the game's first homer, as Lisbet hollered, "That's my guy! What a stud!" Greg and Jimmy pounded ball after ball, and Marlene beamed, "I told you we had natural talent. All we needed was to play together as a team."

We did so well that I began to feel sorry for the Delancey women. They were a real team, after all, and had their first game the next day. We would probably never play together again. But if all is fair in love and war, then, shit, in softball, anything is permissible. So why not humiliate a group of young women?

In any event, the agony didn't last much longer. After five innings the game was called for heat and length. Shaking hands, we wished our opponents luck in their next game, and repaired to a nearby restaurant to savor the come-from-behind victory (if victory it was) over brunch. The team was exhausted but elated, and, surprisingly, I shared in the general merriment.

"Damn, I wish I could have played," I heard myself saying before I remembered I was talking about a softball game. "Fuck the knee. I could at least have batted, and Lisbet could have run for me. What do you say, Lisbet?"

"I say you're dreaming," Lisbet replied with that familiar piranha flash of teeth. "Once a siss, always a siss. You may be cute, honey, but stick to cheerleading. It's what you do best."

Like I said, I hate softball—still.

GOD AND HUMANITY

Too Much Joy: Radiant Light Ministries

NOVEMBER 1987

I DID AN extraordinary thing several Sundays ago, at least for a self-described atheist. I spent the morning, a perfectly good morning when I might have been reading the paper or working out at the gym, in church. Not just any church, mind you, but a church with crystals rather than crosses on the altar and deejays rather than organists in the balcony: a New Age church called Radiant Light Ministries.

I went because a friend told me that it was this year's answer to last year's bingo games and the previous year's jockstrap contests: The Absolutely Latest Thing. Another friend, however, took a more serious view. "I know I've always been a cynic," he confessed. "But I've never been in a place with so much positive energy. It helps me to cope with my ever-increasing anxiety in this age of AIDS."

Intrigued by one friend's cultural curiosity and the other's spiritual quest, I arrived at the church, presently housed in the Swedish American Hall on Market Street, in time for the preservice healing circle. This is a "process" designed to enable congregration members to explore their problems in a group setting, in the hopes of coming to grips with them.

In the healing circle four or five people out of forty asked for help with such problems as sexuality, anorexia, debt, and physical pain. Each time, the moderator, Diane Bechtle, asked probing, albeit leading, questions concerning the source of the problem and its resolution. In every case the origin of the problem was the same—"not accepting myself" or "not being who I am"—as was the resolution: a willingness to accept responsibility for the past and to love one's self in the future.

As tears flowed fast and furious and empathy flooded the room, I found myself wondering if these people really expected to solve their problems, some quite serious, in the course of a fifteen-minute public confessional. I also objected to the moderator's assertion that we were all responsible for everything that had ever happened to us, including, in one instance, a particularly ugly case of child abuse. What I admired, however, was the emphasis on free choice and on the future. The overriding theme was joy, not guilt; love, not sin. "In the name of God, my higher self," the group promised itself, concluding, "And so it is."

A few minutes later I was browsing the literature in the foyer downstairs. Brochures, flyers, and pamphlets advertised stress reduction massage, spiritual counseling, AIDS mastery seminars, gourmet cooking, and cosmetic tattooing. "Experience Bliss!" headlined one. Others promised "body harmony" and "living orgasm." In an adjacent room, tapes and books by "Reverend Matt" Garrigan, the church's dynamic founder, were displayed for sale.

The church service itself, which was termed a celebration, was structured surprisingly like the Methodist services of my childhood. Following a welcome to visitors, morning announcements, and an opening meditation, Reverend Matt gave "today's message." This was followed by an offering, an affirmation, and a closing song. But although the structure was familiar, the style and substance of the service was something else entirely.

For one thing, there was a lot of clapping, cheering, hugging, and laughing the morning I attended. The celebration began not with hymns or processional music, but with the theme from *Chariots of Fire*. To release their energy, the congregation stood up and roared. Moments later they danced in the aisles to disco music. Next, during his message, Reverend Matt paced in front of the altar, mugging and cracking jokes. At the end the celebrants formed a large circle and filled the room with Alleluias. It was a kaleidoscope of ecstatic cries, hushed silences, and determined intensity. My grandmother, a staunch Methodist, would have died (were she not dead already).

The focus of Reverend Matt's message was simple. "We are children of God," he said. "We are guiltless and free of sin." He delivered this message in a rambling barrage of platitudes, epigrams, and amusing anecdotes. Typical Garriganisms included, "All these years of waiting for the Second Coming, and you're it. There is no one like you"; "Your brain doesn't understand *can't;* it only understands *more";* and "They say you've got to be an airhead, out of your mind, to believe all this. It's true. We are." The point of "all this" seemed to be to convince his followers, You can be, do, and have anything. The message was entirely upbeat, positive, and his listeners ate it up like candy.

As Garrigan spoke, I found myself reacting the same way I had reacted to Diane Bechtle. I objected to the simplicity of his philosophy: "You're fabulous just the way you are. There is no remedy to love but to love more." I also opposed his assertion that "Everything that's been going on in your life up to this point is exactly what you've needed and wanted." But my hostility waned in the face of Garrigan's emphasis on self-reliance and the possibility of change. There is no one else out there, he instructed. Love yourself and all else falls into place.

If all this sounds unfocused, well, it is. But this doesn't bother Garrigan, who says, "What we don't need is another dogma, another religion." Although some of his personal beliefs are outlandish—he believes in immortality, for instance, not just of the soul but also of the physical body—it is not the particulars that attract his following. Rather, it is his charisma, and, as my friend had said, the "positive energy" of the celebration. Followers believe what they want, within a wide range, at Radiant Light Ministries. Its embrace is inclusive, not exclusive.

Perhaps too inclusive, I thought before I visited Radiant Light. Having long worshiped at the altar of rationality, I found it hard to understand people who believed in "manifesting" their rent payment through prayer or conquering a virus by wishing it away. As one who viewed crystals, another popular New Age phenomenon, as the mood rings of the 1980s, I wondered, How can intelligent people possibly believe all this crap? Yet many of the people I admire and respect most in this world swear by the new ministry on Market Street, and I think I see why. Although I still don't share their enthusiasm, at least I no longer belittle it.

Even so, one doubt remains. That this church should have grown out of the gay community, with its shared history of guilt, struggle, and eventual acceptance, is not at all surprising. What *is* surprising, however, is that so many people still need to hear the church's message. Is there that much self-doubt lingering in the community that people need to be told, over and over, that they are good, loving, worthwhile individuals? It seems so. Yet what of it? Better a Matt Garrigan to serve that need than a Jerry Falwell to deny it.

After the service a friend hugged me and asked if I was coming back the next week. I hesitated. "What's the matter?" he needled. "Can't you handle this much joy?"

"Oh, I can handle it," I replied. "I'm just not sure that this is the way I choose to express my own joy."

As my friend himself would say, "And so it is."

In the Name of God: Becoming a Gay Pastor

AUGUST 1988

IN A COUNTRY where nearly everyone is told he or she can be the president someday, few want to be preachers—much less gay preachers. But such individuals do exist, according to Reverend Jim Mitulski, the pastor of the Metropolitan Community Church of San Francisco (MCC–SF), the second oldest gay congregation in the country.

The reasons the future ministers give for choosing this occupation are many and varied. "Most are interested in spiritual matters, such as teaching, preaching, and counseling," explains Mitulski. "Others are interested in social affairs, such as community organizing and gay and lesbian issues. Still others want to be involved in people's lives in a more intimate way than they have been before." Whatever their motivations, all must undergo some kind of training. It is not simply a matter of being called by God and hanging out a spiritual shingle.

Because each congregation of the Metropolitan Community Church is a sovereign entity with a different worship style and a different organizational structure, the training process for prospective pastors in the MCC varies widely from congregation to congregation.

"The main reason for this," notes Mitulski, "besides the independence of the local congregations, is that we're a relatively young church, and our training program is still in a state of development. Twenty years ago, for instance, when the church was founded, people became pastors who had little training, but who felt called by God, the way the Pentecostals did. Since then we've become much more organized.

"Still, we are more flexible than other churches. Many of our pastors are second-career people. Others are pastors who transferred in from another church (although they still have to do a year's work with a local congregation before they are fully ordained in the MCC). Then we also have congregations that are led by laypersons, who have no training and are not ordained, but who perform many of a pastor's functions. This is usually because the congregation doesn't have the funds to pay for the training. Still, approximately 80 percent of our pastors do undergo MCC-sanctioned training."

Although each congregation sets its own training requirements, typically the pastor-to-be must have a bachelor's degree or relevant work experience. At MCC–SF, a year's internship is also required. All MCC congregations require the recommendation of the local congregation for prospective ministers. And all require that he or she pass a standardized exam, developed by the MCC, involving biblical knowledge, church history, counseling matters, and the like.

In order to pass the exam, advanced study is usually necessary, either at a mainstream seminary or at Samaritan College, an MCC institution. There are significant differences between the two.

Seminaries are generally three-year programs intended for those interested in general religious studies, as well as for those interested in becoming ministers. MCC–SF usually sends its students to the Pacific School of Religion in Berkeley, where the tuition is $4500 a year and the rewards include a master's degree. It is one of the few seminaries in the country that accepts openly gay and lesbian students.

Samaritan College, on the other hand, offers a one-year program that is more focused, concentrating on pastoral skills, rather than on general studies. It also costs less but does not award master's degrees.

Whichever route an individual takes, when he or she has completed the training and passed the exam, landing a job with the MCC is never a problem. Says Mitulski, "At present there are probably 250 MCC ministers altogether. Twenty or twenty-five people become ministers each year. But any MCC minister who wants to work can. There are more jobs than there are people to fill them.

"Of course, sometimes they don't pay very much. What we offer are full-time jobs with part-time salaries. The minimum salary for a pastor at MCC, for instance, is $12,000. A few make twice that, which is still only two-thirds of what a Methodist minister with similar experience would make. So most pastors supplement their incomes with part-time jobs. Our challenge is to develop these positions so that we can pay better."

The future minister should also be aware, continues Mitulski, that there is far more involved in pastoring than ministering to spiritual concerns. "You have to be as interested in community organizing as you are in being a pastor. This is because many of our congregations have a lot of potential but aren't very large. So you have to build as well as maintain an institution. Things such as mailing lists, advertising, and community networking are a part of the job."

In spite of this—and for some people, because of it—the rewards of being a pastor are great, claims Mitulski. The proof, he notes, is in the number of people who continue to undergo the training. His own congregation has just graduated two students from the Pacific School of Religion, and they are now serving as pastors in Redwood City and Mill Valley. Four others are currently seminarians there.

If further proof is needed, Mitulski points to the example of another of MCC–SF's student interns, who is not a lesbian, but who wants to be an MCC minister anyway. For her it is a chance to work within a progressive organization for a group of people whose spiritual needs have long been ignored by other churches. Like her political counterparts, she might have chosen to empower this slighted minority by becoming president herself—but doubtless she feels this is a better and a surer route.

PEOPLE AND PLACES

How To Meet Lesbians

DECEMBER 1984

WHO WAS THE FIRST dyke I ever knew? Ah yes, Miss Diezel. Miss Diezel—honestly—was my seventh grade French teacher, without a doubt the strictest, meanest woman in the world. With her short-cropped, jet black hair, her pointed, heavy-rimmed glasses, her menacing stare, her thickset build, and her threatening stance, she was not only a fearsome and formidable presence, but also the very picture of a stereotypical bull dyke. The woman would have made a perfect Marine drill sergeant.

Of course, I didn't know she was "that way" at the time. I didn't find that out until years later, long after I had learned to see past the gruff exterior to the heart of gold beneath and to value her as one of my all-time favorite teachers. Poor Miss Diezel. I was in college when the news rocked the church congregation at home that my former French teacher was having an affair with the wife of one of the most respected businesspeople in the community. This was a woman who sang in the church choir, for God's sake, whose sons had been in Boy Scouts with me. But this respectability didn't stop her from leaving her husband when Miss Diezel beckoned. (Many are called, but few are chosen.) The congregation was scandalized, naturally, but I, for one, was delighted.

I don't think I met another lesbian until my college days, when I joined the university's Gay Alliance. There were only a few brave souls in the Gay Alliance, alas, and because there were so few of us, we drew together quickly and didn't bother to discriminate among each other on the basis of minor differences such as sex. Men got along with women and women with men. And that was the way I liked it, the way it should be, I reasoned—but not the way it was for long.

When I moved to the Big City, I found that men and women rarely socialized with one another. There was no need. With greater numbers came greater opportunity, and this usually meant the opportunity to specialize. Women went to women's bars, and men went to men's bars. Most gay people I met were too busy pursuing their own particular visions of utopia to bother about the larger picture. Boyfriends and girlfriends came first, and the gay community as a whole came second.

That, I thought, was a shame, but I soon found myself playing the same game. In my address book there were many Steves and Pauls and Bobs, but not too many Sallys or Janes. (There were plenty of Miss Velmas and Sister Girlenes, of course.) I began to fear that Miss Diezel was fated to be the sole lesbian friend I would ever have. That, I realized, was my own fault: if my interests extended to areas other than the crotch, I might have women friends.

One day I resolved to change all that. "I am going to meet lesbians," I said.

The trouble was how to do it. I knew that lesbians hung out in political clubs, but that seemed a dull prospect, and I was a bit afraid to enter dyke bars. I had little chance of being invited to a potluck dinner, and in the papers I saw no notices for literary groups gathering to discuss *Rubyfruit Jungle*. At last, however, I saw an ad for a play at Fort Mason produced by a women's theater group, Lilith. The play seemed harmless enough, and I knew I'd feel at home in the theater. So I called my friend John and dragged him along.

Did I feel the least bit uncomfortable because John and I were the only two men in the theater? Not me. Did I feel at all out of place? Not a bit. I did squirm a little, however, when one of the actors onstage brandished a gigantic pair of garden shears and sang a little ditty about how she'd like to castrate all the men in the world. Not just rapists, mind you, and not just straight men, but all men. That included me.

"You know," I told John at intermission, "when I was in high school I was forced to take a course on human sexuality, and my teacher, lovely dimwit that she was, taught us emphatically while discussing homosexuality that all lesbians hated men. It had something to do with their fathers. If I took that little number we just saw seriously, I'd have to believe that there was some truth to that."

A gorgeous young woman to my right flashed her fiery eyes at me and snarled, "Yeah, I heard that, and some of us do hate men!"

I decided to try an avenue other than the theater to make dyke friends.

It was then that I saw that the Strand was to feature a movie I had always wanted to see. This time I called my friend Lionel and said, "Lionel, there's this great movie we have to see, and it'll be the perfect place to meet lesbians. It's called *The Women,* and you *know* the place will be swarming with them."

The place was swarming, all right, but not with women. The place was filled with gay men, and there was nary a woman in sight. No wonder. Self-respecting women could hardly be expected to enjoy a movie that portrayed females as vicious, catty, spiteful, mean-spirited, and low, or a movie in which the heroine's mother summed it all up by saying, "I *know* my sex." No wonder too that my "sisters" enjoyed it. "We seem to have a different sense of humor than the dykes," I told Lionel. The gap, instead of narrowing, seemed to widen.

It was a sense of humor, however, that drew me into a women's bar at last. A group called Pussies on the Prairie, a lesbian country and western band, was scheduled to play at Maud's on Cole Street, and this time I enlisted my friend Russell for support. "You'll love it," I promised him. "Besides, I need you."

Russell did not love it, but I did, mostly because right away I felt at ease. Nobody cared that we were there. They were all having too good a time to bother about us. So when Pussies on the Prairie sang (to the tune of "Skip to My Lou"), "Hey, hey, the gang's all here / Same old crowd every year / What do you do with a bunch of queers? / Have a good time, cowgirls," I sang along and had a ball. I also ran into every woman acquaintance I had in town that night—both of them—and they were delighted to see me. Or so they said.

On a subsequent trip to Maud's, I took note of finer details that indicated the character of the place. The bar kept current copies of the *Bay Area Reporter* and the *Sentinel* by the door, for instance: papers that purported to serve the entire gay community, but were directed mainly at men. That's nice, I thought. That's either broadminded of them or desperate. I also learned that the bartender's roommate was a gay man: proof that my high school sexuality teacher was a liar. Finally, I saw that not everyone was a woman. In fact, at my end of the bar stood three gay male couples. I was glad that they were welcome, but I began to worry about the sanctity of the place. Commingling *was* my object, true, but I couldn't help thinking that women might resent this invasion of their privacy. If heterosexuals visited a gay bar, for instance, I wouldn't mind, but I wouldn't appreciate their taking over the place. Perhaps women needed a place to call their own as well. But as Maud's seemed in no imminent danger of attack by men in chaps and alligator shirts, I decided to let the matter drop.

Clementina's Baybrick Inn was the next stop on the Road to Integration. Buoyed by my successful night at Maud's, I took my friend Tom to hear a jazz group—a coed jazz group, mind you—perform. Because Clementina's featured live entertainment, it was a perfect place for well-intentioned souls seeking Harmony and the Greater Good of Mankind and Womankind (such as myself) to go. The entertainment provided the means to avoid standing around feeling foolish and out of place. It also provided the opportunity to mingle with those nearby. "Having a good time?" you might say casually to a neighbor.

"Having a good time, boys?" a woman danced over and asked Tom and me. We replied in the affirmative and introduced ourselves. She in turn told us that her name was Hey Lynn—or Helene, I couldn't tell which. Whatever, at last a chance for a lesbian friend! One thing soon led to another (as it always does): cocktails led to life stories, life stories led to dancing, and dancing led to . . . No, it was impossible, but I could have sworn I saw Hey Lynn copping a feel from my poor, unsuspecting sister Tom. Before long it was obvious. There was no escaping it. Hey Lynn was definitely trying to pick Tom up.

"What gives?" I asked Tom. "Just how gay is this girl?"

"Who knows?" he returned. "But let's scoot before we find out."

So much for my lesbian friend.

The incident with Hey Lynn pointed out something that should have been obvious all along. Although we have much in common, gay men and gay women have two fundamentally different objectives in life: they want women and we want men (even if Hey Lynn seemed to want anybody). This point was further emphasized on a recent ski trip to the mountains with my friend Bob.

Stopping off in Sacramento on the way, we decided to hit the nearest gay bar for a little fun and excitement. This turned out to be the Forum, a dreary, Greco–Las Vegas atrocity peopled largely by women. Whatever attracted them to such a place I cannot imagine, but attracted they were, and Bob and I soon found that in a sea of women the problem was that there was little to attract us.

Even though neither of us was looking for Mr. Right that night and perhaps could have found fun and excitement with any number (or kind) of people, we realized that despite the best intentions, any evening's entertainment value is largely controlled by what we dubbed the cruise factor (i.e., even if you don't wanna fuck, it's still fun to look). Unfortunately, there wasn't much for us to cruise at the Forum.

I gave up the search for women friends soon after that. Oh, I may still drop into Maud's or Clementina's, maybe even Amelia's, from time to time, but I learned a few things during my lesbian odyssey. I found that it was easy to feel comfortable surrounded entirely by women, but that comfort wasn't enough. Creating significant bonds depends on shared interests and experiences, and at present, despite the things we do have in common, there is more that sets us apart. Oh, some lesbians and gay men get along, certainly. God knows, the boys and girls down at Valencia Rose, the cabaret and comedy club, seem to get along great. But I honestly believe that they are the exception to the rule.

I suppose that someday some lesbian will walk up to me and say, "I wuv you. Will you be my fwiend?" In the meantime, though, I'll just have to be content with my friend Keaton. She's straight, true, but at least she drives a pick-up truck.

Chariot of Fire: Tom Waddell and the Gay Games

APRIL 1986

FOR MOST PEOPLE, being a doctor would be enough, but not for Tom Waddell of San Francisco. He was already a practicing physician with the Army in 1967 when he decided to train for the United States Olympic Team. Waddell made that team and placed sixth in the decathalon in Mexico City, but still it wasn't enough. It was then that he first began to think about establishing another kind of Olympic Games—an Olympics just for other gay people like himself.

The road to the first Gay Games was a long one. First Waddell had to come out publicly—which he did in 1976, in the pages of *People* magazine. Then he had to commit himself publicly to the idea—which he did when he received a Cable Car Award as the Outstanding Athlete of 1980. It was then that Waddell quit his job as the medical director for a large corporation, organized a board of directors, and began raising money for what was termed the first Gay Olympics.

Working with an entirely volunteer group, Waddell and Company struggled through the first year financially until help came from an unlikely and unwilling source. When the United States Olympic Committee, seeking to disassociate itself from the Gay Games, obtained a court injunction forbidding the gay group the use of the word *Olympics,* contributions began pouring in for the first time. Says Waddell, "That got us the credibility we needed. It was David versus Goliath, and people love an underdog." At the heart of the matter, although the USOC tried to deny it, was homophobia, and as a result of the USOC's intervention, people began to see the Gay Games as Waddell envisioned them: as a way for gay people to express pride in themselves and to counter this kind of thoughtless, arrogant prejudice.

At a cost of $397,000 (with no more than $1000 coming from any one donor), in August 1982 the Gay Games began. More than 1300 athletes (700 men and 600 women) from 179 cities in 12 countries converged on San Francisco to compete in seventeen sports. The most popular of these, says Waddell, were the "skin sports": swimming, wrestling, and physique, for instance. But the most exciting events, he adds, were the opening and closing ceremonies in Kezar Stadium (at which rock star Tina Turner performed). To see the athletes marching under the banners of their respective cities in a line that stretched the length of the stadium and more was a sight that filled Waddell with pride—and one that he will long remember.

Although hundreds of medals were awarded, competition was anything but the point of the first Gay Games, says Waddell. "Participation was the key," he explains, "not competition. There were no minimal standards. You didn't have to be great, just serious about your sport. We knew there were going to be better teams elsewhere, but we didn't care. Instead, we wanted to redefine winning. For us, it wasn't beating anyone else, but doing your best." Although it took some of the athletes a while to grasp this concept, in the end most of them were enthusiastic about it. Some even filled in for athletes on other teams when needed. Concludes Waddell, "These athletes saw that the games weren't about high-level competition, but about being together with their brothers and sisters and having a good time."

This emphasis on participation rather than competition is only part of Waddell's broader philosophy about the games. At the heart of the philosophy, of course, is gay pride. When he was growing up, he explains, "We [gay people] weren't seeing ourselves as complete, fully vested citizens. We were stereotyping ourselves, buying what the dominant society was feeding us. What we needed was a venue that was totally nonthreatening, one that led to positive esteem: athletics." But for Waddell, this was only a beginning. According to the founder of the games, gaining self-respect and coming out are not ends in themselves, but a process, a continuing transformation. "As a gay man," he states, "I feel particularly advantaged, for I am in a position to continue this process. If we are an ageist, racist, sexist, and nationalist society—and we are—why not continue using this process to bring about change? And why not use the games for that purpose?" To implement these goals, Waddell and the board did more than just deemphasize competition. They also recruited heavily in minority communities, placed emphasis on the participation of women, and tried to erase unnecessary boundaries, such as age differences, wherever possible.

As a result of the first games, there was a resurgence of interest in sports in the gay community nationally and a growth in the number of gay sports organizations, such as the International Gay Volleyball League and the International Gay Bowling Organization. Demand for a second games was so great that planning began almost immediately after the conclusion of the first. The second Gay Games are scheduled to take place August 9 through August 17 of this year, again in San Francisco, at a projected cost of $800,000. More than 5400 athletes, four times as many as in 1982, are expected to participate, and because there has been advance planning and publicity by a staff of 150 volunteers, attendance is also expected to increase dramatically.

The major difference between this year's games, however, and those four years ago, is that this year the specter of AIDS looms heavily over the community, which is making fundraising especially difficult for the organizers of the games. Last time, explains Waddell, fifty-five nonprofit gay organizations were all chasing the same dollars. This time AIDS organizations are receiving most of the money that is available. "I'm all for that," Waddell contends, "but people ought to realize that there is more than one approach. We are starting to see ourselves as diseased, depressed, negative individuals, and we've got to stop that. We need a different perspective, and the games can help us to gain that perspective."

Assuming that the money will come in and that they will receive the large donations they need between now and August to produce this year's games, the board of directors must soon begin thinking about the future. They must consider many questions, including the following: Should the games continue? Where will they be located? Who will have control? How can responsibility for the games be transferred? How can the present organizers ensure that the philosophy of the games remains the same? This last question is the one that is most important to Waddell, who, above all else, is interested in heightening people's awareness. "We, as gay people, have a great opportunity to become teachers," he says. "We have opened up that first door. Let's continue to open up those doors."

Rita Rockett: Powered by Love

MARCH 1986

I MET HER AT the Cable Car Awards, shortly before she won the Dorothy Langston Award for Human Rights. She called me Mark all night long, even after I had won an award of my own and thought she should have known better. But I didn't mind, for until I met her I had been making a faux pas of my own: I had always thought she was a drag queen. With a name such as Rita Rockett, I had reasoned, what else could she be?

Known throughout the local gay community for the brunches she serves to people with AIDS at San Francisco General Hospital, Rita even looks like a drag queen—when she dresses the part. On the Sunday after the Cable Car Awards, for instance, she struts into Ward 5A wearing a scandalous French maid outfit, complete with lace gloves, black fishnets, frilly white socks, spiked heels, and, to top it off, red heart-shaped glasses. "Ooh, Rita, your hair looks great," coos one of her co-workers. "Thanks," Rita replies. "I just took it out of the box."

She does look great. But how she manages it, God only knows, for she spent most of the preceding day cooking fifty-two pounds of chicken with her friend and partner Terry Scott. The chicken, however, is only part of the day's menu. Also included are seafood mousse, tossed green salad, potato salad ("half yogurt, half mayonnaise, in case anybody asks"), homemade peach ice cream, and a host of other desserts (brownies, orange cheesecake, marble pound cake, and cherry almond tart, to be specific). There is enough to feed a small army—and a small army is ready to eat it, including sixteen patients on Ward 5A, twelve scattered around the hospital, their friends and family, and various doctors, nurses, and staff people. Rita usually plans on sixty, which leaves lots of room for leftovers.

While Rita races around the hospital inviting people with AIDS to brunch in the patient lounge and taking orders from those who would rather stay in their rooms, a staff of dedicated volunteers serves in the lounge. These volunteers—on this day it is Tony, David, Johnny, and Richard—have been with Rita for periods ranging from a few months to more than a year. Without them her job would be infinitely more difficult. It is Rita, however, who is always the center of attention. Every few minutes she storms into the lounge and exclaims, "Hey, everybody, it's a party! And so high tone!"

Rita began doing brunches on the ward almost two years ago, at Easter 1984. A good friend of hers, Dennis Yount, a bartender at the Eagle, was sick at the time, confined to his room, and feeling very bitter and alone. Rita planned a big party to cheer him up, but Dennis died before the day of the party. Undaunted, Rita threw the party for the other people on the ward. At first she was concerned that her presence there would be unwelcome. She was nervous that the people at the hospital might not understand or accept what she was trying to do. But her fears were quickly allayed by an immediate outpouring of love and gratitude from patients and staff alike. Rita's brunches quickly became a standard feature of life on Ward 5B (later to become Ward 5A).

For Rita, the idea of throwing a party to cheer people up comes naturally. A long-time resident of Texas, she says, "If you come from the South, whenever anything is wrong, you bring food. If somebody is sick or has died, somehow that always makes it a little better. It brings people together." Bringing people together is especially important on Ward 5A, where people seldom have the chance to gather, because of limitations imposed by their illness. This applies to family as well as to fellow patients. One person told Rita that the Christmas dinner she gave was the first dinner his family had had together in nine years. Rita was grateful to have helped bring about this reunion. "If you can make people happy for only a few minutes," she says, "you've at least accomplished something."

Cooking and serving are not the only things Rita does at her brunches. She also entertains. At Easter she was the Easter Bunny; at Christmas she was Mrs. Claus. Sometimes she invites local entertainers, such as the Vocal Minority, to perform, and she herself tap dances. This is not unusual for Rita, for she has been a party girl for years, ever since she first moved to San Francisco as an ex-Navy wife from San Diego in 1977. Back then, seeking to establish a new life for herself, she used to dance on tabletops at one of the Castro area's wilder party bars. She also used to throw big parties at her home. But despite bittersweet memories of those times, Rita admits that those were parties without purpose, and she doesn't like to dwell on those memories. "It's different now and people have to realize that we have to move on," she explains. "People have a tendency to hold onto things, but you can't go on the same. You've got to grow."

Rita may still dress up as Nancy Sinatra and grind the heels of her go-go boots on the bare back of some supine leatherman upon occasion, but these days she does it as part of some fundraising event and not just for fun. ("It's a tough job," she says, "but somebody has to do it.") She also throws her own fundraisers when the need arises. Although she scans the "Greengrocer's Report" in Wednesday's paper for sale items religiously, fifty-two pounds of chicken doesn't come cheap, and her brunches on 5A can cost upwards of two hundred dollars. She raises the money at parties given at Castro Station or some other bar. Recently Mr. International Leather, Patrick Toner, threw a fundraiser for her at the Powerhouse Bar South of Market. Naturally she welcomes this kind of assistance. Because she holds down a regular nine-to-five job at American–Hawaii Cruises in addition to her brunch responsibilities, it is one of the things that helps to make her life easier.

Recently I called my friend Leon, a former patient on Ward 5B, and told him I was doing a story on Rita. Leon, who now lives in Southern California, said, "Be sure to send her my love. Rita is the greatest. Whenever she was around she always made me feel like a million dollars." I promised, and a week later I gave Leon's message to Rita. Although she was glad to hear that he was doing well, I don't think she had the foggiest idea who Leon actually was. She has made so many people feel like a million dollars, how could she possibly remember each one? But if names are not her strong point, love is. And on Ward 5A, that's what counts.

Captain of the Campus

AUGUST 1987

AW, FUCK, WHAT have I gotten myself into? I thought as I entered the dimly lit but densely populated Campus Theater on Jones Street, right across from the Hung Phat Café. In the back rows of the theater, several sexually aroused men were none-too-discreetly beating away at their laps while on screen a beefy black bodybuilder was ramming the butt of his little blond boyfriend. Although I am hardly a stranger to this sort of establishment, I am not—nor have I ever been—an habitué. Consequently, I was a bit nervous when I walked down the Campus aisle. Yet the real show—the live one—hadn't even started.

The last time I had seen an erotic act on screen had been the night before, when I turned on the VCR in the privacy of my own home. But the last time I had seen an erotic act onstage had been eight years before, when I walked into the Gaiety Male Burlesque Theater on Times Square in New York. That night, expecting to find a series of half-starved, spaced-out street hustlers performing for an audience of depraved and pathetic old men, I discovered instead an unending parade of beauties (performing for the same). One of the strippers, a generously endowed young man named Corky, was so talented that during the intermission I asked him for a date. He, exquisite creature, accepted, and a brief affair ensued. But that was long ago and far away, another story entirely.

This time the performer I had come to see at the Campus Theater was not Corky, but Cory Van Patten. Cory, who was announced as "a twenty-five-year-old native of Orange County, a former tennis pro and model," is the captain of the Varsity Strip Squad, the group that Herb Caen calls "eleven strong men, and not a transvestite in the lot." Captain Van Patten made his appearance wearing running shoes, weightlifter's gloves, cut-off sweatpants (emblazoned Phi Delta Theta), a tank top, and a white windbreaker: an outfit similar to that of my friend Corky, eight years before. But there the similarity ends, for Mr. Van Patten's show was something else entirely.

Although Corky had merely danced, quickly shedding his wardrobe and his inhibitions but never leaving the stage, Cory involved his audience on a much more intimate level. Jumping down from the stage, he traveled from seat to seat, grabbing heads, sitting on laps, and wildly gyrating his body against his adoring fans. He did this in various states of undress, which may have thrilled others but disconcerted me. Although I knew I could handle Show and Tell, I simply wasn't prepared for Audience Participation.

Thinking myself safe for having placed myself away from the runway, I soon found out otherwise when Cory headed my way and displayed his by-now untethered and tumescent member inches from my face. Remembering the sign on the door, The City and County of San Francisco Forbid Audience Members from Touching the Genitals and Buttocks of the Performers, I somehow refrained from engulfing the thing. Instead, I merely smiled and said, "This really isn't fair, you know."

The show's climax was exactly that. After a thirty-minute display, Cory jumped back onstage and, with a shudder, condemned several million sperm to a brief but not entirely useless existence. With a gentlemanly wave of his hand, he thanked his audience. They expressed their own appreciation with a generous round of applause. The announcer then invited everyone downstairs for free beer and a live sex show, and that was that, until the next show a half-hour hence. Meanwhile, the music—disco bump and grind for the bare-assed boys of burlesque—played on.

Ten minutes after the grand finale, Van Patten appeared at the downstairs bar. When asked how much of the hype concerning his image was true, he replied that he really had been a tennis pro and model before he had begun to disrobe for a living. Furthermore, he did live in Southern California, although he originally hailed from the Midwest.

He is also a member of the fraternity advertised on his sweatpants. None of his former frat brothers, however, knows what he is doing now. Neither does his family, whose last name is *not* Van Patten. They think he's a business entrepreneur—which, in a way, he is. This ain't no mere stripper, after all. He also acts as assistant to the president of the theater, and, as such, is involved with scheduling, advertising, and other relatively tame activities.

Cory does what he does for two reasons: the money and the pleasure. "I enjoy it," he says. "It's a chance to entertain, to act, to be in the spotlight. I have no inhibitions about giving myself—within the law. I love the applause." Although he performs onstage once a day, seven days a week, he never gets bored. "The only time it gets boring is when the audience doesn't respond. Then I wonder what's wrong. Is it me or is it them?"

To prevent boredom from setting in, Cory changes his act every month or so. "I don't want it to get old," he states. He also tries to keep the act as believable as possible. "I'll never perform in a cop outfit, because that just wouldn't work. But a surfer or a frat boy: that works. I *was* in a fraternity, after all."

This credibility, Cory points out, is one of the main reasons that people enjoy his performance. "Of course it's acting and show," he admits, "but it's also real. I always get hard, and I always come, because it's a turn-on. But I have to get prepared, of course. I have to get mentally psyched up, and that's not always easy." Neither is it easy to deal with the consequences sometimes. "Doing this every night does put a damper on the rest of my sex life," he confesses. "But that doesn't mean I don't enjoy myself outside the theater or at other times of the day."

Sometimes Cory's show gets too real, and audience members are intimidated by his aggressive style. But Cory claims he knows how to handle this. "If I go up to someone and he doesn't want me to get too close, he'll show it somehow. I'm not going to force anyone. But most enjoy the aggressiveness. It's part of the act. It's essential." Nevertheless, it's also essential to contain that aggressiveness within legal boundaries. "If people break the rules, I politely brush their hands away," he shrugs. "It happens."

Because he gets so much publicity, primarily in newspaper advertisements, Cory's fans often recognize him on the street. Most simply express admiration. The few who expect more are bound to be disappointed, for Cory already has a primary relationship. The recognition is nice, Cory states, "but I don't get a head trip out of it." Luckily, he rarely gets what he calls negative feedback. "About 90 percent of the time people are positive and open-minded about it. Those that aren't: To each his own. I don't judge people. If they want to judge me based on what I do, that's their problem. I have no regrets. I'm proud of my job."

Cory is so proud of his job that he wishes more people would watch him work, even straight men and women. "Most people think this kind of thing is sleazy," he acknowledges, "but I take it professionally. I think it's a fun kind of entertainment that everybody can enjoy, people of all ages and types. We try hard at this theater to make it that way, and I think it shows."

In spite of this, Cory does not plan to dance at the Campus Theater forever. "I'll keep doing it as long as my body's healthy, and right now I'm at my peak. But eventually I'd like to be an entrepreneur, to run my own company. I've had other jobs, as a manager of a singles club and as a marketing consultant for a TV network. I've also got a college education. It's important to me that people respect me for what I have inside as well as outside."

For the present, fortunately, no one's complaining about the outside.

The Bigger They Come, the Harder They . . .

JULY 1986

DID YOU SEE HIM? Did you see him?" asked my friend Hadley at the Lesbian/Gay Freedom Day parade a few weeks ago.

"Who?"

"Rick Donovan. He's signing autographs at the HIS Productions booth."

"You mean Rick 'Humongous' Donovan, the porn star?" I asked breathlessly.

"None other. And, honey, he looks even better in person than he does on film. The man is h-o-t hot."

Now I have been a Rick Donovan fan for years, ever since he fulfilled one of my favorite fantasies by fucking his high school teacher on the teacher's desk in the film *The Bigger the Better*. True, the man can't always get it hard and keep it hard, but, face it, he has a lot to sustain. Anyway, it's a minor drawback, compared with his many other attributes. I especially like the way he snarls when he comes: a curl of the lips, a shudder, and then it's over. My hero.

Naturally, then, when Hadley told me Rick was but a few yards away, I ran to introduce myself. I didn't know exactly what I expected of him, but I knew what I *hoped,* and I figured the easiest plan of attack would be to ask him for an interview. It wouldn't be the first time I'd used my position with the paper to further my own sordid aims. At any rate, it beat asking for an autograph.

Unfortunately, when I introduced myself, Rick merely grunted and referred me to his manager, Richard Lawrence (who is also the head of HIS Productions). "We leave for home tomorrow morning," Richard informed me, "but I suppose we could see you early. Will you be free at 9:30?"

It wasn't exactly what I had in mind. 9:30 A.M.? On a Monday morning? With a third party in the room? Whatever happened to intimate rendezvous in quiet little restaurants at dusk? Whatever happened to romance? How the hell was I supposed to get in the man's pants that way?

Ah, well, you take what you can get in this world. Consequently, at 9:30 the next morning, I showed up at the door to Rick's room at the Argyle Hotel. As Rick greeted me in shorts, an open shirt, and a Reebok baseball cap, his manager excused himself to take a shower. We were alone at last, after all! I swallowed and did my best to keep my eyes focused anywhere but below the neck.

Rick gave me his life history first. Born in Germany, he had spent six years in Alaska and "a few" in Texas, where he actually enjoyed two years in a private military academy. (Ooh, baby.) He then attended Pan American University and joined the Navy. Eventually he ended up in San Diego, where he embarked upon his present career.

Now for the nitty gritty. A good friend who owned a bathhouse had asked Rick to pose for a newspaper ad for his place. Obligingly, Rick posed in a jockstrap above the caption, Where the Jocks Hang Out. This led to his first adult film, *The Boys of Company F,* produced in 1982. A cast of authentic military personnel, past and present, was assembled for the film, and Rick used his Navy experience to prepare for his role as a drill instructor.

"It wasn't easy to make the film," Rick recalled. "Under the lights it was 120 degrees, I had to work with a dozen strangers, and the producers kept reminding me how much all this was costing. Just try to get your dick hard under those conditions. I had some problems."

Problems or no, Rick's work in *The Boys of Company F* led to cameo appearances in a dozen or more films and six or seven starring roles in others, such as *Sailor in the Wild* and *The Bigger the Better,* the best-selling adult video of all time, with more than thirty-four thousand copies sold. His most recent film is *On Top,* which Rick calls "the best thing I've done" and which includes an eleven-minute jerk-off scene: the longest on record.

Rick quickly became a porn superstar, but retired temporarily for several reasons. For one thing, producers weren't willing to pay what he felt he deserved.

For another, his career was interfering with his relationship with his lover. ("And that's the most important thing in my life—it *has* to be.") Most important, however, Rick was feeling uncomfortable with what he was doing, because of the AIDS crisis.

"When the crisis got serious," he said, "a lot of people quit the business, and others cut back. I began doing AIDS benefits—I even cooked dinners for twenty or more AIDS patients at a time—and I decided I wasn't going to do something that wasn't healthy."

After a brief sojourn away from Southern California, then, Rick landed a job in LA in administrative operations for VCA, the largest manufacturer and distributor of adult videos in the world. (HIS is the all-male division of VCA.) He returned to acting in those films only when assured that he would have control over his scenes. "We're going to do it my way or not at all," Rick swore. "My way," as it turned out, meant no blow jobs, no coming inside men, no fisting, no toys, and lots of hydrogen peroxide douches for his partners (Rick is always on top)—but no rubbers either. "I've had trouble with condoms," he explained. "I can't find them big enough and they break. Do you know where I can find extra large ones?"

I shook my head. "Unfortunately, I've never had that problem."

Life as a porn star (Rick, incidentally, disclaimed the title) has other drawbacks, continued Rick. "Usually the attention is flattering, if people do it right. I do care about my work, and I like to know that they appreciate it. But sometimes the attention is not appropriate: on buses or in restaurants, for instance. Furthermore, everybody assumes that this is 90 percent of my life. It's not. I get up, I shit, shower, and shave, I work my butt off and come home at night, like everybody else. I have a whole other life." Involvement in the Imperial Court system, fundraising for AIDS causes, and producing shows, such as a Mr. Jock contest, are facets of this "whole other life" to which few people pay any attention.

Perhaps the major drawback to stardom is that Rick never knows, when he meets someone, "if he likes me because of what I do or because of who I am. And how does he know who I am?" To date, Rick has had three lovers in his life. The first relationship ended after a year and a half. The second was with a former Empress of San Diego (four times) and editor of the *San Diego Scene*, with whom he is still close friends. The third disintegrated because Rick was "much too conservative" for the man. "I don't drink or do drugs," Rick explained. "I'm not involved in the party scene." Because these relationships were back to back, this is Rick's first time being single, alas. "It's a completely different world," he sighed.

Sometime in the future Rick would like to go back to school. "The possibilities in my present job are incredible," he said, "but I would like to be qualified to do other things: something in the food industry, the security industry, or theater management, perhaps. Like everybody else, I want to be rich someday, but the main thing is to find something to do that I like." In the meantime, he will continue to make movies.

When his manager, Richard, returned from the shower, Rick handed me two five-by-seven glossies of himself (one clothed and one unclothed), a T-shirt promoting his latest movie, and a dozen red roses. The roses were only part of a bunch left for him by an anonymous admirer. "I don't know what else to do with them," he said. "You want them?"

"Sure," I replied, "as long as I can make up stories for my friends about why you gave them to me." When I got home, however, the roses had wilted, reminding me of a certain someone who had difficulty dealing with 120-degree lights and the presence of strangers. But I didn't care. No, sir. Some things are precious despite their imperfections.

Talking to the Tourists

JUNE 1983

IT SOUNDED LIKE a good idea when a friend first suggested it. "Just go on down to the wharf," he said, "and ask the tourists what they think of gay life in San Francisco. Do they know about us? Have they met any of us? What *do* they think of this city, gay-wise?"

Gay-wise? It's not in the dictionary. But I knew what he meant. Trouble was, how in the world would I do such a thing? How would I go about approaching straight tourists and asking them about homosexuality without being thought forward at best and perverted at worst? Travelers to San Francisco do expect the unexpected, it's true, but most of them would rather observe than participate in all the craziness. They enjoy the mimes, the dancers, the street artists, and the jugglers, but they form wide circles around them and seek safety in the anonymity of the crowd. They laugh, they take pictures, they drop coins in hats and boxes, but basically they keep to themselves. They don't want to be disturbed. I had to figure out a way to break through that reserve.

I decided on a plan of attack. First I chose a nonthreatening outfit, my standard reporter's garb (which also doubles as my Annie Hall outfit): khaki pants, white shirt, and brown vest. I also considered a Bogart hat with a press card made of construction paper stuck in the brim, but that would have looked a little silly. Even if it did fit in with the atmosphere of the wharf, I did want to be taken seriously, after all. Next, after great thought, I chose and rehearsed the following lines:

"Hi. How are you?" (Nice opening, huh?)

"Are you from San Francisco?"

"Where *are* you from?"

"Oh, that's a nice city. I'm a writer for the *Bay Area Reporter,* and I'm doing an article on what tourists think about San Francisco and certain aspects of the city in particular. Do you mind if I ask you a few questions?"

My first question would be, "What have you seen since you've been here?" I decided to warm up to my subject as gently and as gradually as possible. Finally, after talking about the wharf, Chinatown, Coit Tower, and Golden Gate Park, ad infinitum, I'd ask, "Have you been to Castro Street yet?" and, if that answer was no, "Have you ever heard of Castro Street?" If they hadn't, I'd explain that it was the city's major gay neighborhood, and then I'd ask in succession:

"Are you aware that there are lots of gay people in San Francisco?"

"Why do you think they come here?"

"Are there gay people in your hometown?"

"Do you know any personally?"

And finally: "How do you feel about homosexuality? Does it bother you? Do you care?"

I decided not to identify the *B.A.R.* as a gay paper or myself as a gay person until the end, if then. Call me closeted if you will, but it didn't seem like the best way to put people at ease or to get nonprejudiced answers.

It seemed like a good plan. Simple, basic. What could go wrong? So on a gorgeous Saturday afternoon, I drove to the wharf and wandered out to the end of Pier 39, looking for victims. Unfortunately, although I saw lots of likely candidates, once I found myself forced to act, I couldn't work up the nerve. How to begin accosting people? And so I stood at the end of the pier, watching the sailboats go by and thinking how surprised and disappointed my mother would have been with me, she who had been the most gregarious and least inhibited person I had ever known. Thinking about my mother (may she rest in peace) made me feel so guilty that I finally spurred myself to action. Screwing my courage to the sticking point, I walked up to the least hostile-looking people I saw, three women and one man in their midtwenties, and said, "Hi. How are you?"

They were fine. They were from Southern California and had seen "typical tourist things: Ghirardelli Square, the Cannery, Pier 39." No, they hadn't been to or heard of Castro Street, but when I told them about it, one woman replied that she *had* heard about Polk Street. Yes, they knew of San Francisco's reputation as a gay town. Why did gay people come here? To be with other gay people, they supposed. Yes, there were gays back home in Southern California. (I should hope so.) One woman knew "a few" of them. The others didn't know any. How did they feel about it? Two didn't care one way or the other. The other two replied, "I don't like it," and "It's a turnoff."

"Thank you very much," I replied, and I fled. I was nervous. They, I thought, had been uncomfortable. The next people I talked to, a man from Sacramento and his cousin from Fort Worth (both in their thirties), weren't so bad, however, and with each person or group of people I talked to, it got easier and easier to broach the "forbidden" subject. Soon I was accosting all and sundry—everyone except people with kids, for they made me uncomfortable. I was too aware of the cruel and antiquated stereotype of gays as child molesters, and I felt defensive. Also, I was just being practical. People with kids would be less likely to be open about subjects such as homosexuality when their kids were around. They also would be infinitely more difficult to interview, as the kids would be always dragging them somewhere, asking them to buy something, or spilling ice cream on their shoes.

In all, I talked to thirty-five people: people of all ages (eighteen or older), races, and nationalities. Everyone I approached agreed to talk to me. Indeed, some were eager to talk, and when they discovered the gist of the article, none were hostile (although a few *were* uncomfortable). Believe it or not, I had a relatively good time, considering that every other faggot in town was out lying in the sun while I talked to tourists on the wharf. And I learned some surprising things. The results? Listen to this. (We'll skip the "What have you seen?" part. Either you've already seen it or you wouldn't want to, unless you're a fan of souvenir shops, penny arcades, and wax museums.)

Only two of the thirty-five people I talked to had been to Castro Street, and that was by mistake. They had taken a wrong turn somewhere. Two others, a black couple from Cincinnati, thought they might have been there but weren't sure. "I think we may have stumbled on it last night," said the woman. "I told my husband, 'Look, there are so many men here!' " None had taken the bus tour to Twin Peaks, which passes through the Castro neighborhood.

Very few of the people I talked to—only 20 percent—had ever even heard of Castro Street. Most hadn't. One of the women from Southern California said, "I knew about Polk Street, but not Castro." Every one of these people, however, had heard of San Francisco's reputation as a gay haven. Most had known about the gay scene here for some time, either through their TVs and newspapers or through "common knowledge," but a few only recently had been enlightened. One group of middle-aged Australians waiting for the Alcatraz ferry told me that they hadn't known about gays in San Francisco until their tour guide mentioned it. "Oh? What did he say?" I asked. "He said it was a very tolerant city," they replied. "There aren't so many here as in Berkeley, though," an elderly woman from Long Island assured me while watching a group of black dancers. "That's the *real* center for gays."

Why did the tourists think there were so many gay people here? Nearly every person gave me one or both of the following reasons: because there were so many others here ("They want to be with their own kind") and because San Francisco was a more tolerant city ("They are accepted here"). Several people mentioned "a sense of community." Others spoke about "freedom," "a relaxed attitude," and "open-mindedness."

Almost 70 percent of the tourists admitted that there were plenty of gay people back home, but most pointed out that it wasn't exactly the same thing at home as it was here. As one couple from Omaha said, "Oh, sure, we have them, but they're not really comfortable there." A nineteen-year-old female student from Tacoma acknowledged, "There are gay people everywhere, but here it's accepted. Back home in Tacoma, if two people of the same sex walked hand in hand, people would freak out." Another nineteen-year-old student, this one a male (and what a male!) from Boston, didn't believe that there were necessarily any more gay people here than anywhere else. It was just that it was talked about more here, and it was more open as well, a sentiment that was echoed almost word for word by a married couple from Seattle. A few tourists, incidentally, were particularly sophisticated about the gay communities in their own hometowns. One couple from Houston told me about the Montrose section of that city. Another from Salinas discussed AIDS cases in their town.

Eleven of the thirty-five specified that they knew gay people personally or had gay friends. The elderly woman from Long Island, who was on a bus tour of California, confided, "I have some very dear friends that are homos. Most are very talented, well-mannered, lovely people." The student from Tacoma had met gay people through her human sexuality class at school, and the Houston couple had "several gay friends." None of the tourists, however, had met gay people in San Francisco. Only four, the couple from Cincinnati and the nineteen-year-old student from Boston and his friend, had even seen people they thought might be gay. "I was passing by a hotel called the Casa Loma," the Boston student related, "and some guy called out the window to me." "Did he try to pick you up?" I asked. "No," he replied, smiling, "but it would have been interesting to see what would have happened if he had tried." A white-haired woman from Miami, on the same bus tour as the woman from Long Island, hadn't had the same kind of experience, but she had had a gay encounter. "I saw a gay newspaper," she confessed, "but I didn't like it." When I asked her what she had read, she shook her head from side to side and replied, "Oh, I couldn't tell you. Those ads! Awful!"

Surprisingly, only six of the people I interviewed expressed disapproval of homosexuality. One was a twenty-one-year-old sailor off the USS *Berkeley*, who spent the entire time I was talking to him cruising women as obviously as possible. (A definite prequeen, I thought.) Another was an Australian, who said, "I don't like it. I think it's wrong. It shouldn't be publicized or bragged about." Everyone else, however, expressed variations of the same sentiment: "It doesn't bother us. It's their way of life." Many qualified that statement by adding "as long as they mind their own business," "as long as they don't bother me," or "as long as they don't make a spectacle of themselves," indicating that they probably didn't admire or respect gay people very much, but they didn't really care one way or the other. Fortunately, there were others who concluded, "They're just people, no different from anybody else."

For someone who spends 95 percent of his time confined to the gay areas of San Francisco, it was an enlightening experience to spend a day at the wharf. I needn't have been so nervous, after all. Straight people really aren't all that bad. Most of them don't hate us—they don't, they don't—and some can be quite friendly. The boys from Boston and the girls from Tacoma (the student had a sister) were wonderful. We had long heart to hearts, and I eventually told them not only that I was gay but also all about gay life in the city (à la Hippler). I even tried to set the two groups up, and when that fell through, I told them where to find the straight bars in the city (as if I knew). Four hours of the wharf can get old real quick, though, so when the breeze from the Bay picked up, I returned home, a wiser man.

Hymn to The River

SEPTEMBER 1983

A SLEEK YELLOW convertible glides smoothly along Highway 101 north of San Francisco, heading away from the city. The top is down, and in the back a thin blond wearing a leopardskin headband and a diamond earring is fretfully rubbing suntan lotion on his arms and face as he complains about the pallor of his skin. "I look like death on a cracker," he says. "I sure hope this trip does me some good." His best friend, a bronzed beauty with a Kentucky drawl and the body of a Spartan warrior, sprawls next to him in the sun, luxuriating in its steady warmth. In the front seat the driver chats about nothing with his newfound boyfriend: the price of gas, the latest movies, gym routines. Both are wearing mirrored sunglasses, which reflect the rolling brown-and-green landscape around them and the bright white highway ahead. They have been driving for little more than an hour. As they descend into a broad, quiet valley and cross the county line, the driver turns toward the back seat and says, "This is it, boys. The Sonoma County line. Won't be long now." Their destination: the Russian River.

The Russian River is only sixty-five miles north of the city, and the four take every opportunity they get to escape to there. Sometimes they drive up for the day, sometimes they stay longer. This time they haven't decided how long they'll stay or what they'll do. The driver wants to rent a canoe and spend the day paddling upstream. His boyfriend would rather lie by the pool at one of the gay resorts, where he can cruise to his heart's content. The bronzed beauty suggests hiking through the redwood forests at the river's edge. His best friend, she of the leopardskin headband, favors floating motionless on a sky blue raft in the middle of the cloudy green river—within view of a nude beach, if at all possible. And, of course, it is possible. The four debate until they reach the River Road turnoff, but in the end, as usual, the driver gets his way. He appeases the group by promising to stand for cocktails at Fife's or the Rusty Nail afterward. "This is *my* car," he proclaims, "and we're going to do it *my* way." Nobody really minds. The main thing is not what to do but to do it. The main thing is to be there.

The first time I went to the Russian River I didn't see another faggot anywhere, except for my friend David, lying at my side. I couldn't believe this was the gay paradise I had heard so much about, the sylvan utopia I had waited a year to see. To my right, a fat woman in curlers and a hairnet, lying under a multicolored beach umbrella, shouted, "Billy, I *told* you not to go in past your knees!" To my left, a group of rambunctious teenage boys in cut-off jeans and worn sneakers amused themselves by slipping ice down the bikinis tops of their nubile young girlfriends, who were screaming with horror and delight. The river's waters were murky and uninviting. The beach was a bed of rocks, impossible to lie on, impossible to cross barefoot. "What *have* we come to?" I questioned David in despair. "What *have* we found?"

What we had found was Johnson's Beach, the major swimming and sunning area for the town of Guerneville, California. Lying adjacent to the one-lane bridge that leads into town from the south and only two or three blocks from the central business district, it is the first beach you see when you come into town from that direction and a favorite watering hole for straight tourists and local youths. David and I stopped there after driving up from San Francisco for the day because we didn't know where else to go. We knew that there must be gay beaches somewhere, but we had no guide book to The River, and we were too lazy to search gay beaches out. Instead we spent the day dodging little kids and avoiding splash battles, vaguely uncomfortable and distinctly disillusioned.

Had David and I opened our eyes or wandered just a little farther in any direction, we might have found what we sought. This was in 1980, and ever since 1978, when one of the nation's leading newsweeklies had dubbed Guerneville a "gay boom town," gay people had flocked up to The River in droves. They established resorts and shops, bought cottages and houses. What had once been a sleepy, neglected little town barely able to support itself suddenly became a thriving, vigorous resort area again. Guerneville was transformed into a home away from home for thousands of Bay Area gay people, a pastoral retreat from the heady pace of big city life, an oasis of tranquility. Some of the locals didn't appreciate the change, of course, and for a while Guerneville's bucolic reputation was tarnished by the threat of roving gangs of belligerent thugs, but things have calmed down since then. These days the number of tank tops and tight Levi's equals or surpasses the number of polyester double-knit slacks on Main Street, and nobody seems to mind.

Why do we go there? Isn't it enough to live in San Francisco all year long, the city so enchanting that we call it Baghdad by the Bay? Sometimes when I return from a driving trip to the north or east, and I see the gleaming towers soar above the sparkling waters of the bay, or I watch the fog roll in toward Alcatraz, I think I must be in Oz. The magic of the place is palpable, its allure irresistible. So why leave? Because . . . Because despite its hills and parks, despite its cool climate and its storybook Victorians, San Francisco is still a big city, and any city gets tiresome after a while. Deep within most of us is a need for the open air, a cry for the wilderness, a longing to escape to the woods. San Francisco can't really satisfy those urges, but The River can, and it's only sixty-five miles away.

There are other places we might go that are close, but we choose The River for several reasons:

1. It is hot. We find the summer sun there, which we rarely see in San Francisco. It is nice to walk outdoors without a shirt on. It is nice to lie by a pool and get a tan.
2. It is picturesque. So is the rest of Northern California, but The River is so charming as it flows past vineyards and apple orchards, meandering through redwood-covered hills on its way to the ocean. It has a subtle beauty, entirely unlike the spectacular grandness of Yosemite: its beauty has the power to soothe rather than excite, to subdue rather than invigorate.

3. We can *use* The River. Unlike New Yorkers and Los Angelenos, we cannot use our ocean, for the water is too cold and the surf is too dangerous, and if that isn't enough, the sharks are mean and nasty. But at The River we can swim, we can canoe, we can float around all day and do nothing. I suppose we can fish, but few of us do.

4. There are others of us there. When I graduated from college nine years ago, I moved to the Allegheny Mountains of Virginia to teach, thinking the wilderness would be all I'd need. I quickly discovered that it wasn't enough. I needed companionship. I needed love. I needed sex. And in the Virginia mountains, it is nearly impossible for a gay man to find those things. But not at The River. There it is possible to enjoy all the bounties Mother Nature provides without sacrificing emotional and sexual needs. It may even be possible to fulfill everyone's favorite fantasy there—retiring to a vine-laden cottage with the man of your dreams—but don't count on it.

Shortly after my disillusioning trip to The River with David, my friend Jim gave me my first gay glimpse of the place. He took me to the private cabin of a friend of his, and although I saw only a few more gay people than the first time, *this* was how I had imagined life at The River would be: quiet, serene, inviolate. The cabin was perched on the side of a steep slope far, far above The River. One end was anchored firmly in the ground. The other was resting precariously high on a pair of rickety stilts. The roof and deck were buried in redwood needles. Inside, a fireplace rose from the center of the main room, and in the kitchen mismatched china plates adorned an otherwise empty cupboard. It was dreamily romantic, and Jim and I spent all our time there when we weren't on The River itself, smoking joints and listening to classical music on the radio.

Jim was my tripping buddy. While others did their drugs at late night dance places such as Dreamland and the Trocadero, Jim and I confined our acid to the daylight hours. A few times that fall and then again the next summer, Jim and I dropped acid and spent hours on the beach about a mile upstream from Wohler Bridge. I never could have found it myself. It was one of those places I wanted to find but that required a friend to show me the way. Why *do* we choose the most inaccessible sites for our playgrounds? I wondered as we trudged up the road to the beach. Just because they *are* inaccessible, I answered myself, which gives us the freedom to do what we want.

Did I say we spent our time on the beach? Hardly. Rather, we spent it all in the water, examining the rocks covering the bottom and splashing about to watch the spray sparkle in the sunlight. If we left the water at all, it was to swing on branches hanging low over the river. Jim and I were like two little kids when we did acid—or, more aptly, two aging flower children—discovering, wondering, appreciating the beauty and terror of everything. It was a perfect way to spend the day until we retreated back to the cabin at night, promising never to go home—a promise we never kept.

My second summer the cabin was no longer available, so I turned to the resorts. There at last I found all the faggots I could ever have hoped to see, and some that I would rather have not. At The Woods, I discovered, the disco set turned The River at night into a miniscule replica of the city: a lovely place, but one to be avoided at all costs for those seeking peace and quiet. The Willows, on the other hand, was like a big, sprawling family home, with its communal kitchen, overstuffed furniture, and baby grand piano. Other places featured other attractions, ranging from little more than a fireplace and a hot tub to the works: sports facilities, restaurants, live entertainment.

Of all these, the Russian River Lodge was my favorite for a while, despite its reputation as Folsom in the Woods. The chosen haunt of the Levi's/leather set, its chicken coop, treehouse, and campgrounds were notorious for nocturnal ramblings, but I enjoyed the rustic atmosphere of the main lodge and the glorious swimming pool more. Later my gym friends introduced me to Fife's, the granddaddy of all the gay places and the most complete resort on The River. The set at Fife's was less rough and tumble than the Russian River Lodge crowd and was divided into two camps: those with muscles and those without. Those with oiled their bodies and glistened by the pool. Those without sat in the shade and sipped cocktails, eyes gleaming. When not posing or voyeuring, the guests wandered acres and acres of pristine, manicured grounds. Fife's is so well ordered that at first I was a bit taken aback, but I soon grew used to the place. In fact, one of my favorite memories involves a porn star, my sleeping bag, and a bottle of poppers in the campground there. Ah, you and the night and the music. . . .

Shall we talk of love? The best trips to The River were those with Paul, Paul of the English accent and rippling stomach muscles, whom I met, I must confess, at the St. Mark's Baths in New York City. Paul was enamored of simple things—of butterfly wings and dragonflies, of dew on the grass and the shape of a stick—and I was enamored of Paul. We made love on beds of eucalyptus leaves, in overheated cabin bedrooms, under the redwoods, and at the water's edge. There are those who are fervent devotees of lovemaking in the great outdoors, and for them The River is a garden of sensual delights. I too enjoy the caress of sun and wind, but I think the reason Paul and I fucked so much at The River had far more to do with Paul himself than with anything The River could offer. He was simply a marvel. A paean to Paul.

At times The River reminds me of the river of my childhood, the Chattahoochee. The Chattahoochee tumbled "Out of the hills of Habersham, / Down the valleys of Hall" on its way from the mountains of North Georgia to the Gulf of Mexico.

I lived a mile from its green and leafy banks, where it formed the boundary between the wooded suburbs of North Atlanta and the farm country beyond, and where I lived the river was wide and shallow. Its waters were still ice cold from the mountains, and there were plenty of rapids to shoot and cliffs from which to dive. There are few rapids or cliffs at the Russian River, but it too is wide and shallow, and its banks are leafy and green. Sometimes when I'm standing in midriver and the water still isn't over my head, or when a group of teenage boys floats by in a canoe—Boy Scouts perhaps?—I am reminded of the Chattahoochee and home, and The River is dearer to me for that.

Oh, but I always paint too glowing a picture. The River isn't paradise. In spots it's downright homely. Jim calls it funky. Its beaches are rocks or dirt rather than sand, and the water isn't as clean as it might be. (Last summer there was a major formaldehyde spill in The River, which closed it for days. This year vandals broke off the valve of a large sewage pipe and flooded The River with tons of treated sewage, closing it again.) In the winter it turns into a raging torrent and frequently floods the area for miles around, causing hundreds of thousands of dollars' worth of property damage. There is little work to be had for the year-round residents in the winter, and many who move there "permanently" because of the summer madness move back again when the rains come and the party ends. (But is that The River's fault?) Some people still call you a faggot, and there's nary a movie theater in sight. Despite these drawbacks, however, The River is a special place, and those who discover it rarely stay away for long.

I haven't been up to The River as often as I'd like this summer. I'm having skin troubles and the sun isn't good for me. I suppose I could sit in the shade and drink Margaritas, but that isn't my style. I'd rather be on or in the water. Someday it would be nice to buy a house there, if only I could afford it. I've even thought of teaching there, but I'd rather not teach anywhere if I can help it. There ought to be some way to make The River a more integral part of my life. In time I'll figure out what it is.

A sleek yellow convertible glides smoothly along Highway 101 south of the Russian River, heading home. The night air is cool and moist, but the boys inside are too sunburned to appreciate it. To them it hurts. Anything does. The two in the back are soon asleep despite the pain; the sun absorbed their energy earlier in the day. After a while, the driver's boyfriend puts his head on the driver's lap and lets the motion of the car gently lull him to sleep. The driver hums quietly to himself as the radio plays a soft country ballad. Oddly enough, he does not mind going home. He loves the dark and the feel of the open road. He loves letting his imagination wander as the others sleep. His favorite time to return, however, is in the evening, as day turns to night. If there is fog, he ignores his passengers' pleas to put the top up. The drop in temperature is abrupt and severe. It is hard to believe that the merciless sun of noon and the dense fog of evening are part of the same day. But if it is clear, he slows to enjoy the blazing vision before him: the city aglow with the last rays of the sun, with fiery oranges and golden reds.

In the city the four climb clumsily out of the car and dig in the trunk to find their things. In gym shorts and sandals, carrying beach towels and deflated rafts, they feel like aliens in a strange land. The night is cold. Their skin still hurts. They want only to sleep. But the driver detains them. "Next week?"

Of course.

Ode on a Grecian Yearn

MAY 1986

WHEN I WAS twenty-one I visited Greece for a week as part of a two-month Grand (Backpacking) Tour of Europe. I slept on cottage roofs by the moonlit sea, picked blood red poppies in olive groves, feasted with peasants by clear mountain streams, and ran shirtless and barefoot through sun-bleached ruins. Wildly infatuated with the land and its people (at twenty-one, I was wildly infatuated with everything), I vowed someday to return, Fate and the gods willing.

Thirteen years later I fulfilled that vow—not for the year I had promised myself when I was younger, but for a mere three weeks, all I could afford. If I was afraid when I left that I expected too much, that Greece would necessarily disappoint the second time around, it was an unreasonable fear. The trip was all that I could have asked for and more—for this time, unlike the last, the trip had a homosexual dimension.

I swear I didn't expect it. When friends asked if I was going to Mykonos, that renowned international party mecca of the Mediterranean, I said I doubted it. I live in the gay capital of the world, I pointed out. Why, then, plan a specifically gay vacation?

In Athens, consequently, I spent my time exploring archaeological ruins instead of homosexual nightclubs—and I wouldn't have known where to find the latter if I tried. But although gay night spots are easy to ignore, a gay sensibility is not, as I discovered when I went to Nafplio, a small coastal resort in the Peloponnisos. Passing by chance a sign advertising the Nafplio Gym, I decided on a whim to check it out, to see (among other things) how it compared with the gyms at home.

As it happens, the Nafplio Gym is nearly a carbon copy of any of the gay gyms in San Francisco: the same equipment, the same music, the same tasteful (if understated) decor. The only significant differences were kilos instead of pounds and heteros instead of homos. I felt right at home. I felt even more welcome when a kid named Vangelis was assigned to me as guide and interpreter.

At first I thought his name was Angelis, and he certainly looked the part. His beauty was heaven sent: dark, curly hair, olive skin, smooth, sculptured chest, tiny waist, and tight, firm ass. He wore no shirt, and at one point he even dropped his sweatpants to see how he looked in his briefest of bikinis in the mirror. At home I would have laughed, but in Nafplio I nearly swooned. Vangelis, as friendly as he was beautiful, had me completely under his spell. After our workout, at my urging, he agreed to meet me "at the blue chairs by the water."

Following a quick shower at home, as the sun set over the castle in the harbor, I stared into Vangelis's baby blues while we discussed politics and love. To my amazement he told me that he was only eighteen but that he had been "on the streets" since he was twelve. "There isn't anything I haven't tried," he said with a teasing smile, "except getting fucked in the ass, and I won't try that because I'm afraid I would like it." Later, in an ice cream shop, he asked if I was gay. When I replied in the affirmative, he said, "I knew it. I can always tell, even if you don't act 'that way.' But be careful whom you tell here, because most people don't think the way I do."

After the ice cream shop came dinner with friends (one of whom has hopes of becoming Mr. Hellas someday), dancing at a nearby disco, drinks at a Greek tavern, and late night pizza. When at last the moment of truth arrived, Vangelis let me down easy. "Sex is one thing," he said, "and friendship is another. Besides, just because I've tried everything, that doesn't mean I still do it."

A week later, miles away, I was still pining. That's when I resolved to go to Mykonos after all. Like sex and friendship, fantasy is one thing and reality another, and pining away for an eighteen-year-old, however godlike, just isn't my style. Besides, I had met one Greek god in Nafplio; in Mykonos I might easily meet another, one who, unlike Vangelis, had not only tried everything but was *still* trying—and succeeding in the attempt.

Mykonos has two major nude beaches: Paradise for the straight people and Super Paradise for the gays. (At last, someplace in the world with its priorities in order.) At Super Paradise Beach on my first day there, I met Dimitris, a twenty-five-year-old blond with striking green eyes. As we baked in the sun, we too talked of politics and love, but this time the conversation was less circumspect and more pointed, for this time, when it came to love, at least, Dimitris and I shared a common understanding.

Back in town we explored the fabled Mykonos night life together, and as I watched well-dressed young people from all over the world dance to American rock videos, seemingly without a concern in the world, I felt locked in a time warp. Here once again was a world of instant gratification, a world of pleasure, sex, and drugs: a world, in a phrase, without AIDS. I asked Dimitris and his friends about AIDS, in fact, and amazingly one of his friends hadn't even heard of it (or so he claimed). He and Dimitris, he explained, were "yuppie junkies," party queens interested mainly in good times. Safe sex was a foreign concept to them. They felt much more comfortable discussing lighter matters. For one night only I was willing to oblige—and later, fortunately, Dimitris obliged me also.

Two islands later I found myself in Rhodes, and there I met two Frenchmen, Martin and Laurent. They had come to Rhodes for a sailing vacation on Martin's father's boat and asked me to join them for as long as I liked—until Martin's father arrived. Schoolgirl gushing aside, Martin and Laurent were TCFW (Too Cute for Words), and although they were outwardly straight, I wondered if secretly they could be boyfriends.

I didn't wonder for long. Although in Martin I sensed a kindred spirit, it was he who, on our second night together, suggested we visit the discos to look for "chicks." Ever one to oblige, I agreed to go. (If I ran into anyone I knew, I could always say I was doing research for a psychology term paper.) Unfortunately, the rumors I had heard about Rhodes—that the ratio of women to men was five to one—proved to be true, so any hopes I had of pouncing on my drunken, frustrated friends at the end of the evening were laid to rest. Nevertheless, I stayed with the Frenchmen until I saw a group of English couples with their legs tied together hop by in the middle of the street. "Heather, you silly sod, wait up!" cried one Englishwoman. "See you back at the boat, boys," I immediately told my friends. "Believe it or not, this isn't why I came to Greece."

There were others as well who caused my heart to skip a beat—Craig, the gay Australian on Mykonos, who promised to come to San Francisco before the year was out; Dinos, the straight man who shared my cabin on the ferry to Rhodes (and whose sheets had a way of slipping alarmingly to his crotch); the unnamed raven-haired youth on the boat to Aegina, who was the cynosure of all eyes; and an entire French soccer team on a mountaintop near Sparta—but, if you'll remember, if I did not travel to Greece for the night life on Mykonos, neither did I go there to lust after sex objects, attainable or not.

Consequently, when I came home and developed my pictures, I found scores of pictures of broken columns and not one to remind me of a broken heart in Nafplio. But I will not soon forget the man with the angelic name, the blond with the striking green eyes, or the boys on the sailboat—and that is as it should be. For even if I did not plan to spend my time in Greece yearning, yearn I did, and hallelujah for it. Vacations are not a time to plan, after all, but a time to let go. And letting go is just what I'm hoping to do, once again, as soon as the poppies bloom in the olive groves.

THE FINAL WORD

A Stonewall Retrospective

JUNE 1989

MACON, GEORGIA, is the armpit of the South. Sultry, hot, and humid, it is no place to spend the summer. Yet that's exactly where I spent the summer of 1969, the year of the Stonewall rebellion, studying French in a special summer school for high school students while drag queens and others protested decades of oppression in New York City.

Wesleyan College, where I joined three hundred other seventeen-year-old scholars from across the state, is renowned for its architecture, its magnolias, and its most famous graduate, Madame Chiang Kai-shek. But what I mostly remember is the friends I made: Reuben, an incipient hippie who couldn't wait to escape his fundamentalist parents by moving to San Francisco; Suzanne, a free-spirited artist who did her best to introduce me to the joys of heterosexuality; and Jay, a sweet-natured football player with whom I fell in love.

I was too young, alas, to realize I was in love with Jay. Or perhaps I was too afraid. The school's only obvious homosexual, after all, was a notorious queen named Tommy, who used to dance the Charleston in a 1920s-style bathing suit at the head of the dormitory stairs for all the world to see. I fled in terror whenever Tommy, interrupting his Ruby Keeler fantasies, winked conspiratorially at me—which he did with alarming regularity. Condemnation as a faggot, suspicion of faggotry, or even guilt by association was something I did not believe I could afford.

Whether I actually heard about the riots in Greenwich Village that summer I don't recall. Of more immediate concern in 1969, at least to the general public, was the first flight to the moon, which I watched on TV one night after performing the red, white, and blue musical extravaganza "The Testament of Freedom" with the Men's Chorus that afternoon. Patriotism was big that summer—but not gay liberation.

It is likely that I heard about the riots when I returned to Atlanta, my home, that fall, but whether my memories are real or invented, I cannot say. Neither can I say when Stonewall began to affect me personally. Perhaps it was during my senior year, when Mr. Yates, the "bachelor" English teacher, assigned *Tea and Sympathy* in English class. To this day Mr. Yates maintains that afterward I thanked him for the assignment by declaring, "*Now* people will understand what it's like."

What *what* was like? Gay life? How would I have known? I didn't come out until 1972. In the meantime, the sense of oppression that gay people had felt for centuries was something I knew all too well—until the breath of freedom that was sweeping the nation at last blew my way, enabling me at age twenty to recognize, accept, and respect the thing I had feared so long: my own sexual nature.

To be a part of those early years of gay liberation was a heady, exhilarating experience. Because we knew little of early pioneers in the homosexual emancipation movement, such as John Addington Symonds or Dr. Magnus Hirschfeld, we thought we were the first homosexuals since the ancient Greeks to proclaim our right to live and love as we saw fit. Following in the footsteps of blacks and women, we became the new vanguard of a great historical movement: a people whose time had come.

True, I played little part in that movement personally, for I lived far from the centers of emerging gay culture—New York, San Francisco, and Los Angeles—and I wasn't yet willing to sacrifice other important goals simply to be gay. "To be gay," you see, was an overriding, all-consuming passion in those days, one which often necessitated the abandonment—or at least the subjugation—of home, family, and career. I wanted to finish college first, and then to teach, perhaps to travel. Later, I thought, there would be time to lead an intensely gay life.

Voluntarily trapped in the provinces, I nevertheless shared in the excitement of the movement and benefited from its achievements. When prominent gay people came out publicly or when cities passed gay rights bills, I cheered. When homophobes denounced us or thugs attacked us, I choked with rage. I found out about these things the only way I could: through gay newspapers, visits to other cities, and letters to friends. Meanwhile, I pursued my own goals and desires.

Mainly I wanted what so many others wanted then and now: to fall in love and live happily ever after. I was told when I first came out that it would never happen. Without the blessings of church, state, and society, gay people had no choice but to lead lonely, miserable lives of heartbreak and despair, culminating in pathetic old age—but I never believed it. I believed we could do whatever we wanted. With Stonewall the old rules were overthrown.

Romantic that I was, my particular scenario for falling in love was to move to the city (any city), find a likely candidate, and then drag him back to the woods, where the two of us would enjoy a blissful existence for the next forty or fifty years. I'm not sure how I expected to achieve it, but I also assumed that kids would magically appear somewhere along the way. Perhaps eventually I would return to my hometown with lover and children in tow to lead a lavender version of the Ozzie and Harriet story. I was nothing if not naive.

Other gay people more radical than myself wanted to transform society completely, to break the bonds of capitalistic, patriarchal, heterosexist tyranny by redefining family structure, gender roles, and all the rest. This was okay by me. Then, as now, I was easy. A world of men in flowered skirts was equally as appealing as a world of men in flannel shirts. The essential thing, I believed, was to create a world where all things were possible and acceptable. That, to me, was the fundamental meaning of Stonewall.

Unfortunately, it didn't work out that way. As the 1970s progressed, the clone look (and attendant perspective) drove all others from the field, and gay society took on more and more of the traits and manners of mainstream society. To our dismay, we discovered that we could be just as intolerant, narrow, and selfish as those around us. There were differences, to be sure, between us and the world at large. We held bigger parties, did better drugs, and had more sex than our straight counterparts—supposedly—but these differences were superficial at best, and, if anything, served to diffuse our energies, rather than to concentrate them.

By this time I had left the provinces for the ghetto and found my own values changing rapidly. Love, children, a career, the future: all that was still important, but I couldn't help getting carried away by the giddy whirl of ghetto life, first in West Hollywood, and then in New York, and finally in San Francisco. Finding a lover took a back seat to finding a trick for the night. Planning the next five or ten years fell victim to planning the rest of the weekend. If there was a point to it all, it was hardly fulfillment or contentment, but experience. I was determined to get jaded.

All that changed when a virus called HIV invaded the community. The exhilarating rush and mad frenzy of our lives—which seemed to be the only way so many of us knew to say yes to life—came to a crashing halt when this mysterious and frightening intruder made its presence felt. Soon, all too soon, friends sickened and died, and those who survived wondered, Yes, but for how long? Shocked and disillusioned, we began to question our past and to reevaluate the direction of our lives.

There are those who say we eventually would have questioned the path we were taking with or without AIDS. Perhaps so. But too many add that we needed to mature as a community, and that AIDS, as an agent of that transformation, was a blessing in disguise. Despite my criticisms of the past, of a way of life I once willingly shared, I cannot agree. Such an attitude is not only smug; it is facile and shallow.

To indulge in revisionism, to impose a 1990s morality on the past, is too easy. People forget that we were charting new territory in the 1970s. Certainly we made mistakes—but we did the best we could, and at least we faced our lives without trepidation. I, for one, will never apologize for doing what we did, especially when we could not foresee the consequences. We acted in good faith. All we wanted was to find a place for ourselves.

In the early years of the crisis, I was concerned not so much for myself as for the community at large. I recognized AIDS as a serious threat from very early on, yet I always believed that somehow I would survive. I couldn't imagine my own death. I couldn't envision a crisis so profound that an entire generation—the Stonewall generation—might be lost.

As time passed, however, the likelihood of escape seemed more and more remote. AIDS stole one friend after another. Finally it threatened me. Even then I preached optimism and survival. I still do. But in recent months, I must confess, my faith has begun to falter. I suffer more frequently from depression and fatigue now than I ever have before. I continually wonder, What is to become of us?

There are many disturbing things about the AIDS crisis, but one of the worst is that it seems to have overwhelmed all our other concerns. In our desperate and valiant attempt to save lives, we seem to have lost sight of many of our original goals: federal equal rights legislation, for example. Although the national media has tidily reduced us to a one-issue subculture—it is convenient, if despicable, for them to equate gay people with disease—we must not do this ourselves. We must not abandon the demands we made at Stonewall.

And let that demand be an angry one. As a friend reminded me recently, we are celebrating the twentieth anniversary of a riot, not a political garden party. Stonewall was an act of violence, an act that the vast majority of us who march proudly in the Gay Day parade every year would probably not have condoned at the time. Such events are rare. The only other time gay people have felt so abused that they spilled into the street in righteous fury was the White night riot of 1979, ten long years ago.

I often wonder what I would have done had I been at Stonewall or the White night riot. Would I have thrown a brick or torched a police car? I'll never know. I only know how I felt when I read about these events from afar, particularly the latter one. I was excited and proud that gay people were rebelling, yet fearful of the consequences. Fortunately, we have a better way to express our anger now, a way many of us chose when we protested the Supreme Court's sodomy decision in 1987: nonviolent civil disobedience. But nonviolence works only when others are capable of sharing our outrage. Thus in the past this wasn't always an effective option.

Years have passed since Stonewall, since White night, since the discovery of AIDS. It sometimes amazes me just how much time has passed, how much history I have experienced. There are those, I suddenly realized one day, who, unlike myself, don't remember life before Stonewall, who never enjoyed the "good old days" of the 1970s, who can't even imagine a world without AIDS. An entire generation of gay people has grown up in the shadow of a preexisting gay culture—a culture that may have baffled them at times, but that must have made their way easier. I sometimes feel alienated from these people, I sometimes envy them; but most often I view them as I do the generation older than my own: as partners, brothers and sisters, in an ongoing struggle for a just society.

A just society. As the idealism of youth merges with the pragmatism of middle age, I grow ever more realistic about what I can expect to see accomplished in my lifetime. I honestly thought, when I was younger, that an ideal world, a world without rejection, discrimination, harassment, or brutality, was within reach. Now I recognize that I may die before sexual orientation ceases to matter, ceases to turn people into second-class citizens. Naturally, this is hard to accept. But I take comfort in the belief that someday we will create such a world. It may take another twenty years, or twenty more than that, or even twenty more, but it will happen. Stonewall was just a beginning.

ABOUT THE AUTHOR

Mike Hippler has been a columnist for the San Francisco *Bay Area Reporter* since 1982, and his work has appeared in a number of other journals, including *The Advocate* and the *San Francisco Chronicle.* He is the author of *Matlovitch: The Good Soldier* (1989) and the recipient of three consecutive San Francisco Cable Car Awards for outstanding journalism. A native of Atlanta, Hippler graduated magna cum laude from Duke University in 1974 and received a master's degree in education from San Francisco State University in 1980.